445
MICHAEL PALIN
BRAZIL

MICHAEL PALIN

BRAZIL

PHOTOGRAPHED & DESIGNED BY BASIL PAO

WEIDENFELD & NICOLSON

CONTENTS

INTRODUCTION

AFTER COMPLETING *New Europe* in 2007 I found many good reasons to take off my travelling boots and put my feet up on the sofa. Almost twenty years had passed since I'd set off on *Around The World In Eighty Days*. Since then I and my tireless crew had travelled every continent and seen so much that, rather than keep on doing it, I felt it was time to sit back and take in what we'd done.

But once a traveller, always a traveller, and I realized that however happy I might be at home, as long as there were maps and guide books and airline schedules I was still fatally susceptible to the lure of the open road. And although I had visited every continent there was one country, almost as big as a continent, that I knew nothing about, and that was Brazil.

Apart from being in a film of the same name, directed by Terry Gilliam in 1985, all I knew about Brazil was that it represented sun, sea, samba and the most successful national football teams in history. But as our Western world tipped into recession, Brazil emerged in a more serious guise. It was the 'B' of the BRICs, one of those economies surging forwards as fast as we were sliding backwards. In 2012, they leap-frogged the UK to become the world's fifth-largest economy. Suddenly there were lessons we could learn from them, there was an export market we desperately needed. Trade delegations were being hastily assembled and shipped out to São Paulo and Brasília. Economists were writing glowing essays and environmentalists beginning to nod approvingly. As London began to plan for her own Olympics, the venue for the next games was highlighted. It was of course, Rio de Janeiro, Brazil. The 2014 World Cup was going to be hosted by the country that had won the trophy more often than any other: Brazil. As all roads once led to Rome, it now seemed that all roads led to Rio. A second New World was opening up.

It became glaringly obvious that in all my travels, I'd missed a bit. And a very large bit too. Twice the size of India, for heaven's sake. Not only must I go to see Brazil, but I would probably need to go several times, just to take it all in. And given the size and scale and beauty and vivacity of the place it seemed a good idea to take a television crew as well. I asked around. Most of the old crew, and some new faces, leapt at the chance. The BBC nodded agreement and in June 2011 we set off on the first of four shoots, which were completed in April 2012.

Brazil, I now know, is a lot more than sun, sea and samba. It's the home of the greatest rainforest in the world, as well as the greatest river system in the world and the biggest waterfalls, by volume. But more than the abundance of natural wonders, it was the extraordinary diversity and richness of its inhabitants that struck me most forcibly. There are the descendants of those who settled the country thousands of years ago. There are the descendants of those millions of slaves brought to Brazil from Africa, and of the Portuguese landowners who enslaved them. Then there are those who came to Brazil voluntarily, and in huge numbers, from the late nineteenth century to the present day. Italians, Poles, Lebanese, Germans, Japanese, Koreans and many more, all bringing their skills and their culture to what has become an impressively united nation. Brazil is not a loose federation, or a polyglot conglomerate; it is a remarkably effective collection of different people who are happy to see themselves first and foremost as Brazilians. The process of integration has fostered one of Brazil's most marked characteristics, tolerance. There are others, such as loud music and very cold beer, a soft and languid delivery which makes them sound as if they've just woken up, and a feeling among the majority of Brazilians that the work-life balance should definitely be weighted on the side of life.

There is a famous old Brazilian saying, *'Para ingles ver'*, 'for the English to see'. It's been wryly defined as 'the difference between legal requirement and actual behaviour', and for many Brazilians this relaxed attitude to the law is still a guiding principle. But, especially in the more Europeanized south of the country, where the economic boom is being managed, I detect that times, and national stereotypes, may be changing With BRIC prosperity comes responsibility, a strong voice in the world economy, a seat on the UN Security Council perhaps. And this, some think, demands a new discipline, a new work ethic. The Brazil of beach and carnival is also a Brazil of banks and billionaires. Will it, I wonder, become more like the Western world, wealthy and worried? I hope not. Socrates, the footballer, not the philosopher, described his fellow Brazilians as 'a shrewd, vain, happy people'.

That certainly accords with my own observations. And I can't think of any other nation that it could apply to. Welcome to Brazil.

Michael Palin London, June 2012

Notes on the text.

The Day Numbers refer only to those days on which we filmed. Travelling days spent on planes and days off are not recorded. For those who like fine detail or may be encouraged to see Brazil for themselves, our filming trips were as follows:

Amazónia and Brasília in January 2012 - The North-East in June and July 2011

Minas Gerais and Rio in October 2011 - São Paulo and The South in April 2012

For Wilbur

Page	Places Visited
104	Alcântara
79	Alto Paraíso de Goiás
33	Ariaú Towers, Rio Negro
243	Barra da Tijuca
301	Barra Mansa
91	Belo Horizonte
49	Blumenau
96	Barreirinhas
291	Belém
28	Boa Vista
75	Brasília
159	Cachoeira
300	Campo Grande
169	Cardeal Mota
286	Curitiba
15	Demini
44	Fordlândia, Rio Tapajós
310	Foz do Iguaçu
124	Juazeiro do Norte
92	Lençóis Maranhenses National Park
36	Manaus
186	Mina Alegria
290	Morretes
114	Olinda
180	Ouro Preto
246	Parati
126	'Pega de Boi'
293	Pomerode
116	Recife
192	Rio de Janeiro
124	Salgueiro
132	Salvador
41	Santarém
281	Santos
159	São Félix
254	São José dos Campos
259	São Luís
262	São Paulo
170	Serra do Cipó National Park
60	Wauja Village, Upper Xingu River

ATLANTIC OCEAN
FRENCH GUIANA
URINAME
AMAPÁ
Macapá
Amazon
Belém
Alcântara
Lençóis Maranhenses
São Luís
Barreirinhas
Parnaíba
Fortaleza
Santarém
Fordlândia
Tapajós
PARÁ
MARANHÃO
CEARÁ
Teresina
RIO GRANDE DO NORTE
Natal
BRAZIL
Juazeiro do Norte
PARAÍBA
João Pessoa
Olinda
Recife
PIAUÍ
'Pega de Boi'
Salgueiro
PERNAMBUCO
Araguaia
TOCANTINS
Barragem de Sobradinho
Maceió
ALAGOAS
Xingu
Tocantins
Palmas
BAHIA
Aracaju
SERGIPE
ATO GROSSO
Wauja Village
Cachoeira
São Félix
Salvador
Alto Paraiso de Goiás
São Fransisco
Cuiabá
DISTRITO FEDERAL
Brasília
Rondonópolis
Goiânia
GOIÁS
MINAS GERAIS
Serra do Cipó
Barra Mansa
MATO GROSSO DO SUL
Paranaíba
Cardeal Mota
ESPÍRITO SANTO
Belo Horizonte
Mina Alegria
Campo Grande
Ouro Preto
Vitória
SÃO PAULO
Campos
Paraná
São José dos Campos
Parati
RIO DE JANEIRO
AY
Barra da Tijuca
Rio de Janeiro
São Paulo
Santos
PARANÁ
Curitiba
Morretes
oz do Iguaçu
Pomerode
Blumenau
SANTA CATARINA
Florianópolis
RIO GRANDE DO SUL
Porto Alegre
0 200 400 600 800 kilometres
0 100 200 300 400 500 miles
Rio Grande
URUGUAY

PART 1 | AMAZÔNIA & BRASÍLIA

ATLANTIC OCEAN
VENEZUELA
GUYANA
SURINAME
FRENCH GUIANA
Boa Vista
RORAIMA
Demini
AMAPÁ
Mouths of the Amazon
Macapá
Negro
Branco
Trombetas
Monte Alegre
Amazon
Belém
Ariaú Towers
Manaus
Santarém
Xingu
Fordlândia
Gurupi
Amazon
AMAZONAS
Tapajós
Madeira
Purus
Iriri
PARÁ
Marabá
B R A Z I L
Porto Velho
Araguaia
TOCANTINS
Palmas
RONDÔNIA
Xingu
Tocantins
MATO GROSSO
Wauja Village
Alto Paraiso de Goiás
BOLIVIA
Cuiabá
Brasília
Rondonópolis
DISTRITO FEDERAL
Goiânia
GOIÁS
0 200 400 600 kilometres
0 100 200 300 400 miles
Paranaíba
MINAS GERAIS
MATO GROSSO DO SUL
Campo Grande
PARAGUAY
Paraná
SÃO PAULO

Day 1 · Demini, Roraima

Above · *A tribal welcome. The Yanomami greet their link with the outside world.*

Preceding pages · *Flying into the rainforest near the border with Venezuela.*

THE DOGS are the first to welcome us. As the pilot, Francisco, eases our plane to a halt at the end of the bumpy grass runway, they race towards us, roused to a frenzy of barking and capering by the sound of the engine and the arrival of an interloper. Behind them figures appear at the doors of the two or three buildings that comprise Demini airstrip.

Here in the remote rainforest of North-West Brazil, any arrival from the sky is greeted with expectation. There are no roads that lead here, or even a navigable river. Aeroplanes are the lifeline to the outside world.

At the end of the airstrip are refuelling facilities and a small clinic, staffed by nurses on a monthly roster. There is a kitchen and communications equipment, and some fresh coffee to greet us.

As we unload, figures begin to emerge from a narrow path that leads out of the forest. First come curious little boys in long red shorts, looking, with their black hair, dark eyes and light brown skin, as if they might have stepped straight from the other side of the Pacific. Indonesia or even China. They're followed, a little more warily, by young girls and, with them, older women, most of whom wear nothing but a brief decorated red apron round their waists. The young men, like young men anywhere, make an entrance of self-conscious swagger. They carry bows and very long bamboo arrows with thorn-sharp wooden points. As the women stand and watch from beneath the shady eaves of the clinic, the men gather around appraising us curiously. Sensing I might make a good foil, one of them arches back his bow and sends an arrow flying high into the air. Then he gives me his bow and bids me do the same. Amidst much chortling I unleash one of the arrows, which thuds into the ground about five metres away. They seem to like me for having a go and when I take out my notebook they gather round it with great interest. The man with the bow asks for my pen and writes something in my book, in his own language, in fluent longhand. Another likes my straw hat and pops it on his head as unselfconsciously as an MCC member on a hot day at Lord's.

1

2

3

I'm quite relieved by their affability, for my new friends are from the Yanomami tribe and have a history of being fearless and often ferocious fighters. The Yanomami are one of two hundred or so indigenous tribes still left from the days when the first Europeans set foot in the country. There were estimated to be some five million Indians in Brazil when the Portuguese began to settle here early in the sixteenth century. Today, after the depredations of slavery, disease and loss of land to loggers, farmers and miners, they number no more than 300,000.

It's a walk of just over three kilometres (two miles) from the clinic to the *maloca*, the home of this particular group of Yanomami who are to be our hosts for the night. We leave the modern world behind at the end of the airstrip and follow them deep into the forest. A very beautiful walk it is too, with sunlight filtering through the foliage and a great quiet, broken only by low voices and the

4   5

occasional screech of a bird. After forty-five minutes the *maloca* appears abruptly, at the end of the trail. A long circular construction similar in dimension to a small football stadium, which, despite its size, seems to melt into the surrounding forest. Rising protectively behind it is the smooth grey bulk of a granite outcrop, fringed with scrub.

This huge circular house, which they call a *yano*, measures some 400 metres in circumference and twenty-five metres across. The outer wall, a jumble of beams and planks, is topped with a palm-thatch roof which slopes down at a sharp angle towards a central, sand-covered plaza. Beneath the roof is a beamed and pillared space about fifteen metres deep, accommodating beneath it about 180 people. The hammocks and living areas are at the back, leaving the front clear as a walkway. There are no partitions. Everyone can see everyone else around the circle. Privacy is respected without the need for separate rooms or enclosures and as they help me sling my hammock no one makes me feel conspicuous.

Until the 1950s no one knew much about the Yanomami. Their isolation from the rest of the world enabled their way of life to continue as it must have done for thousands of years: hunting, fishing and living off the fruits of the forest like bananas, yams, manioc and maize. Then, as John Hemming writes in *Tree of Rivers*, his history of the Amazon: 'That tranquillity was destroyed by three inventions: the plane, the chainsaw and the bulldozer.' This combination pushed the Yanomami to the brink of extinction. In the late 1980s this remote border area saw a gold rush, which drew thousands of *garimpeiros* – gold prospectors – into the forests, far outnumbering the Yanomami. Trees were felled and streams and rivers poisoned by the mercury needed to extract the gold. Alcohol, prostitution and diseases like syphilis accompanied this new invasion. Despite a demarcation area being drawn up to protect the tribal land, the lust for gold continued unabated until, in 1993, the killing of a number of Indian men, women and children and the attempt by the perpetrators to burn their bodies led to serious attempts to expel the *garimpeiros*. In the last twenty years a local NGO, working closely with the Yanomami, has improved their conditions and things are looking better for them, with numbers rising to some 20,000 on either side of the border with Venezuela.

***Opposite:* 1** · *At Demini airstrip. At least someone's interested in my holiday snaps.* **2** · *Yanomami children wait for health checks at the clinic.* **3** · *At the maloca. Me, dog and guidebook.*

***Above:* 4** · *In my mosquito-proof hammock. I look as if I'm waiting to hatch out.* **5** · *Keeping the communal walkway clean.*

1

2

3

4

I have complicated feelings about being able to just fly in here. Three hours door-to-door from my hotel in Boa Vista. I have no motive other than curiosity about how these people live, but I feel I have nothing to offer them in return. As it turns out this is not entirely true. Over the years the Yanomami have learnt a lot about public relations. They know that some outsiders are bad and some are good. They must impress the good ones to keep out the bad ones. Davi Kopenawa Yanomami, who welcomed us to the *maloca* wearing his traditional paint and feather adornments, has been promoting the cause of Brazilian Indians all over the world. He appreciates that people like ourselves who come here in good faith will hopefully paint an attractive and sympathetic portrait of the Yanomami to the world outside and this will make them less easy to exploit.

They are getting together some dancing for us. Nothing moves very fast here, but the preparations themselves are fascinating. The participants gather in a sunlit glade in the forest, men at one end, women and children at the other, to prepare themselves for the afternoon's celebrations. A tree stump, covered with brushes and paints, acts as a make-up table. As a basic decoration, they rub each other with a red dye from the ground-up seeds of the *urucum* flower, which also protects their skin from insects and sunburn. Over this, other designs are painstakingly applied. Parallel stripes are drawn on the faces of the children and, with the aid of pink plastic hand mirrors, much attention is given to the hair. Necklaces of yellow plastic beads are carefully adjusted. The boys have thin wooden needles inserted into their noses and round their mouths and they walk about sharpening their arrows as if halfway through an acupuncture session. The men wear anklets and armbands adorned with clusters of toucan feathers. As a final touch the men and boys have a coating of white feathers from the breast of the harpy eagle stuck onto their heads.

They prepare unhurriedly, and eventually the procession sets out along the track to the *maloca* led by one of the tiniest boys of the village. He's followed by the women, a number of them holding their babies, followed in turn by the men striking fierce poses as they go. They assemble beneath one of the giant mango trees, but only when they've moved into the communal house does the procession

5

6

***Opposite:* 1-4** *· In the forest, preparing for the dance. Palm spines through the nose and mouth, toucan feathers and red dye for the body.*
***Below:* 5** *· Harpy eagle feathers for the men.*
6 *· The women lead the procession out of the forest.*

1

2

3

become a dance. The women lead, moving gracefully, six steps forward, two steps back, as they circle the house. The men, representing the hunters, follow, stamping their feet, waving spears and chanting menacingly. The dance goes on for some time, despite the great heat, and when the women have finished the men gather in line in the central, unshaded plaza to shout and jump. At the end of the dancing everyone, from the oldest to the youngest in the village, is rewarded with a thick brew of fermented peach palm, *pupunha* juice, dispensed from huge buckets. The red berries, with their peach-coloured flesh, are rich in protein, starch and vitamins. The result must be quite potent and there's much competitive drinking among the men. No one is reproved for taking too much; in fact the young children take fresh supplies to their elders. It's a big communal treat and I'm offered a taste, and gratefully accept. After my refusal of another brimming bowlful their curiosity about us wanes, and they get on with enjoying themselves. This is their party.

It's the end of the day. The celebrants have dispersed back to their hammocks to sleep off the effects of the *pupunha*. Some will have taken a pinch or two of the hallucinogenic snuff which keeps hunger and thirst at bay. It's made from a tree resin called *epena* and little jars of it hang from the timber pillars, for public use. As if parodying the mood in the *yano*, a baby tree sloth which is being kept as a pet eases itself extremely slowly along one of the beams. The only outside activity

4

5

6

is a woman with a broom chasing a black-bristled peccary, or wild pig, that has been shuffling round the place all day, getting the dogs very irritated. She ushers it fiercely out through one of the doors, where it stands, snorting resentfully, before lowering its great round snout and resuming its hoovering in the dust.

Once night falls there is little to pierce the darkness other than the embers of small fires which are lit around the *maloca* to keep the insects away and provide some warmth in the early hours. Like everyone else I sleep in a hammock. The man next to me is wild-haired and a bit confused. He has a black wad of chewing tobacco permanently lodged in his lower jaw. He seems generally ignored by the others in the community, and swings gently in his hammock murmuring to himself. Cockroaches scuttle around by the fence as I clean my teeth.

I wake in the middle of the night. It's very dark and very quiet, but I need to answer the call of nature. I switch on my torch and head for one of the entrances, only to find all the doors shut and fastened. I ease one open and walk to the nearest bushes. Fireflies dance around. Then a grunt and a snuffle nearby makes me freeze. It's the peccary, a few paces away and eyeing me with malevolence. By the time I return to the *yano* I find a woman standing by the door. She lets me in, smiles, pushes it shut and secures it with a peg. It's a hostile world out there and I feel embarrassed that I might have momentarily jeopardized the collective security.

Opposite:* *1 *· Young children are always held close.* ***2-3*** *· The dancers circle the* yano, *the roundhouse. Women and men in separate groups.*
Above:* *4 *· The warriors end up at the centre of the plaza for a hunting dance.*
5 *· The reward at the end of the dance. Huge quantities of fermented peach palm.* ***6*** *· How do you say 'I've had enough'?*

1

2

3

4

Day 2 · Demini, Roraima

I'M WOKEN BY what sounds like torrential rain but is in fact a powerful wind rushing through the thatch roof above me. A voice starts up, loud and clear, not far from me. A man speaks for almost half an hour, as if delivering a sermon. No one reacts and later I can find no one who can tell me what he was talking about. The man who was lying next to me last night has gone and someone else is in his place. I swing myself out of my hammock, take my towel and washbag and walk across the plaza to a stream that runs at the back of the village. No one else is about. I strip off, leave my clothes on a granite boulder and lie flat in the cool, clear, shallow water. Yellow butterflies flutter just above the surface and the tall trees lead my eyes to a distant blue handkerchief of sky.

I'm washed and dressed by the time the first Yanomami come down to the stream. The young men walk with arms folded, and they greet me with an amused smile. Some of them bid me good morning in Portuguese. Back at the *maloca* the peccary's found its way in again and is being harried by the dogs. It stands its ground: ugly, surly, but impressively unafraid.

The community seems depleted this morning. I'm told that many of the young men and women are out at the gardens some way away. One or two of the older women have begun to prepare their staple diet. Manioc, or cassava, is one of the oldest cultivated foods known to man but it requires careful preparation as it contains toxic elements. Rendering it safely edible is a laborious and time-consuming process involving peeling, grating, grinding and boiling. When the manioc pulp is ready it's rolled into thin white discs which are thrown up onto the thatched roof to dry.

I'm struck by how well the *maloca* seems to work. Everything they have is potentially shared. There are no walls behind which things can be hoarded unnoticed. The bond between mothers and children seems particularly strong. Small babies spend most of their time in flesh-to-flesh contact with their mothers and I have hardly heard any of the crying or scolding that we in our enlightened world might take for granted.

There are elders but no bosses in the *maloca*. Davi, who is their shaman and the spokesman for many Indian tribes, is a man of dignity and a very clear sense of what the future holds. He wears a fine feather headdress for our interview, which begins inauspiciously.

'Davi,' I ask, 'You live here in one of the most remote parts of the world…'

The remainder of my question is drowned out by the sound of an aircraft coming low over the trees. Much laughter. Start again.

'Davi, being so cut off from the rest of the world, do you…'

'Sorry, we'll have to stop,' says Seb, our sound man. He motions upwards. 'Another plane.'

When this airline hub of north-western Brazil finally quietens down I ask Davi

Opposite: ***1*** *· Mothers and children bathing in the stream.* ***2 · 4*** *· Taking it easy. In foreground, manioc tubers.* ***3*** *· Discs of manioc bread have been dried on the roof.*

Preceding pages *· A Yanomami family on the path to the airstrip.*

1

2

3

if he sees himself as Yanomami or Brazilian first. Though his answer is Yanomami, he concedes that there are some aspects of integration with the wider world that have been of great benefit. In health, particularly. The clinic and the airstrip have ensured that far fewer of the Yanomami are dying from diseases like measles and malaria. There have been no deaths from malaria for several years. But the threats remain. There are still those who see the rights of the gold prospectors as equal to those of the Indians. There are farmers who want to start clearing the forest to raise cattle, military who want to take land to secure the border area, and big dams are planned which will cause their rivers to dry up. He is glad that we have come here to show the world how his people live; but if we truly want to defend their way of life then we must go home and protest to our governments who support companies investing in Brazil's abundance without a thought for the tribes.

'We are the people of the forest,' he says quietly and insistently. 'We are the ones who know how to look after it.'

Before we leave there is further evidence of how rapidly the world outside has changed the Yanomami way of life. Not far from the *maloca* they have cleared the forest to create a football pitch. It might not be level, but there are two goalposts and two very keen teams. The kit consists of footwear (optional) and a pair of shorts. Striped shirts are painted on their upper bodies and striped socks painted on their calves. Despite the punishing heat they throw themselves into the game, everyone chasing for every ball. It's a happy image but it's also a confirmation that their old way of life is changed for ever and now, for better or worse, the days of isolation are over.

We walk back slowly, reflectively, through this sylvan peacefulness until we reach the airstrip. Francisco, our pilot, is already waiting, looking anxiously at the sky.

We bid our last farewells and climb aboard. The clearing and the cluster of buildings recede into the distance. For the next hour there is nothing below us but rolling rainforest, swathing the land in every shade of green, broken occasionally by vivid dabs of purple and yellow blossom. Thin spidery rivers appear, then peter out. I can see no sign of a track or a trail. Then the landscape changes, levels out, and where there was forest there are wide fields of grass and some soya and ahead of us is a proper airport and soon we're down to earth again.

Opposite: *1 · Bedtime story.* ***2*** *· With Davi, spokesman for the Yanomami around the world.* ***3*** *· Yanomami FC. Nowhere in Brazil is too remote for a soccer match.*

Below *· Last sight of the maloca, our home for the past two days.*

Day 3 · Boa Vista, Roraima

RORAIMA is Brazil's newest state, created in 1988. It's about the same size as the UK. The capital, Boa Vista, lies beside the broad waters of the Rio Branco, recently bridged by a road carrying Highway B-74 which connects it with Manaus and the Amazon 750 kilometres (470 miles) to the south. It's an unsentimental frontier town. Though the state is home to twenty indigenous tribes and a huge area of protected land, the sympathies of Boa Vista appear to lie elsewhere. The statue that dominates the main square is of a kneeling gold prospector and there are shops painted gold where the produce of the *garimpeiros* is openly traded. A big American I talk to at the hotel buffet is here to look at some farmland he's bought in the north of the state. Despite the demarcation of land for Indians and the restrictions on the *garimpeiros* there's money to be made here. Boa Vista sees itself as the gateway to a land of opportunity.

The Public Prosecutor of Roraima State is an unequivocal supporter of the rights of the indigenous people and says that a lot of those living in Boa Vista are civil servants administering government funds on their behalf. We talk down by the river near a portentous mural depicting the great Brazilian explorer Colonel Cândido Rondon. He it was who, at the turn of the twentieth century, accompanied the ex-American-President Teddy Roosevelt and his son Kermit on many of their intrepid travels through the Amazon headwaters. Rondon had great admiration for the indigenous tribes he encountered and in 1910 he helped create the Indian Protection Service. A state called Rondonia was named after him, and indeed there are, somewhere, two small tributaries of the Amazon, one called Rio Roosevelt and the other Rio Kermit.

1

2

Rodrigo the Prosecutor and his wife Tatiana are young, bright lawyers from the South. They both manfully defend their posting up in the far North, though there's clearly not a lot going on here. He quotes a local saying: 'If a lion came to Boa Vista on a Sunday afternoon, it would die of hunger.'

Last year he suspended all mining activities in the state, but admits that it is very expensive to police such a vast area and the boundaries of protected land are difficult to pin down. Fifty gold miners have been arrested but the penalties are weak; and with the world price of gold at an all-time high there are those who will always take the risk.

He sees the future of the Yanomami being secured not by separation but by an increasing two-way exchange, with tribespeople coming to the city and outsiders visiting the *malocas* to get to know their way of life. Lasting protection, he feels, can only be based on mutual respect and understanding.

Opposite *· The Rio Branco at Boa Vista. Recently built bridge at top of picture.* ***Above: 1*** *· With the Public Prosecutor and his wife. He's taking a strong line against the miners.* ***2*** *· Shops like this show the gold prospectors are still in business.*

Day 4 · Beside the Rio Negro

WITH ONE BOUND we've crossed the Equator and are now in a small village on the banks of the Rio Negro, a few kilometres upstream from where this already mighty river joins the Amazon. The houses are modest, clapboard constructions built on stilts, for in the flood season the river can rise by at least ten metres. The odd thing is that they all seem freshly painted in bold, bright colours. I'm told that this is because this village was recently the location for one of Brazilian TV's much-loved soap operas. This one had an ecological twist and catered for the increasingly serious interest being taken in the Amazon.

That was then. Now the TV company has moved on and there is not much left to this small fishing settlement but the glossy colours of the houses and a general air of listlessness. It's here that I meet Elias, one of the last of the old-style rubber tappers, or *seringueiros* – *seringueira* being the Portuguese name for the rubber tree. In his mid-sixties now, Elias's deeply lined face, weathered and pinched, betrays a hard life, or possibly a hard-drinking life. He was nine years old when his father took him on his first rubber-tapping expedition. Like

1

2

3

4

the gold prospectors of Roraima, the *seringueiros* worked in small self-employed groups, often far from home for long periods. He showed me one of the rubber trees, the *Hevea brasiliensis*: short, slender and with its grey bark scarred with incisions. The cuts are made close to the base of the tree where the latex runs more plentifully. Elias draws his blade diagonally across the bark and as the white sticky juice oozes out he collects it in a small metal pot. This is heated to a temperature of 800°C over an open fire, which contains sulphur to keep the latex malleable. This vital part of the process, called vulcanization, was discovered by the American inventor Charles Goodyear in 1839. Elias adds the vulcanized latex to a growing ball weighing several kilos. In this form the rubber would have been shipped downstream by the *seringueiros* to the middlemen in Manaus or Santarém. In the late nineteenth century a lot of Brazilians grew immensely wealthy as the world demand for their rubber increased.

It was a French explorer named Charles Marie de La Condamine who first drew attention to the valuable properties of *Hevea brasiliensis*, but ultimately it was the British who benefited most from his discovery. Sir Joseph Hooker, the industrious botanist who was Director of Kew Gardens from 1865 to 1885, was fascinated by the exotic plants and trees of the world. In the 1860s he had encouraged Richard Spruce to bring seedlings of the cinchona tree, the source of quinine, out of South America and had them transplanted to India, providing an antidote to malaria and one of the essential ingredients of gin and tonic. Hooker then turned his energies to the rubber tree. In 1876, at Hooker's instigation, a man called Henry Wickham, now much reviled in Brazil, smuggled out enough seeds to germinate rubber trees at Kew Gardens. By 1900 they were successfully transplanted to Malaya. A most skilful botanist called Henry Ridley – 'Rubber' Ridley, as he became known – persuaded tea producers to raise *Hevea brasiliensis* on their Malayan plantations. His perseverance paid off. By 1908 there were ten million rubber trees in Malaya producing rubber at a fifth of the cost of the Brazilian product. By 1920 Brazil's most profitable export business had collapsed. Elias's father, like other *seringueiros*, continued to tap but the days when you could get seriously rich from Brazilian rubber were over.

As one of Henry Wickham's countrymen I feel almost embarrassed as Elias demonstrates the process for us, albeit without much conviction. Everyone looks up in some relief as the skies darken and we just have time to race across the village football pitch and into the Pousada Jacaré (Alligator Guest House) as the first thudding drops of a tropical deluge descend. For a few hours there's nothing much we can do. It's one of those tropical storms of such intensity that, as the writer Álvaro Mutis put it, 'they seem to announce the universal flood'. We eat from a basic buffet of fish, chicken, rice and salad and then take to the hammocks that hang on the veranda.

Elias sits at the table with a succession of beers, pouring out the story of his life to anyone who'll listen. And a sad story it is too. He'd married at the age of

***Opposite:* 1** · *Tropical storm approaching Elias the rubber tapper's village.* **2** · *The village was spruced up for a soap-opera location. They've since moved on.* **3** · *Elias and me and the rubber tree,* Hevea brasiliensis. **4** · *Elias shows me the kiln in which he vulcanizes the rubber.*

nineteen and they had one son. Then for some reason he left home. Walked out. He says now that he left the one woman he'd ever really loved, and never found her again.

When the rain eases we tramp across the duckboards and out along the rickety wooden jetty to pick up our boat. It's an open boat and a very wide river, and the wind whips what's left of the rain into our faces as it carries us back down the Rio Negro to the hotel where we'll be spending the night.

I've never come across a hotel quite like it. From the river its collection of round wooden towers, painted a murky, undergrowth green, looks like a row of abandoned gasometers. There's something ominous about its appearance, as if we might have stumbled upon some abandoned jungle laboratory where an experiment went terribly wrong.

This is not that far from the truth. The Ariaú Towers complex was built in the 1970s as one of the first eco-lodges in the Amazon. The famous French naturalist and explorer Jacques Cousteau had come here to study the river dolphins and wanted to create some sort of centre, something that would blend in with its surroundings, in which visitors could experience the richness of the rainforest without damaging it. The buildings would be made from local materials, which is why there is no steel or concrete to support the framework that carries the six-storey accommodation pods and the network of walkways that connects them, high above the riverbank.

Though it's a little run-down these days, it's a playful sort of place, with more than a touch of eco-kitsch. A big, colourful snake rears up beside the swimming

1

2

pool. There's a three-metre-high Disney-like Indian with bow and arrow and a pair of painted wooden leopards clinging to tree trunks outside the Aquarium Disco and Bar. To get to my room, Casa do Tarzan – the Tarzan House– I have to cross two bridges and climb four flights of precipitous steps to the top of a tree. I could have done without the dainty white curtains, the bedspread and the towels rolled up in the shape of a snake, but I sorely missed a liana to swing myself down to the ground, not to mention a distorting mirror in the bathroom to make me look like Johnny Weissmuller.

It was only as I lay back on the bed to take it all in that I became aware of the potential disadvantages of a tree house in the Amazon rainforest, a constant chorus of scuttlings, scratchings and peckings from the walls and the ceiling. It was like lying in a nesting box. I'm all for being close to nature, but not this close.

Opposite *· Giant Indian hunter towers over a walkway at the Amazon's first eco-lodge.*
Above: 1 *· My tree house. The nearest I'll get to being Johnny Weissmuller.* ***2*** *· A squirrel monkey lurks by the breakfast room.*

Day 5 · Ariaú Towers, Rio Negro

UP EARLY after a night of weird dreams which I put down to the malaria tablets. The squirrel monkeys are already scooting about waiting to find their way through the netting and into breakfast. They have distinctive tan fur on their backs and faces that seem to consist only of two big eyes. They're hugely appealing and very naughty.

With a bit of luck we shall be looking at more unusual wildlife as we head off up a side river to a rendezvous with *Botos Cor de Rosa,* pink Amazon dolphins. My guide is a young man called Gabriel. His family are *caboclos,* people of mixed Indian and European blood for whom life has never been easy. Gabriel has created his own luck. He taught himself English in the 1990s, qualified as a guide for the Ariaú Towers and moved his wife and young family to Manaus. But the recent fall in tourist numbers, especially from North America, has just cost him his regular job, and he now works part-time.

The trees that crowd the still, reflective surface of the creek seem strangely silent. Gabriel explains to me that the water of the Rio Negro is acidic, which means fewer fish and less food for the birds. Almost as he speaks a largish bird

detaches itself from the tree cover and flaps lazily up ahead of us, its wings silver in the pale morning sunlight. It's an osprey.

The wind catches us as we emerge from the sheltered side channel onto the wide, lake-like waters of the Rio Negro. Ahead of us, on its platform of lashed-together logs and a threadbare thatched roof, is the pink dolphin viewing-platform. There are two main species of river dolphin in the Amazon. The grey dolphin is shy of humans, but the more plentiful pink dolphins have been courted over the last few years by a local boy who has won their trust by feeding them sardines. He's already thrown a few in and as I slide into the water I can see fins coming closer. This is not something I've ever done before and I'm a little apprehensive. Then the first of them makes contact beneath the water, a cool, hard, strong back, a soft skin and a bulbous neck like that of a walrus. And then a spectacular jaw, as long as a chainsaw and lined with twenty or thirty teeth, breaks the surface and snaps at a sardine. There are five of them circling now and as they come in closer I can see them gliding towards me, then I feel them twisting and turning, giving me a whack with their hard flippers or probing the water awfully close to my lower body with their long, scissor-like mouths. They're agile but sightless and I feel quite pleased that they trust me enough to bounce off my body and still come back for more. And I trust them enough not to mistake anything of mine for a sardine.

For fifteen minutes or more I rub along with dolphins, until the bait runs out and they swim slowly away. When we're back in the boat Gabriel tells me that the

1

3

2

4

pink dolphin plays a very important part in the folklore of the Amazon villages. At party times, when there is drinking and dancing, he is believed to swim up to the village and, taking human form, impregnate the local girls, before disappearing as the daylight comes. I'm all for local legend, but blaming it on the dolphins is such a blatant cover story. I check with Gabriel and no, he's never seen a half-dolphin child.

We carry on up the river to a more substantial floating platform on which Gabriel's parents have a shop and a small hotel. They're known as *ribeirinhos* – the small businessmen of the riverbank – and they live by fishing, growing fruit, gathering brazil nuts, running a small bar and shop and trying to attract eco-tourists. They've no guests at the moment and they're doing work on the rooms. Gabriel's mother makes us Amazon coffee and we sit and watch the world go by.

'There is no road here. The river is our road,' says Gabriel, and I think he's quite happy with that.

The Rio Negro is a clear and clean river without much alluvial content. It sustains 1,300 species of fish including twenty-five species of piranha. One's blood runs cold, or is it hot, at the very mention of piranha, but Gabriel reassures me that none of them are dangerous. Not here on the Rio Negro. And there are no mosquitoes here either, unlike on the Amazon. He likes this time of year (it's January) as the rains come and the river starts to fill. By June it will be the time of plenty for those who live off the rivers, as the levels will have risen by anything from ten to fifteen metres, creating a vast and fertile flood-plain called the *várzea*.

Opposite *· Swimming with the pink river dolphin. He's rather more interested in the sardine.*

Above: 1 *· Gabriel, the caboclo, takes me to meet his family.* ***2*** *· Gabriel's father brings DIY supplies.* ***3*** *· Gabriel's mother and father on their floating bar, hotel, shop, and satellite dish.* ***4*** *· A customer from across the river.*

Every fifty years they have freak conditions. In 2009, the highest the river rose was twenty-nine metres, followed the year after by a drought.

The sound of outboard motors hums around us as small boats come up alongside. His father unloads two empty fuel drums which will be lowered down to give extra support for the platform. A lean and quietly dignified old man wearing a wide-brimmed straw hat ties up, waits patiently to collect supplies from the shop and steers his boat back across the stream to the far bank. The pace of life is gentle. The sunlight sparkling off the river makes me deliciously drowsy. I could stay here for ever.

Day 6 · Manaus

ANYONE who visits Amazônia must at some point pass through Manaus. It's the capital of Amazonas State, a major transport hub, with a busy airport, docks and a brand-new, four-kilometre-long (two and a half miles) road bridge over the Rio Negro. Its population is growing fast and has just topped the two million mark. Declared a Free Trade Zone in 1967 Manaus has become Brazil's biggest manufacturer of white goods and electronic appliances. People come from hundreds of kilometres away to buy their cheap TVs here. And from beneath the nose of its rival Belém, it's won the right to host the only World Cup games to be played in Amazônia in 2014.

Manaus has known the good times before. A hundred years ago it was at the centre of the rubber boom and, briefly, one of the wealthiest cities in all the Southern Hemisphere; the first city in Brazil to have trolley-buses and the second to have electric light. Then the rubber boom ended, as fast as it had begun, and for many years Manaus went back to being a hot, sticky backwater which no one wanted to visit. The bars and brothels emptied and the grand old buildings became too expensive to maintain. Apart from one. An icon that bestrides two boom times, the internationally renowned opera house. The first thing I discover as I stand marvelling at its creamy three-storey facade is that it's not actually called the Opera House. It's called the Teatro Amazonas.

1

2

But the confusion is understandable. When it came to spending money, the Brazilian rubber barons of the 1890s looked across the Atlantic for their inspiration. Spurred on by the indefatigable ambition of the Governor, Eduardo Ribeiro, palatial houses, public buildings, clubs, bars, restaurants, banks and brothels set out to turn Manaus into the Paris of the Tropics. No self-respecting *hommage* to the French capital was complete without a nod to their culture and that meant, at the very least, one opera house.

They imported Scottish ironwork, English china, Portuguese architects, Italian marble, French mirrors and curtains. The only ingredients from Brazil were timber and the rubber that was used to pave the driveway outside so as to soften the sound of carriage wheels during the performance. The whole majestic edifice was opened in 1896. Governor Ribeiro, whose vision had transformed Manaus, died by his own hand in 1900, coincidentally the same year that the first Kew-raised rubber trees were planted in Malaya, marking the beginning of the end of Brazilian rubber domination and the Paris of the Tropics.

Looking at the Teatro Amazonas today, built on a mound above the attractively restored square of Largo de São Sebastião, it's hard to imagine it in hard times. Its pink and white exterior, restored fifteen years ago, glows in the sunshine, lavish detail piled on lavish detail and crowned with sumptuous stucco personifications of music and drama. In contrast to the neo-classical facade is the magnificent mosaic-tiled dome that rises behind it, less like Paris and more like a mosque in Isfahan or Tashkent.

I step inside, glad to be out of the blazing sun, and suddenly find the sweat pouring from me. Manaus is notoriously sticky – I think the reading for today was ninety-four percent humidity – and there's a problem with the air-con inside the

Opposite: *1 · 'The Opening of the Ports'. Bronze statue reminds us that Manaus was once at the centre of international trade.*
2 · The Opera House aka Teatro Amazonas. Symbol of one golden age, hoping to herald in another.
Below · Inside the Opera House. The Amazon Philharmonic prepares to rehearse.

Above · *Magnificent excess. The greatest auditorium in the Amazon. Steel from Glasgow, decoration from Italy.*

theatre. Members of the orchestra, gathering for a rehearsal, fan themselves with their scores as they take their places on a long, deep stage. The interior is very fine indeed. The 700 seats are all separate and upholstered in plush, ruby-red velour. They're set mainly in the stalls, above and around which three narrow galleries of boxes rise in a beautifully graceful curve, giving the auditorium intimacy and grandeur at the same time. Busts of great cultural figures, Schiller, Shakespeare, Goethe, Mozart and the like, decorate the balconies. On the interior of the dome is a spectacular piece of *trompe l'oeil* which gives the impression that the Eiffel Tower is springing out of the roof above us.

Luiz, the portly conductor from São Paulo, taps his baton to bring the sixty-strong Amazon Philharmonic Orchestra to order. They're rehearsing the overture to *O Guarany,* an opera by Carlos Gomes from the hugely popular nineteenth-century novel by José Alencar. The Guarany are, or were, an Indian tribe and the hero of the story is an Indian who saves the life of a white girl. Gomes died in 1896, the year the Teatro Amazonas opened. A painting of his bust, with a winged angel protecting it, appears on the inside of the dome, next to the Eiffel Tower.

It's a lively and inspiring piece, but Luiz has things he's not happy with. As they go over it again I look into the handsome ballroom, whose parquet flooring is of such quality that visitors – and there are many – have to slide into absurdly large furry slippers before they enter. Feeling like a troll on steroids, I swish my

1

2

way across and out onto the mighty, pillared balcony. The view of Manaus is quite depressing. The high-rise blocks of the 1970s are grimy and neglected. The opera house is an ornate jewel in a rough and ready city.

With rehearsals over for the morning, I've a chance to meet some of the players. They're from all over the world. Wolfgang, one of the horn players, is from Germany. '*East* Germany,' he adds with deliberate mock horror effect. There wasn't much work at home for a classical musician – too many competing orchestras. In 2004 he answered an advert for a tuba player to come and play Wagner's *Götterdämmerung* in the Amazon.

'I looked at Brazilian culture and I loved it.' In 2005 he came over and stayed. He married a girl from Manaus and they have a son. 'Here we work to relax.' I ask Wolfgang if he spends much time up in the jungle. He screws up his face. 'I don't need to. I have snakes at home.' He explains, with much laughter, how he had to get someone to dispose of two green cobras in his garden. Which didn't sound that funny to me.

Classical music is a relative newcomer to the Brazilian music scene and when he's not playing in the Amazon Philharmonic, Wolfgang, along with Elena, one of the violinists, teaches classes of youngsters in a small room at the Sambadrome, a huge stadium where all the Carnival preparations and events take place.

Elena is from Plovdiv in Bulgaria. She's in her mid-fifties, short and stocky,

Above: 1 *· Luiz the conductor urges on his orchestra.* ***2*** *· In the ballroom at the Opera House.* ***Below: 3*** *· Wolfgang, one of the musicians from the orchestra, encouraging young Brazilians to learn an instrument.* ***4*** *· Elena from Plovdiv teaches the string section.*

3

4

with close-cut fair hair and an easy, relaxed manner. She's lived in Manaus for twelve years and has seen it change a lot. 'When I came Manaus was like a village.'

Now it's grown bigger, more expensive and, she thinks, more violent. But the young cellists and violinists she and Wolfgang are trying to interest in Bruckner this afternoon are all given their tuition for free and she hopes that in a small way what they provide is some alternative to the streets. I ask her how different she finds Brazil from Europe. She spreads her arms. 'It's like another universe. The mentality here is a *tabula rasa*. With these children you have to begin at the very beginning. It's quite a responsibility.'

Which, clearly, she's happy to take on.

Our hotel is north and west of the city centre, near two large army camps and the affluent strip of beach called Porto Negro, where Manaus's millionaires live. I take a walk through the car park and down to the riverbank. The Rio Negro, which rises up in Yanomami territory, has swollen spectacularly. The far bank is nearly five kilometres (three miles) away. It's just too big to take in, and it hasn't even become the Amazon yet. I content myself with nature at its more intimate, watching Oriole blackbirds, flashes of vivid black and yellow, as they chase each other in and out of the trees.

Day 7 · Manaus ✈ Santarém

Above *· Riverside chat with Paulo Adário of Greenpeace.*

BEFORE WE LEAVE and head east I'm given an overview of what is happening in this vast Amazon region, the size of Western Europe, from someone intimately concerned with the health of the world's largest rainforest. Paulo Adário lives in Manaus and works for Greenpeace. We sit and talk beside the river. He sees cause for cautious optimism. When he first came here the annual rate of deforestation was 'a Belgium' per year. That's 30,000 square kilometres.

'We use Belgium as a unit of measure,' he explains. 'Now it's less than a third of a Belgium. That's good news.'

As far as the indigenous population of the Amazon is concerned, there is, on the face of it, good news too. The principle of Customary Rights ensures that if a tribe can prove that they have lived in a certain area for sufficient time it becomes theirs. Twenty percent of the Amazon is now Indian land.

At the same time the world demand for Brazilian resources, be they soya, iron ore, gold, oil, aluminium or timber, is apparently insatiable. Brazil is the largest exporter of beef on the planet and seventy-five percent of the deforestation has been to clear the ground for cattle. At the Copenhagen Climate Summit in 2009, President Lula's government committed Brazil to reducing deforestation by eighty percent within ten years. Yet, only a few weeks ago, Dilma Rousseff,

President Lula's successor, signed off on a huge series of dams which will have a profound effect on the rainforest in the Xingu River area. I'm glad that on balance protection is winning over reckless deforestation, but while there is so much demand and so much land one feels the debate will never be over.

Flying east from Manaus further emphasizes the size and scale of Brazil. Just under two kilometres downstream of the city is the spectacular phenomenon of the Encontro das Águas, the confluence of two mighty rivers where the dark, acidic flow of the Rio Negro meets the sediment-filled Solimões River to form the Amazon proper. For several kilometres they run side by side until the muddy flow of the Solimões wins the battle and the Amazon becomes a mighty sheet of caramel-coloured water. Manaus is 1,600 kilometres (1,000 miles) from the sea, but only thirty-two metres above sea level, which is why the land below us is a great weaving mass of water, spreading itself over hundreds of kilometres. Seeing it from above I can almost comprehend the extraordinary statistic that twenty percent of all the world's fresh water is contained within the Amazon Basin. I settle back into my aeroplane seat as all that moisture curls upwards. Clouds like big and billowing white sails merge, turn dark and suddenly the water that was down there is all around us.

Halfway between Manaus and Belém is Santarém, the third and most intimate of the big cities of the Amazon. With a population of less than 150,000 souls it lies close to a confluence twenty-five kilometres (fifteen miles) wide where the clean, green waters of the Rio Tapajós join the alluvial flow of the mother river. The vast quantities of water that swirl around it make the shores fertile, and there's a museum in the town with a rich collection of pre-European ceramics, some dating back 10,000 years. Together with nearby discoveries of cave and rock paintings, they bear witness to a creative and sophisticated indigenous culture which was virtually wiped out. What replaced it was the European taste of the settlers. Santarém is another rubber boom town with a legacy of handsome colonial buildings and a big cathedral dominating the dockside. It's also infamous in Brazilian history as the home of Henry Wickham, the rubber seed hero, or villain (according to whether you're British or Brazilian) who arrived here in 1874.

But Santarém nearly had a second chance to get rich. Twenty-five years after Henry Wickham's seeds switched production to the other side of the world, emissaries of the legendary American car maker, Henry Ford, arrived in the city, hoping to initiate a second rubber boom in Brazil. It would be sustained by the demand from his motor car factories and, more importantly, it meant that no longer would he have to rely on rubber from the British Empire which he so despised. In the 1920s a town was built on the forested shores of the Rio Tapajós and christened 'Fordlândia'. Despite huge investment, this attempt to recreate the values of the American Midwest in the Brazilian jungle was a spectacular failure. To see what remains of Henry Ford's dream I'm doing what his cohorts did eighty-five years ago. I'm taking to the river.

A flyblown dockside road leads to Santarém's small, squeezed, massively busy ferry port. I pass a big plastic rubbish container with the word CLEAN, partially obscured by the rubbish in front of it, inscribed in large letters on the side. A turkey vulture stands astride it and dogs are nosing around in the overflow. Ahead of me is a muddy track on which are drawn up serried ranks of trucks carrying cargo for the twenty or so ships jostling for position around one single floating jetty. The vehicles are not allowed any closer, so from here everything has to be carried on by hand. Enormous loads are borne by staggering porters. Four dozen litre-bottles of beer on one man's shoulders, two-metre-long gas cylinders on another's. The loads are so heavy that the men must keep running to prevent their knees buckling under the weight.

Opposite: ***1** · Various forms of waste disposal by the ferry port at Santarém. **2** · No trucks allowed on the pontoon, all cargo has to be hand-loaded. **3** · Beer is in big demand. **4** · The São Bartolomeu I takes on last-minute supplies. **5** · The big squeeze. Amazon ferryboats wait for an opening at Santarém's congested terminal. **6** · Lower-deck passengers have to share with the cargo. **7** · Upper-class, a multi-coloured forest of hammocks.*

I dodge out of their way as we wait to find out which ferry is going towards Fordlândia. Eventually we're directed to the *São Bartolomeu I*, heading up the Tapajós on an eighteen-hour journey to the town of Itaituba with four stops on the way. A hundred people are crammed on the two small decks and twenty-five tonnes of cargo is stacked around them. The only way that so many people can survive an overnight voyage is to take to their hammocks. I've bought one in Santarém and I'm shown the space allotted to me, cheek by jowl with several families and their children.

Despite the apparent chaos the *São Bartolomeu* leaves dead on time, with people flinging themselves aboard even after we've cast off. One man hurls his bags a full metre before leaping on after them. Getting out onto the river requires extraordinary navigational skills, as the boat has to be reversed from the jammed jetty, inch by meticulous inch. When we have eventually prised ourselves free, two incoming ferries race each other for the vacant space.

The skyline of old Santarém gradually recedes and we run alongside a complex of silos and soaring conveyor belts that dwarf everything else around. This marks the presence of the American grain company Cargill who, in 2003, invested a Ford-like fortune to build a terminal for the produce of their soya plantations in the area. Apart from the forest cover removed for soya production, an upgrading of the road system to transport the soya to the silos at Santarém created a corridor of deforestation and development. The losers in all this were the *caboclos*, the general term for smallholders and traders . Despite having little legal or financial clout they fought for survival, and still are fighting. Only three months previously a man was shot dead in Itaituba for passing on information about illegal logging. In the last six months of 2011, eight people have been murdered for opposing forest clearance in Amazônia.

There is a tiny bar in the stern of the ship, with cans of beer and booming disco, but this is largely a family boat and most people are already enveloped in their hammocks like so many pupae waiting to hatch out.

Ahead of us the huge skies darken and jagged storm clouds hang over the mouth of the Tapajós. Another mighty river, as wide as a Swiss lake.

1

2

3

4

5

6

7

Day 8 · Fordlândia, Rio Tapajós

DURING THE NIGHT we transferred to the *Aruã*, a smaller riverboat, and took our time to travel down the Tapajós so that we could approach our destination in daylight. A storm hit in the middle of the night, with wind and torrential rain lashing the boat. This morning the last shreds of the rain clouds are disappearing, but it's grey and cool. The riverbank is an endless wall of tangled, intertwined greenery, from which the occasional screeching bird darts out, dips, swings and vanishes again. There's a disappointing lack of colourful wildlife. A flash of blue in the reed beds is more likely to be a plastic bag or chip off a water tank. The forest cover is broken every now and then by a modest *caboclo* cabin sitting in a clearing, with maybe a horse or a couple of cows grazing, a white egret patrolling the shore and, always, a dog stretched out across the threshold fast asleep.

It's mid-morning when there's the first unmistakable sign that we are in sight of our goal. Rising above the trees like some great bird is an elegant grey pod perched on top of tall triangular stilts. It's a 1930s water tower, and if it looks as if it should be in some industrial plant outside Detroit, that's exactly the intention. Fordlândia was Henry Ford's industrial dream town in the middle of the Amazon jungle.

In the mid-1920s, thanks to the huge success of the Model T, the world's first mass-produced car, Henry Ford's company had sixty percent of the truck and automobile market in Brazil. Hearing rumours of Ford's interest, various Brazilian entrepreneurs approached Ford with offers of cheap land for rubber production in the Amazon. Ford liked the idea. It appealed on more than merely commercial grounds. He had his own, highly individual way of running a business and was

becoming frustrated by what he saw as interference at home. As Greg Grandin writes in his book *Fordlandia*, the Amazon adventure offered a fresh start for Ford in a place 'uncorrupted by unions, politicians, Jews, lawyers, militarists and New York bankers'.

He acquired a million-hectare site beside the Tapajós River and in the late 1920s the company began to impose his dream of orderly, industrial efficiency on the untidy, disorderly profusion of a rainforest. After a disastrous start everything began to work rather well, with the single exception of the sole reason they were out there in the first place – to grow rubber.

Due to a combination of ineptitude, impatience and the ravages of South American Leaf Blight, the rubber plantation failed. Ford belatedly employed agronomists as well as business managers, on whose advice he moved the plantation to nearby Belterra, whilst still keeping Fordlândia as a company base for research and development. But disease, difficulty in training and keeping a workforce, and import and export restrictions gradually took their toll and in 1945 the company moved out altogether. The Brazilian government briefly tried to operate what was left, but that fell through and Fordlândia, as an industrial enterprise, was abandoned in the 1950s. The ghost town that was left behind is what we see now as the *Aruã* rounds the bend of the river.

It's clear that people still live in Fordlândia. There is a church a little way up the hill, houses along the bank and a ferryboat at the jetty. But it's the buildings that have been abandoned that dominate the town. Beside the jetty rises the Turbine Hall, some twenty-five metres high and one hundred and fifty metres long, and on the brow of the hill behind it are two more enormous industrial sheds. Walking ashore past the cramped little shack that serves as a ferry-port shop and

Opposite · *The Itaituba ferry heads into the night.*
Above · *Fordlândia at first light. 1930s water tower rises above the trees. The Turbine Hall at left of the jetty.*

1

3

2

4

*Above: **1** · Henry Ford's follies. In the empty Turbine Hall. **2** · State-of-the-art hospital, now terminally ill itself. **3** · Workshop No. 2 Some of the old machines survive, but there's still plenty of room for the school bus. **4** · Workshop No. 3. Still in use. But only just.*

into the empty, glass-walled space of the Turbine Hall you begin to get a sense of what Ford meant when he said 'The man who builds a factory builds a temple. The man who works there, worships there.' It's not that fanciful to feel that you're in an industrial cathedral.

The workshop up the hill has quite a lot of the old equipment, if not working, still intact. A dismembered clocking-on board for punching cards, an adding machine, a Junkers generator, ovens with dials and the maker's stamp: 'Weston Electrical Instruments Co. Newark, New Jersey, USA'. Workbenches are still in place, with vices half open as if the operator's hand had just left them. The almost completely glassed walls at either end must have been state-of-the-art at the time and still feel very modern. A yellow school bus is parked inside.

An overgrown concrete roadway connects this shed with Workshop No. 3, which is the largest of them all, with floor space on two levels. Stout steel columns support a long, tall A-frame roof. There are workbenches and a row of abandoned lathes. A cast-iron staircase, big enough for busy factory-floor traffic, leads upstairs. I climb it cautiously at first and then with more confidence, the clang of my footsteps echoing round these deserted walls. A wide wooden floor is covered with piles of desiccated Brazil nuts, and it's as I'm bending down to inspect them that a noise comes from below that makes me freeze. One of the lathes has come to life.

The whizz and the whirr of a drill takes me back to the top of the stairs and,

Above · Small-town America survives in the Amazon. Red fire hydrant, bottom left. Trees trained across to provide shade.

looking down, I see a man working away, black, middle-aged and completely preoccupied. It's an unforgettable image. One man working in a room intended for thousands.

We go for lunch at the Pousada Americana, run by an optimistic man called Guilherme who came down from Santarém a year and a half ago, hoping that Fordlândia's past would be his future, luring curious Amazon tourists down the Tapajós. He admits it hasn't happened yet. Most of his guests are film crews, so he hopes that bit by bit the word will get out. The rooms are clean and brightly painted and the food is good, but there's a very noisy parrot that shouts for coffee all day long, and five turkey vultures are lined up on the fence outside.

Fordlândia is a treasure trove of industrial archaeology. This transplantation of the American Midwest to the Amazon jungle is unique and has left some remarkable things behind. Clapboard houses with neat verandas are set back from a road that has sidewalks, elegant lamp standards, fire hydrants and a roof of trees with branches deliberately trained to create a protective tunnel of shade for the managers and their families who, all too briefly, lived there. A sadder fate has befallen the hospital. Designed by Albert Kahn, who had masterminded the best part of a kilometre-long assembly plant at Ford's Dearborn, Michigan, headquarters, it is now a long, low wreck of a place. Where neat lines of spotless beds stood beneath a light and airy roof, there is now just mould and decay. Broken, rain-blackened beams and discarded asbestos panels are strewn across the floor. There are rooms with their names still above the door. Sal de Espera– the Waiting Room, Sala de Raio X, Gabinete Dentário; but the only things moving inside them now are colonies of bats, their droppings piled up on floors that were once immaculate.

The grand dream of Fordlândia from which they all awoke in November 1945 is not entirely a story of waste. The school building, dating from 1931, is still in use, as is the basketball pitch, with its bleachers intact. Today's inhabitants of Fordlândia still live in some of the houses the Ford Company built, and raise chickens and watch white rabbits lolloping about and gather to talk beside the red water hydrants the Americans left behind.

Ironically, the big companies of today, making their money from logging and soya, seem to have passed Fordlândia by. It's a small town with a huge ghost in the middle of it. The ghost of Henry Ford's ego.

On an almost perfect evening we head down the Tapajós and back to the Amazon. The sun seems to linger, and the fading colours of the day create kaleidoscopic patterns in the bow-waves As darkness falls, the trees lose their rich diversity and merge into one solid, inky-black wall. The only thing that's missing is the sense of being on a river. Though we're snug against one bank, the other is over one and a half kilometres away.

Below · *Sunset colours the Tapajós River.*

Day 9 · Belém

YOU HAVE TO make an early start to catch the fish market in Belém. But it's worth it. In keeping with the Brazilian penchant for nicknames, the market complex is called Ver-o-Peso – 'See the Weight' – for it was here in the days of the Portuguese that goods for sale were weighed to assess the taxes payable. Now it's a wonderland of stalls selling fruits of the Amazon, religious charms and potions, T-shirts, jewellery and as rich, exotic and complex a selection of *polpa de frutas* – fruit juices – as I've ever seen. But it's the fish that are the stars of Belém Market.

Belém stands at the southern portal of the Amazon delta. Its opposite number, Macapá, is 350 kilometres (220 miles) away to the north. A casual look at an atlas will show that it is the last city on the river. A closer look will show that Belém is in fact not on the Amazon at all. The wide stream that flows past the market is the Rio Guamá, a tributary of the mighty River Tocantins, which is itself a tributary of the Amazon. Not perhaps so surprising, then, that the Amazon's outflow is of greater volume than all the rivers of Europe put together. Over 770,000 cubic metres (170 billion gallons) of river water is disgorged into the ocean every *hour*. Nearly fifty-seven million gallons every second. The clay-brown plume of the Amazon stretches 400 kilometres (250 miles) into the Atlantic.

Geographically epic as its location might be, Belém is a place of few pretensions. Its long history has created a multi-layered city which has some grand buildings but no grand gestures. Like a well-lined face it betrays a life of hard-earned experience rather than easy comfort. Nowhere is this better demonstrated than down by the jetties where the fish are brought in. On two sides of the waterfront are old colonial houses with tall first-floor windows, ironwork balconies and colourful, tiled exteriors. On the roofs of these bright facades the black turkey vultures gather, shifting from leg to leg and occasionally opening their wings as they wait for the fish to be unloaded. Some are already down on the ground, tearing away at piles of discarded entrails on the side of the solid stone jetties. The fishermen's boats are small and, like the houses, brightly coloured. They will have come in from the scattering of islands to the north and west of Belém, bringing the produce of the *ribeirinhos* – not only fish, but fruits and vegetables too. All around baskets are being unloaded, often by chains of men tossing them ashore. Much of the produce is sold from upturned boxes beside the boats themselves. The fish is either gutted on the spot – skin scraped, tails chopped off, innards flung into the water or snatched in the greedy beaks of the vultures – or sold untouched, the lines still sticking out of their mouths. The jetties are hosed down by council workers in the orange overalls of the Prefeitura de Belém, but the water is treated like a rubbish dump, with all manner of filthy debris sloshing around, trapped between the boats and the harbour wall.

Set back a little from the quayside and looking like a small fortified town is the covered fish market, constructed of Glaswegian ironwork and opened in 1901. It

1

2

3

has a wide, square, floor plan with silver-grey iron walls, cormorants perched on the roof, and, at all four corners, pointed iron turrets covered in fish-scale tiling. Despite the jauntiness of its appearance, there is an air of serious purpose about the Mercado Ver-o-Peso, to which I'm initiated by my guide to Belém, Priscila Brasil. And that's her real name. Priscila is quite short, with a pale complexion, dark hair and lively dark eyes. Born and brought up in Belém, she's at one time or other been an architect and a documentary film-maker, and currently she's managing one of the hottest properties in the local, and hopefully national, music business.

With us is a tall, well-built youngish man with a fine head of hair and a broad brow which overhangs deep, coal-black eyes. With his wide shoulders tapering to a wafer-thin waist, Thiago Castanho looks like a film star but is in fact a culinary

4

5

star, owner of two of the most fashionable restaurants in the city. He's here to buy lunch for us and a couple of hundred others. There is plenty of choice, with 2,000 species of fish in the Amazon Basin. This profusion is reflected in the overflowing white slabs that fill the main hall. The *pirarucu* is over two metres long and so big that it hangs down over the front of the stall. It has a lung which enables it to survive in oxygen-depleted water, but only at the expense of having to break the surface more frequently to take in air, which of course makes it a sitting target for fishermen. Others of impressive proportions are the *tambaqui* and the *filhote*. The latter is Thiago's favourite – big, fat, thick, juicy – and he discusses the finer points of today's catch with his regular supplier before buying some enormous fillets. There's a constant coming and going beneath this great iron-ribbed roof. Men and women tasting the prawns, looking quizzically at the *surubim* with their intricate black and silver stripes, gauging the freshness of the piranha, sampling *tacacá*, shrimp soup straight from the bowl, or admiring the shining gold and black *tucumari*. One man, wearing a beatific smile, walks around banging two lavatory seats together. I'm mesmerized but no one else seems to give him a second look.

Having made his choice, Thiago leads us through to his favoured fruit stall. It's run by a large lady in late middle age, wearing the cling-wrap hair cover obligatory for anyone involved in the food trade. She's stacking a pile of what look like coconuts but actually are brazil nuts still arranged, like segments of an orange, in the hard shell in which they grow. I'd never seen them in their natural state before, but as I make to touch she waves me away, fiercely. And the camera even more fiercely. But once she knows we're friends of Thiago she warms up and starts to ply us with all sorts of exotica. I recognise the *pupunha*, the fruit from which the Yanomami made their celebratory brew, and also the little hairy red fruits from the juice of which they made their body paint. I try a *cupuracu*, a soft, rather heavy taste, *acai*, the so-called wonder-fruit whose fame has spread far beyond the Amazon, and something embedded inside the tendril of a liana which has to be twisted open to reveal the fruit beneath. I'm sure there is huge goodness in all these rainforest fruits but it's an acquired taste, and I found some

***Opposite:* 1** · *Unloading fruit on the waterfront at Belém. Turreted market building in the background.* **2** · *Fish-gutting is popular with the turkey vultures.* **3** · *Fishing boats from the mouth of the Amazon crowd in.* **4** · Filhote*, pride of the Amazon.* **5** · *Thiago talks big fish to Priscila and me.*

1

2

of them rather smooth and glutinous compared to the crispy citrus with which I'm more familiar.

Leaving Thiago to make his purchases we move on, sampling many of the Amazon fruits in juiced form, at the popular *polpa da frutas* stalls. *Bacuri, murici, graviola, tucumã, manga, maracujá*. Not a single one I'd ever heard of. And not a single one was I allowed to miss out on by the large, persuasive ladies who made them up.

It seems that most of the Mercado Ver-o-Peso is run by big, assertive women of a certain age. Priscila nods. 'You're right. Women are strong in the Amazon,' she tells me.

Which is how the Amazon got its name in the first place. In the early 1540s, a Spanish expedition under Francisco de Orellana, in the course of a remarkable river journey *eastwards* from the Andes to the sea, found itself fighting a tribe, large numbers of which were women. So effective were they that Orellana likened them to the legendary warriors of Greek literature, known as the Amazons, women who were so honed to warfare that they had no right breast, enabling them to hold their bows and arrows with greater control. This encounter made such an impression on Orellana that he named the river after his adversaries.

As if to emphasize the fact, Priscila takes me to another part of the market where African and Indian charms, herbs and potions are sold by two more strong Amazon women, a mother and daughter. They have bottles, powders, natural oils, barks and leaves. 'Preparations for the body and the spirit,' as Priscila, a frequent user of these traditional medicines, puts it.

She's a great believer in one mixture which can be used for almost anything from shampoo to the relief of arthritis. Their top sellers, somewhat predictably, are 'natural Viagra' and an oil that provides 'baths for love'.

We meet up with Thiago again for lunch at his newly opened, very chic restaurant, Remanso do Bosque, opposite the Botanic Gardens. By this time he is in his starched white chef's apron with his name embroidered on it. He describes our starter. Shrimp with *acai* sauce and fried tapioca. All traditional ingredients, but the way of cooking is his own creation. As we eat, I ask Priscila about her city, and once again the word 'traditional' comes up. Belém was the first city of the Amazon.

3

4

Founded by the Portuguese in 1616 as the City of Our Lady of Bethlehem, it grew rich from slavery long before it became rich from rubber. Though the port of Belém was the indisputable hub of Amazon trade, it was, on the land-side, cut off from the rest of Brazil. Blown north by favourable trade winds, ships from Belém could reach Europe faster than they could Rio, and there was no overland alternative.

'We are very traditional because of our isolation,' Priscila maintains. 'We keep our things as they were. We talk different. We use the old Portuguese that people in the south don't use any more.'

After the rubber boom ended Belem fell into serious decline. Manaus, its great rival, was made a Free Trade Area in the 1960s, and is now connected to the south via a fast new road. And just to rub it in came the decision that Manaus would be the only Amazon city to host a World Cup game.

None of this worries Priscila that much. Brazil's great quality, as she sees it, is its tolerance. The country is vast but its diversity is a source of pride. The North is 'totally different' from the South and yet they are all first and foremost Brazilians. And she does detect a growing interest in the Amazon from people in the rest of the country. They are no longer just looking north for exploitation of the resources. They are seeing in the vast state of Amazonas a rich mix of tribes and a respect for their way of life which they hadn't appreciated before. Our talk turns again to a familiar topic.

'Most of the strong people in the Amazon are women. The power is in them. Men don't talk so much. They keep their place.' She laughs, and stabs a fork in my direction. 'Tomorrow you're going to meet Gaby' – Gaby Amarantos is the name of the rising musical star she represents – 'and you are going to understand the power of Amazon women. You will see, it's not only a legend. It's true.'

The dashing Thiago makes his way over to ask our opinion of the meal so far.

And I realize that throughout our short acquaintance it's Thiago, as fine a specimen of Brazilian manhood as you could wish to meet, who has been the quiet one, and little Priscila the one with the opinions and the confidence to put them across.

***Opposite:* 1** · *Ver-o-Peso Market, Belém. Thiago's favourite fruit and veg stall.* **2** · *'Preparations for the body and spirit'.* ***Above:* 3** · *Fresh produce isn't a problem in the Amazon delta. New arrivals from the fertile islands.* **4** · *How it all looks on the plate. Thiago serves us at his restaurant.*

Day 10 · Belém

FIRST THING THIS MORNING I take a stroll in the Praça da República, a sort of open-air museum of what the rubber boom meant to Belém. Although it can't seem to make up its mind whether it's a park or a tropical rainforest, it has an evocative air of celebration about it.

As in Manaus, there is a fine opera house at its centre, called the Teatro da Paz, with columned porticoes and loggias. In front of it is an impressive, if somewhat neglected, statue celebrating peace. On top a woman in swirling cloak brandishes a sword and on the plinth below are commemorated heroes of Brazil's struggle for independence from Portugal. Though independence was granted in 1822, Brazil didn't get rid of the monarchy and become a Republic until 1889. All the old buildings in the Praça hark back to Europe. In celebrating their break from nearly four hundred years of Portuguese rule, the burghers of Belém chose to make their city look more like Lisbon than ever.

There are two bandstands, both of elegantly fashioned green ironwork. The finest of them has been beautifully restored with a wood-block ceiling and an elegantly curved roof with a cupola above it, topped by a wrought-iron harp. As I walk past, marvelling at its elegance, a foot rises slowly above the parapet, stretches, then withdraws. A moment later a thin column of smoke rises from the same place. I peer tentatively round the side and there's a young homeless black man lying on the floor with a thin sheet over him and the first cigarette of the day between his fingers.

Beyond the Praça, multi-storey apartment blocks seem to have taken over the city. Stained and grimy from the heavy rainfall, they make Belém look less like Lisbon and more like Calcutta. Both are at the heart of big river deltas, and concrete and high humidity don't mix well, creating the impression of cities going mouldy.

At street level though, life is vibrant, visible and noisy. To sample it, Priscila takes me to meet her very special client, the Queen of Technobrega, Gaby Amarantos. Gaby lives in a side street in a predominantly black area of town. Outside her house, boys are kicking a football about and two men are loading up a wooden cart with what look like old circuit boards. There's a constant procession of people being dropped off by the private Kombi-taxis that pull up at the junction with the main road. Cars go by with huge speaker systems on their roof-racks, blasting out invitations to listen to a new radio station, or visit a new club or, more often than not, just go to a party. Every door, window and balcony on every house has a security grille attached.

Gaby owns two houses in one and access is through a warren of rooms in which various members of her family live. There are religious pictures on the walls of the rooms we pass through on our way up to the first floor. From there we step out onto a spiral staircase bolted, rather perilously, to the outside of the

Above · *Gaby Amarantos, Queen of Technobrega, in one of her dressing rooms.*

building. This leads us up to the top of the house and at last I see a few glimpses of Gaby's profession: a rail of costumes, a clock with the Beatles' *Abbey Road* album cover on its face, a wicker frame for a skirt, feather headdresses and, on a low table, a music magazine with what I assume is Gaby's likeness on the cover. A well-built woman with arm raised and fist clenched, her strong, striking features contorted into a mock snarl.

We eventually find Gaby in a cramped dressing room, entirely surrounded by clothes on rails, shoes on racks and props on shelves. The camera has not lied. Even sitting amongst all this stuff she is a powerful physical presence. Her glance is shrewd and penetrating and a little guarded. As she looks me up and down I feel as if I'm being frisked, and only when she breaks into an unexpectedly warm smile do I feel I've passed the test. I'd expected a younger woman. A starlet. Instead I'm looking at a mother not far short of forty, someone who's seen an awful lot of life already and for whom fame is something that happens to other people.

I ask her if, growing up here in Belém, she'd ever expected to be a national star, featured in magazines and selling out concerts. She turns her big, wide eyes towards me. 'I was born a star,' she replies, without an ounce of conceit. 'We were a samba family. There was music everywhere. I grew up with the sounds of the neighbourhood.' Her mother was a pillar of the local Catholic church, another element in her musical upbringing.

Success didn't fall from the sky. She'd been working and playing for fifteen years before pioneering Technobrega, a fusion of Brega, a style of fairly cheesy romantic songs from the North and North-East, with computers, keyboards and

Above · *Gabby at work. Stomping, shaking and gyrating.*

electronic music. Now she's being dubbed the Beyoncé of the Amazon, profiled in *Elle* and *Vogue* and in demand in Rio, São Paulo and as far south as Porto Alegre. She remains very proud of her Amazon Indian heritage. It's given her *a força*, the Force, that self-belief which kept her going and is now exciting the audiences across the country.

'It's like the power of nature,' enthuses Priscila, 'which explodes on stage, and makes everyone fall in love with her.'

Priscila, I have to remind myself, is Gaby's manager, but when we all assemble for a show at the Club do Remo, backing onto the river, I see exactly what she means. A crisp, six-piece backing band warms up the audience – mostly female, early twenties, with more than a smattering of gay men. Gaby strides in like a goddess, wearing hot pants, shiny red high-heeled boots and a tight grey-and-white Lurex bodice. Her already impressive height is emphasized by a plume of feathers and her long hair hangs low down her back. Stomping, shaking and gyrating, she pounds out the numbers with a defiant sexiness that leaves no doubt as to who's in control. The audience dance frantically, single women miming her movements with an electric intensity, flinging themselves about, charged up and released by the rousing imperiousness of her delivery, and the exhilaration of her message.

This is indeed a force of nature at work. She's like a Boadicea for our times. An Amazon warrior reborn.

Day 11 · Belém

OUR LAST MORNING in this beguiling city. As we drive away from the hotel, police are clustered around a vagrant on one of the benches outside the Teatro da Paz. As I look closer I see the vagrant is a woman with a patch over one eye and a baby in her arms. A tall, well-dressed man walks by without breaking step. He's reading a piece of paper very close to his face and has a tiny dog on a lead far below him. Then they're lost behind the mango trees that line Presidente Vargas Avenue, as we turn and head for the waterfront. We're joining a boat which will be taking a twenty-strong cello orchestra out across the river to some of the nearby islands. The cellists are all teenagers, many from tough, poorly educated backgrounds, who get together every now and then to visit outlying areas of the city to introduce people to their music.

They're called the Orquestra Juvenil de Violoncelistas da Amazônia, or the Amazon Cello Choir for short. It's the brainchild of another force of nature, male this time, called Áureo de Freitas, a, wiry, restless, forty-five-year-old cello teacher. He has persuaded a company to sponsor a mini-ferry on this voyage to the islands and he is fussing about arranging the chairs and the speaker system on which he'll be playing a backing track. The children, whose only qualification is that they should have had no previous musical training, are dressed in uniform black T-shirts with a green cello on the front and their names on the back. It's already hot and many of the cellos lie propped up against the chairs, with towels over them for protection, looking like elderly sunbathers.

Once out into the stream, with the fancy turrets of the Ver-o-Peso Market receding behind us, they rehearse their repertoire. It consists of a beautiful Bach Prelude, which suddenly, violently, and for no reason I can see, breaks into Led Zeppelin's 'Kashmir', at which point the young musicians leap to their feet and thrash away at their cellos in rock and roll style. On paper it sounds pretty ghastly but on the boat in the middle of the river, with the sun on the waters and the forested shores of the first island coming closer, it is actually quite thrilling. Proud parents are on board to film their children. The local TV channel is reporting on it. And the cellos, for some inexplicable reason, are a job lot of 300 sent out by Kent County Council.

'They were all messed up,' says Áureo. But repairs were made and he was able to offer them very cheaply to the families of the children.

We've crossed the wide river and entered a narrow channel which leads into the heart of the island. After so many days on the wide open spaces of the Amazon system this is a revelation. The narrow waters wind, most picturesquely, past small clapboard houses on stilts from which the local fishermen and their families come out to watch us pass. Children are diving off wooden piers, nets are drying, clothes are being hung out on a washing line strung between two palm trees. Some of the braver children race alongside us through the trees. Then,

1

2

3

Above: ***1*** *· The Amazon Cello Choir. Each player has their own named T-shirt.* ***2*** *· The Choir in Led Zeppelin mode.* ***3*** *· On the waterway through the islands.*

as we round a bend, Áureo raises his bow, nods his head, and the music begins, augmented by a pumping playback track. The boat slows, the sound of massed cellos sends birds flying out of the trees. Ahead of us is a small settlement of palm-thatched huts beside a green-and-white-painted Pentecostal church. A group of villagers gather curiously as, suddenly and explosively, Led Zeppelin crashes out over the forest. Áureo leads from the front, urging, cajoling and flinging himself into the music.

Mouths and eyes are open wide as we chug slowly towards the village, but it's hard to tell if it's inspiring them or scaring the life out of them. To me it's a little too close to *Apocalypse Now* for comfort, and I think everyone's a lot happier when they go into their Beatles medley.

Áureo is unashamedly Messianic about what he's doing. 'The cello has become the most popular instrument in Belém,' he raves. 'The other night in the

4

5

6

Praça da República 10,000 people cheered for us. It was wonderful.'

He echoes what Priscila was saying about Belém's feeling of isolation from the rest of Brazil. Indicating the orchestra behind him, he asks, 'Our window opens to Europe and to the US. Why is it that only last year we go to São Paulo?' He grins at the memory. To save money they'd gone by bus. It had taken them two and a half days.

Though we've only come as far Belém's offshore islands, this glimpse of rural riverbank life is tantalizing. Once the cellos are stilled there is a peace and serenity and intimacy about these settlements that I haven't sensed anywhere else on the magnificent but overwhelmingly huge rivers of the Amazon.

It's all over too soon. The skies are darkening ahead of another deluge, and we're turning and heading as fast as we can back up the channel and onto the wide grey waters of the Guamá. The huts on stilts lie behind us. Ahead is the high-rise skyline of the city and a plane rising slowly from the airport.

*Above: **4** · Bringing music to the backwoods. **5** · Not everybody listens. **6** · But many do.*

Day 12 · Wauja Village, Upper Xingu River

YET ANOTHER of the many tributaries of the Amazon is the Xingu, which flows for almost 2,000 kilometres (1,240 miles) north from Mato Grosso, in the very heart of Brazil, to join the Amazon some 400 kilometres (250 miles) west of Belém. A combination of serious rapids and a lack of gold and other tempting minerals effectively kept adventurers and prospectors at bay and it wasn't until the 1880s that anyone from the outside world permeated the Upper Xingu. John Hemming gives an account of the twenty-nine-year-old German anthropologist Karl von den Steinen, on the day he and his expedition first made contact with the indigenous people. 'They walked up a forest trail away from the river for almost an hour, in silence and increasingly apprehensive about what awaited them. The expedition suddenly entered a clearing with three enormous thatched huts. An Indian youth emerged and came towards them. One of Steinen's frightened Bakairi (guides) spoke in Carib and, to everyone's relief, was understood and answered. The two young men walked forward, leaning against one another and embracing, "both talking at once, and both trembling all over their bodies from a mixture of fear and excitement"'.

Much has changed for the peoples of the Xingu between then and now, but as our single-prop plane drops down towards a thin, cleared strip in the midst of hundreds of kilometres of rainforest I experience some of that same apprehension that gripped Steinen's expedition 128 years ago. There are still no roads below us and, apart from a clearing at the end of the runway, the forest seems all-encompassing. We touch down, bounce and rumble to a halt at the point where the runway meets the village. There must be twenty huts ahead of me, and they are indeed, as Steinen found them, enormous, every one as big as an upturned ship's hull, thatched from roof to ground, and none with any apertures save a tiny triangular entrance cut in front and back.

For a moment all is quiet. Then, as I clamber out onto the wing of the aircraft, I hear a distant chanting, growing louder by the minute. I jump down onto a surface of dried mud and look up to see what appears like a war party coming towards me. All men, their nearly naked bodies covered with red and black markings and adorned with clusters of leaves and feathers on their ankles, upper arms and through their ears. Impressive in their unity and harmony, they move towards me, swinging from side to side, with a menacing, crouching stance, an insistent, thumping step and a high-pitched chant. Then, when they're almost upon me, they break step, becoming instantly amiable and welcoming, talking and shaking hands with me and all the crew. Curious women and children, also almost naked, watch from the sidelines. In the middle of the welcoming party is a pale-skinned Western woman wearing a billowing blue shirt, black pants and a floppy straw hat.

__Opposite__ · Bird's eye view of the Wauja village as we approach its red-earth runway. __Below: 1__ · Is it a welcome? Is it a war dance? __2 -3__ · The children stay cool as I meet the Wauja elders.

1

2

3

Her name is Emi Ireland, an American anthropologist who lived with this Wauja community fifteen years ago and has learnt their language. With her are two other non-Wauja, one of them a visiting American, photographing everything, and the other a Brazilian film-maker, his pale legs covered in bites. From being nervous of meeting the Wauja I now find myself feeling a twinge of disappointment that the outside world is much more visible here than amongst the Yanomami.

The difference, of course, is that the Wauja have had seventy more years of contact with the outside world. And they were fortunate enough to be infiltrated by anthropologists rather than gold prospectors. In 1945 two brothers from São Paulo, Orlando and Claudio Villas Boas, came to the Upper Xingu on a government project and were so taken with the people and the way they lived that they made their homes amongst them. In 1961 the Villas Boas brothers were instrumental in setting up a protected area and now the Xingu Indigenous Park covers 22,000 square kilometres (8,500 square miles). Their policy of change 'but only at the pace the Indians want' has been largely successful and the number of indigenous people has increased fourfold since the 1960s.

Emi walks us through the village to the hut where we shall be staying, first of all correcting me quite severely for calling it a hut. And of course she's right. Some of these constructions, clad from rooftop to the ground in thatch, are as long as a manor house and as tall as a church nave. They're laid out in a wide circle facing onto a central arena. Much of the domestic activity takes place where the houses back onto the forest. From here tracks lead to the gardens and to the washing pool. There are also the 'alligator paths', so called because these are where young men of courting age lie in wait for girls coming out from the houses and home in on them like the proverbial alligator. The hardy reptile, unattractive as it might look, is often used as a sexual image among the Wauja.

The only house in the middle of the central plaza is the men's house, where the ceremonial flutes are stored, and where the men gather daily to chat, make jokes and prepare for various ceremonial activities. It has more elaborate decoration than the others, with a web of tree roots sticking out horizontally from each end of the roof beam. These are called the 'earrings' of the house and they are the architectural equivalent of the sharpened wooden pins that the men wear through their ears and whose tips are decorated with feathers.

We sit on one of the long tree trunks laid on the ground to watch a ceremonial dance. This is performed by men, women and some of the children. Everyone has their bodies painted, but the men and boys have flamboyant extras like multi-coloured belts and toucan and macaw feathers attached to leggings and armbands. Their hair is like the Yanomami, covered in the brilliant red paint of the *urucum* flower. It's cut in identical black fringes and their faces have black line markings. The women, more modestly decorated, wear their long hair down to the waist and have swirling abstract black patterns painted on their legs.

Women are banned from the men's house and are, for instance, forbidden to see the sacred flutes. The men catch the fish that is such an important part of the diet, but it is all taken to the men's house and divided out amongst them before being distributed to the women. In practice this means that women do not always get the food they need to feed their children properly.

Opposite *· With Emi Ireland, who has known the Wauja for thirty years, outside the men's house.*
Above *· The dance of the Kagapa. All about catching fish.*

1

2

3

4

It's now the start of the wet season, a difficult time of year for the Wauja. Though manioc is available all year round their fish stock is low. As the rivers swell and rise it is, as Emi puts it, 'like shooting fish in the ocean'. Come the dry season, on the other hand, 'it's like shooting fish in a barrel'.

The dance they perform for us is, suitably, a dance about catching fish. Some of the dancers are wearing leaves and grass skirts as they enact the search for a small bait-fish that hides amongst the leaves. If it can be found it is auspicious because it will lead them to the big fish. This dance of the Kagapa is usually performed in the dry season. I ask Emi if they're laying it on just for us. She nods. 'Sure. For them it's like celebrating Christmas in August.'

It's very hot by now and there's no shade at all in the centre of the village. The Wauja, untroubled, continue to move and sing and dance in their sweeping circular patterns and I can only marvel at their persistence. Emi looks on with some admiration. In some respects things are a lot better for the tribe than when she came here thirty years ago. 'They haven't had a village this big for 100 years.'

The numbers of the Wauja are still small, 400 altogether, in three villages. But thirty years ago they were down to 200. Watching them now, swirling and turning in the dance, it seems almost inconceivable that they should have come that close to extinction. But though epidemics of measles and influenza and the depredations of malaria are a thing of the past, tuberculosis, diabetes, drug and alcohol abuse in the border towns were all unknown to the Wauja when Emi first came here.

Opposite: ***1*** *· The percussion team.* ***2*** *· The dancing can last several hours.* ***3*** *· Women join in to help the men in the search for the fish.* ***4*** *· Itsautaku.*

Itsautaku, the shaman, is a shortish man with a yellow feather headdress and a string of white shells around his neck. He has a serious, almost pained expression and holds a clutch of arrows and spears slightly taller than himself. He, more than anyone, embodies the continuity of the Wauja. His grandfather was a great chief at a time when the tribe had been practically wiped out by a series of epidemics which Emi likens to the great plagues in Europe during the Middle Ages. The people were left too weak to bury the dead and those who survived gathered together in one village for protection. Even then they were not immune to further outbreaks of disease, such as a devastating measles epidemic in 1954. But now they have vaccines and the numbers have begun to build. Emi smiles as she remembers when she first came here. 'Many of the people I knew as children now have ten or eleven children of their own and they ask me, "How come you only have two?"'

The dance goes on much of the afternoon, with varying numbers of participants. When it finally stops refreshments are brought out. I find myself included and offered chicken and chilli in a manioc pancake. Itsautaku gravely invites me to visit his house and talk with him tomorrow.

In the early evening a most important part of our visit takes place, the giving of presents as thanks to the tribe for their hospitality. Once upon a time weapons, like guns for hunting, would have been a popular choice, but now it's something different. The Wauja have become so used to being filmed that they have become curious about the process and want to make films for themselves about their own culture. Marcelo Fiorini, the Brazilian who came out to greet us this morning, is here to teach them how to do it. A mat is laid out in front of the men's house and our director, John-Paul, displays what he has brought, including a laptop, an editing programme and various other video and computer accessories. The Wauja men investigate them quite critically. The days when a few lengths of cloth and some biscuit tins would have been accepted unconditionally are long gone. As Emi points out, many of the tribe have learnt Portuguese at school, and some have been to university. The village has its own communications centre, with a satellite dish powered by solar panels and a short-wave radio, vital, among other things, for keeping in touch with their villages and those of other scattered tribes.

1

2

Above: 1 *· Our director, John-Paul, and Emi with the computers they wanted us to bring as gifts.* ***2*** *· Food on offer outside the men's house.* ***Opposite: 3*** *· The morning after. Repairing the roof after a downpour.* ***4*** *· Cooking fires inside make the long-house look like a bonfire.* ***5*** *· Bikes and motorbikes have changed life here.*

By the time the presents have been assessed and accepted, darkness is falling and the flies are biting. We cook ourselves some food in our guest house and sit outside on tree stumps in the moonlight until one by one we wash at our single standpipe and take to our hammocks. It's too hot inside the house to close the entrances at either end and, as I lie gently swinging, I'm aware of bats swooping in and out and around the tall-beamed roof above me.

I find food for thought in a book Basil has lent me, *The Adventures and Misadventures of Maqroll*, by Álvaro Mutis. 'There is no mystery to the jungle, regardless of what some people think. It's just what you've seen. No more, no less. Simple, direct, uniform, malevolent...Time is confused, laws are forgotten, joy is unknown and sadness has no place.'

In the middle of the night there's a terrific downpour and water drips in through a hole in the roof.

Day 13 · Wauja Village, Upper Xingu River

I GET UP EARLY and walk into the village. Past the schoolroom, with desks laid out on a concrete floor, past a pick-up truck and a tractor in a state of disrepair. Two children, one pushing the other in a metal wheelbarrow, giggle as they catch my eye. A solitary figure rides a bicycle across the plaza. Overnight fires are still burning in several of the houses. There being no central chimneys, the smoke finds its way out from any available hole in the thatch, giving the impression of entire buildings gently steaming. On one of the houses a man is repairing the roof. A tiny figure against a wall of thatch. There is a ladder below him up which his young son carries fresh lengths of dried grass. The houses look so solid and secure that I'm surprised to learn that they only last about ten years before having to be rebuilt again.

After breakfast I accompany Emi and the women and children on a washing party. A well-trodden track leads through the manioc gardens for nearly a kilometre before petering out in the swampy banks of a pool, overhung with trees and bushes. The children skip excitedly across the mud and leap into the murky waters.

3

4

5

Emi wades in after them and I follow her, both of us fully clad. I don't think the children see this sort of thing very often and it seems to make them even more animated. Whilst they splash and jump about the women, standing up to their waists in the water, set to the washing. Emi tells me they love soap and shampoo, so there's much washing of hair, clothes and bodies. By the time we wade out the sun has strengthened and dries me out on the walk back to the village.

There had been talk of my accompanying the men on a fishing party, but at this time of year it would mean a half-day's walk, at least. They also hunt birds and monkeys but these are much harder to catch, especially since the Brazilian government passed a law forbidding the use of guns. A law which, Emi points out, was intended to deal with gun crime on city streets. It had never occurred to anyone that it might deprive legitimate hunters like the Wauja of a source of food.

Instead of hunting and fishing I spend the rest of the morning watching how their most staple food, manioc, is prepared. It's grown in the gardens around the camp and can be harvested at any time of the year. The women dig the tubers up and bring them to an open-sided thatched 'kitchen' where the brown-skinned, foot-long tubers are painstakingly transformed into pancakes. There's much suppressed mirth today because I'm going to be helping them out, and men just don't do this sort of work. I'm put on to peeling first and given what looks like a shallow metal dish with which to scrape away the husk. It's quite satisfying work,

Above · *The morning bath and laundry combined.*
Opposite: 1-2 · *Learning the art of manioc-grating.*
3 · *The final touch to my manioc pancake.*
4 · *Waste disposal.*
5 · *Young Wauja tills the soil.*

and soon I've a pile of ivory-white, freshly stripped lengths of manioc beside me. I'm promoted to grating now, and, although I didn't know it at the time, this is rich in comic potential. I'm sat, legs apart, in front of a rectangular metal grille and shown how to grasp the manioc tuber firmly and then to push backwards and forwards in a regular rhythm, until it's whittled away. This I do, to mounting smiles and laughter and, I like to think, a certain muted admiration. The more energetically I grate, the more they urge me on, and it's perhaps just as well that it's only after I've finished that I realize manioc-grating and the sexual act require exactly the same technique.

Such is my entertainment value that I'm moved swiftly on to the next stage of the process. This involves breaking down the hard manioc powder, after which I'm led to the fire and shown how to spread this powder onto a red-hot pan without scorching the tips of my fingers. Not an easy task, as there's a draught coming through, causing the smoke to billow back in my face, so my eyes are running and I can barely see what I'm doing. This is the highlight of the gringo cooking demonstration and is met, not with concern for the welfare of my fingers, but with renewed hoots of laughter. Emi explains, as kindly as she can. 'They say that if the smoke gets in your eyes it's a sign that your wife is with another man.'

Well, whoever my wife is with, I turn out a pretty mean pancake. And, according to Emi, my skills have not gone unappreciated. 'They say you will make a very good husband,' she reassures me, adding, a little unnecessarily, 'for the older women.'

1

2

3

4

5

In the afternoon, Emi and I go to see the shaman. Along with his fellow elders like the Songmaster and the Bowmaster, he is the man with the power in the village. His house is like a great barn inside and dotted around are numerous pieces of beautifully worked local ceramics, as well as ornamental beadwork belts and mats and magnificently woven hammocks. As we talk, a parrot hops about on a carved bench beside us. Like Davi, the spokesman of the Yanomami, Itsautaku has a canny awareness that things are changing. He too embraces the outside world, but only on equal terms. Both sides must understand and respect each other's culture. The Wauja, like other rainforest tribes, believe in a spirit world which controls their lives. The spirits may lie in people or in objects. They are sometimes good, sometimes bad, but they must be constantly propitiated. The dances we have seen are 'vessels for the spirit', and by performing them they propitiate those spirits whose co-operation they need for everything from good health to food, fertility and protection from their enemies. It's what we call religion. When we start to talk about the modern world and the conservation of the environment, Itsautaku speaks on behalf of all the Xingu peoples. Emi translates.

***Opposite:** 1 · The magnificent thatched houses. **2** · With the shaman, Itsautaku, surrounded by the handiwork of the villagers. **3** · A glimpse of their ancestors. The Wauja watch slides from the Rondon expedition of 1924.*

'They know the outsiders want their land. They know that they don't want to be good stewards of it. They know they will despoil it and leave it.'

The damming of rivers in the Xingu Basin bears out their fears. Anything that deliberately cuts off the flow of water to their rivers affects their ability to fish and to grow crops. More worrying is the recent increase in fires caused by the heating-up and drying-out of the 'under-storey': that dark lower layer of the rainforest. Climate change is one factor, but this is aggravated by any artificial constriction of the rivers. And yet this seems to be government policy now. The Belo Monte dam project in the eastern Amazon will be, says Emi, 'The third largest dam in human history,' adding, 'and the scientists say it makes no sense whatever in terms of energy efficiency.'

Whatever the arguments, the Wauja, like every other tribe that has lived in the rainforest so successfully for thousands of years, feel deeply threatened by these operations. They have set up vigilance posts to guard their territory, but as more huge schemes are green-lighted they can sense that there's not much that 400 can do to influence a government needing energy for 200 million.

In other confrontations with the Western world, Itsautaku shows that he and his sons are by no means naive. He talks at some length about what Emi translates as 'intellectual property rights' – that those who come to take pictures of life among the Wauja should enter into some agreement to give the tribe some control over the way their images are used. This is why he is encouraging the young men to learn how to take films and pictures themselves. As he says, the Wauja have been studied by anthropologists for a hundred years now, but though they took their pictures, they never took their names.

Itsautaku fixes us with a look of heartfelt intensity. 'What I want, above all, is a picture of my father.'

1

2

3

Arapawa, the soft-spoken, well-educated son of the shaman, feels very strongly that one of the most important protections for the indigenous people is the documentation of their history and culture, in the same way that the white Westerners document theirs. To this end, he's been working for thirteen years on the compilation of the first ever Wauja dictionary, which he hopes will be translated into Portuguese and then English.

After dark, a screen is set up in the centre of the village onto which Emi and Marcelo project photographs of the Wauja taken by the Rondon expedition of 1924. Most of the village are sitting out in front of the screen, and there are occasional shouts of laughter, recognition and a general buzz of discussion about how they look and how they cut their hair. With clam shells in those days, I'm told. It's quite something, to see a small, once endangered people so absorbed in discovering their past. Emi, Marcelo, Arapawa and Itsautaku have all told me that this sense of their own identity is the Wauja's best defence against an uncertain future. Watching them under a cloudless night sky, with the glow of the screen reflected in their eyes, makes me feel that something quite significant is happening here, something quite inspiring.

Day 14 · Upper Xingu → Brasília

Above · My pilot in the Xingu, Gerard Moss. ***Opposite*** *· Ox-bow lakes everywhere as the rivers wind slowly through the forest.*

AFTER WE STRIKE our hammocks and pack our bags, an impromptu market takes place outside our guest house. It begins with a group of curious boys gathering round Nigel, taking turns at looking down the viewfinder of his camera. Then word gets out that we've decided to leave behind our towels, hammocks and some of the food we brought with us. Soon there is a jostling crowd viewing what's on offer. It's very different from the day we arrived. This is not some official welcome organized by the elders, this is shopping. Instead of feathered armbands and grass skirts there are long shorts and striped T-shirts, and many of the women, almost naked as we made manioc together, are wearing print dresses this morning. Hammocks, blankets, pots and pans are bartered for ceramics, bead decorations, local oil for skin protection. Two Wauja arrows are exchanged for a head-torch.

Our two planes are ready to leave by mid-morning. Emi will be staying behind for a few more days. For her the Wauja are family, and they treasure her too. She tells me that the idea of kinship is very important in the village. There are so few Wauja here and in the two other villages that everyone is in some way related, and everyone is a cousin or an aunt or a brother-in-law. She was made very aware of this when she took a small group of Wauja to São Paulo and every time she met anyone they would ask how they were related to her.

I sense that we have been more deeply affected by the contact than our hosts. They're now back to getting on with their lives and there's markedly less interest in our departure than our arrival. Apart from a last look through the camera for a young Wauja in a Beatles T-shirt.

We climb away from the village and out across the rainforest, an environment which my pilot, Gerard Moss, knows as well as anybody. A tall, pale, mustachioed, rather dashing figure, Gerard is Swiss-born, married to an Englishwoman and living in Brasília. For the last ten years he has been criss-crossing the skies above the world's biggest rainforest for what he calls the Flying Rivers project. This involves gathering data on one of the least understood resources of the Amazon, the huge amount of energy emanating from the trees themselves. The forest as a rain machine.

He simplifies it for me. By process of evaporation every tree in the rainforest gives off somewhere between 300 and 1,000 litres of water each day. Averaging it out, this means that twenty billion tonnes of water is pumped, daily, into the skies above the Amazon Basin. Understanding the science will, he believes, lead to a much greater appreciation of the importance of the rainforest, not just for biodiversity or the world's climate but for the Brazilian economy. He's trying

1

2

Above: **1** · *A river on its way to join the Amazon, 2,500 kilometres (1,550 miles) north.* **2** · *The outskirts of Brasília have dug deep into the forest.* **Opposite** · *Brasília with its man-made lake, Paranoá.*

to push home the message that forest in place is worth considerably more to the country than forest destroyed. Ten years ago, he admits, it was a hard struggle to get any backing for his research. Since then, he says, there has been a 180-degree change of attitude, and people are listening. Unfortunately far too few of them are politicians. It's clear that Gerard has great respect for the power and beauty of the rainforest and an empathy for the people who live there. As we fly south-east towards our refuelling stop at Canarana, he banks the plane and points out the rivers we're crossing as if they're personal friends. The Rio das Mortes, snaking through the trees, clear and serene. The 2,500-kilometre-long (1,500 miles) Araguaia, a river which all Brazilians regard as especially and magically beautiful.

Because of its blessed combination of the Andes and the Amazon Basin, Brazil generates ninety-five percent of its water needs without any recourse to dams or irrigation. This, together with abundant land and generally benign climate, gives it an enviable potential for cultivation on a huge scale.

'They say God is Brazilian,' he smiles, 'and sometimes you have to think it's true.'

By now, the forest cover is beginning to break up. Gerard's pointing out the cleared squares of land right up against the trees, testing the limit of the protected areas.

'What happens is that someone will buy some land that isn't protected, cut down the trees and sell it on to someone who'll put a few cows on it. And cows really don't do well on soil like that, so after a few years he'll sell it on to some big company for soya, which grows just about anywhere.'

I ask him if reforestation is an option, but he shakes his head adamantly. It's just too expensive. Better to use the money to save what's there already.

Below us now is the Planalto, a big, stable ancient rock-mass that covers almost half of Brazil. 'Nothing but farms from here to Porto Alegre,' says Gerard, half in wonder, half in sadness. Porto Alegre is, after all, over 2,000 kilometres (1,300 miles) from here. I look down at the colossal, treeless fields beneath and the sudden steep escarpments with waterfalls spilling off them and realize, to my regret, that after two weeks I've finally left the rainforest behind.

Day 15 · Brasília

MY HOTEL ROOM looks out over a wide stretch of water. Nothing much different there, except that, for the first time since I arrived in Brazil, this is not water that will eventually find its way into the Amazon. Sixty years ago it would not even have been here. I'm looking out on Lake Paranoá, artificially created in the late 1950s to provide precious humidity for a brand-new city called Brasília that was springing up on a treeless plateau, bone dry for six months of the year.

The principle of a new capital had been written into the Brazilian constitution from the earliest days of the Republic, but the idea of putting it in the interior, a long way from anywhere, was a brave and bold, and many people thought completely foolhardy, decision. But not Juscelino Kubitschek, the son of a Czech gypsy, who won the Presidency in 1956 with big ideas for Brazil and the rousing slogan 'Fifty Years in Five'. Within a year of taking office he had set up a planning group called NOVACAP and enlisted two resolute left-wing modernists, Lúcio Costa and Oscar Niemeyer, to design the new city. By the end of his Presidency in 1961 it was up and running. Which was not bad, bearing in mind that when work started the nearest railway was 125 kilometres (80 miles) away and a paved road 450 kilometres (280 miles) beyond that.

Stepping outside this morning, the air tastes and feels quite different from the north. We're nearly 1,200 metres above sea level, and it's dry and clear, with no hint of the lurking dark clouds that were always somewhere in the Amazon skies. And there's a sense of space that cities don't usually have.

Brasília's layout has been compared to an aeroplane, with the long central fuselage, called the Eixo Monumental (Monumental Axis), containing all the government buildings and coming to a point at the western end where Congress and finally the Presidential Palace are located. Along the Axis are the various auxiliary sectors, each one carefully delineated – the Hotel Sector, the Banking Sector, the Cultural Sector and so on. The residential areas, the *quadras*, extend along the 'wings' of the 'aeroplane' and fan out from the Eixo Rodoviário, the ring road. The streets have numbers rather than names, and a typical address might be 573 Norte, Bloco C, Loja 15. It's all rather daunting at first and I feel I need a human voice here.

I take a ride around the city with someone whose own birth just about coincided with the birth of Brasília. His name is Dinho Ouro Preto, and he's the lead singer with a band called Capital Inicial. Moving to Brasília as a teenager, he was drawn to punk rock in the eighties and now, in his late thirties, he's mellowed into New Wave. Slim, with jet-black hair and good-looking in a tidy way, he has lived in São Paulo since 1985. I want to know what it must have been like growing up at the heart of one of the great urban experiments of the twentieth century. Was it all wonderfully exciting?

He grimaces and thinks for a moment. 'In aesthetic terms I didn't like it that much. I thought it was something that separated people. That didn't take into account the individual. It was built by someone who believed in the collective idea.'

Which of course was deliberate. Kubitschek's choice of a brand-new capital was motivated by the need to build a symbol of a united Brazil, a Brazil for all the people, untainted by favour or fiction or past history. Salvador, the first capital,

1

2

Opposite *· Oscar Niemeyer's buildings, like the National Museum, are Brasília's trademark.*
Above: 1 *· With Dinho Ouro Preto in a VW Combi – part of his youth, now a piece of art.* ***2*** *· Visionary architecture. The atrium of the Royal Tulip Alvorada by Ruy Ohtake.*

and Rio the second, both had a weight of history behind them – a history, very often, of slavery and exploitation. Brasília was to be a new start, on neutral ground. Lúcio Costa, educated for a time at the Royal Grammar School, Newcastle, and the man charged with the overall plan for the city, saw it as a chance to build an urban Utopia. Oscar Niemeyer, the chief architect, was a Communist. With these fathers Brasília was never going to be a child like any other.

Dinho recognizes this and says that his initial reactions were probably just the natural responses of a rebellious teenager against the embrace of home. He did, after all, buy his first record here – it was by Jimi Hendrix – and he honed his musical tastes by hanging out near the University of Brasília and listening to bands with names like Electric Abortion.

He laughs and admits that with the passage of time he's changed his ideas. 'I do think it's beautiful,' he says, as we head west, looking out at the Metropolitan Cathedral in the shape of a huge crown of thorns and the smooth white dome of the National Museum, with a single ramp curving into a flying-saucer-like entrance halfway up the side of it. 'But I'm curious to see what time will do to it.'

I can see what Dinho means Niemeyer's wonderfully fluent designs may lie on the Eixo Monumental, but there's nothing monumental about them. There's a filigree gracefulness which will take some looking after. Someone will have to keep the shining white domes shining white.

As Dinho says of the original layout, 'There was always a feeling that this would be enough. Brasília would be this size for ever.' It was a forlorn hope. Costa and Niemeyer built a city for half a million people, and from the start it was never enough. The 30,000 workers who built Brasília showed no inclination to go back to their homes when they'd finished and pretty soon they were joined by others from the North who saw that there would always be more work to do. In 2010, when it celebrated its fiftieth anniversary, Brasília, now settled and successful and with a hinterland of rich farming country, was heading towards a population of four million.

Most of the new Brasilienses live in satellite towns spread far and wide over the surrounding plateau, and though there are very strict controls on new building

Above *· The Ministry buildings in Brazil's fifty-year-old capital.* ***Opposite*** *· The hills at Alto Paraíso. Locals believe crystal strata beneath them create a potent energy field.*

within the original axis, they can build what they want beyond that. The result is that Brasília has lost some of its visual magic, and looks a lot more like anywhere else these days.

If the capital has changed, so has the country. Dinho reminds me that only twenty-five years ago Brazil was facing economic meltdown with three-digit annual inflation and spiralling violence in the cities. Now things have changed. 'We're a long way from social justice – from distributing the wealth – but at least it's top of the agenda now.'

His remains an alternative voice, but he admits his songs are less angry now. We both agree that Brazil doesn't seem to be an angry place. Brazilians tend not to be prohibitive and proscriptive, their inclination is to accommodate each other. I suggest to Dinho that part of the reason might be that, unlike most countries, they don't seem to have a natural enemy to rally against. Since the end of the devastating Paraguayan War of the 1860s, Brazil has avoided any major conflicts.

Dinho thinks there's something in this. 'It may be why we don't go in for American-style patriotism. You won't see national flags hanging out of the windows – except when the World Cup's on.'

Their standing army is small. They have a few fighters, a destroyer or two. He laughs ruefully, 'If Uruguay decided to invade there wouldn't be much we could do.'

It's late afternoon now and we've done more talking than looking. We take a last sweep around the iconic Congresso Nacional with its unfenced white concrete walkways and reflecting pools, and Dinho heads back to São Paulo and I head back to the shores of Lake Paranoá.

Day 16 · Brasília 🚌 Alto Paraíso de Goiás

I'M NOT SURE if it in any way affected NOVACAP's decision to site the new capital where it did, but I'm told that there is an area just north of here where a seam of crystals, 200 kilometres (124 miles) long and 30 kilometres (18 miles) deep, creates a force field of energy which is said by those who live there to have powerful effects. UFOs have been sighted there and on a NASA photo of the Earth from space the area was reported as giving off an unmistakable glow.

It should be a day trip from Brasília to this mystical paradise, but the GO 118 highway due north out of the Distrito Federal – the Federal District – and into neighbouring Goiás is badly pot-holed. The drive takes several hours, through the *chapadas* – the escarpments left by rivers slicing down through the Planalto – and alongside immense fields dotted with the white Asian breeds of cows that survive so well here. We enter the Chapada dos Veadeiros National Park, a large protected area marked by a host of waterfalls. The rolling landscape is covered with typical *cerrado* forest. It's characteristically savannah, with a great diversity of trees, bushes and wildlife.

It's late afternoon by the time we reach our destination, one of four towns at the epicentre of the crystal energy field, and called, suitably, Alto Paraíso de Goiás – High Heaven of Goiás. Six and a half thousand souls live here at 1,676 metres, the highest point on the plateau. On the outskirts of the town a sign welcomes us to 'Alto Paraíso de Goiás. Homem Harmonia e Natureza' – Man in Harmony with Nature. This fine concept is somewhat at odds with a clumpy, unfinished concrete abstraction which occupies the centre of a roundabout. On the other hand it is extremely apt for the *pousada* where we're staying, which seems to be a working farm with rooms. A peacock is in full display outside the window of my rondavel, and processions of chicken and geese are constantly coming and

going. As I'm walking before supper I'm delighted to see a toucan in action. I've seen their feathers adorning the shins of the Wauja, and when we were in Manaus I became very envious of our director, J-P, who had two of them tapping at his hotel window every morning. This was the first time I'd seen this colourful whizz of black, yellow, red and green actually on the move. A beak with a bird attached.

Day 17 · Alto Paraíso de Goiás

ON THE carved wooden table beside my bed, one of a number of heavy, Hobbit-like pieces that furnish my room, the clock shows 5.15, as I eventually succumb to the combined shrieks of peacocks, geese, chicken, crows and toucans.

A few hours later we're into town to meet a witch called Tatiana. It's quite a disappointment. Tatiana and her fellow enchantresses are nothing like the pinch-nosed women in pointy hats and broomsticks with which we frighten our children. The witches I meet are sitting around taking tea in the wide, comfortable armchairs of a very big, very well-appointed modern house. They're well-travelled and well-off. Most are in their late thirties, early forties and comfortably rounded. It would need strong broomsticks to carry some of them.

Copies of *Architectural Digest* lie around and Tatiana's husband, a big, forceful man from São Paulo, is taking the crew on a guided tour of the house he's still building. I sit around with the ladies, talking about Celtic influences, the potency of Glastonbury and the Avebury Circle and I'm beginning to feel nothing more than mildly homesick. When Tatiana appears the atmosphere subtly changes. There is an aura of power in the room. Tatiana is a tall, striking woman with piercing dark eyes. Eyes that I can easily see blazing. She wears a turquoise-blue kaftan with a decorative band on her head. She clearly sets the agenda for the programme of rituals which have been taking place over the past few days. Today is called the 'Ritual of the Waters'. It's a celebration of the African goddess Yemanjá and involves a series of ablutions in which the basic chakras – liver, spleen, throat, heart, head, chest – will be cleansed one by one, as they process up a series of pools and waterfalls. The location is a nearby beauty spot called the Cachoeira das Loquinhas. The path alongside the seven waterfalls is well laid out, with wooden bridges and walkways. It's pretty rather than spectacular. As we walk I ask Tatiana if it's quite acceptable to be a witch in Brazil. She nods briskly. The Brazilians are very tolerant of witchcraft. In fact they're tolerant of almost everything. Especially in Alto Paraíso. 'It's very open-minded here,' she assures me. 'The Dalai Lama was here. We have ashrams, ayahuasca [the hallucinatory jungle drug], Krishnas. Mysticism in Brazil is very important.'

Opposite: ***1*** *· With Tatiana at the first waterfall.* ***2*** *· The Ritual of the Waters. Tatiana instructs her followers.* ***3*** *· The highest waterfall and the highest state of enlightenment.*

Modern witchcraft seems to be less about spells and cooking-pots and more about oneness with nature, of celebrating Gaia, the Great Mother, and the seasons and the solstice and the equinox. 'And the new belief of the new era that you have to respect nature.'

These wealthy witches sound an awful lot like the Wauja.

'I used to live in big towns,' Tatiana tells me, 'but the energy is so confused. Here we just have the nature and the sun. Love comes from the earth.' I nod. It would be rude not to. I rather want to get back to witchcraft. 'Is there a concentration of witches here in Alto Paraíso?'

'Oh yes. This town has a very strong female energy. Men go, but the women stay. Women make things happen here.'

'Like?'

'A woman runs the supermarket. Women run the restaurants.'

We're at the first pool by now. The stream is quite narrow here and it's a bit of a squash getting all the witches close to the water. When they're in position Tatiana, looking in her element, stands on one side of the pool, tree branches forming an arboreal halo behind her, and issues various incantations and leads her followers, who now number about ten, in various stretchings of arms and raising and lowering of haunches.

At the next waterfall there's more room and most of the witches opt for total immersion. Rose leaves are scattered on the waters and scented oils are dispensed. By the time they reach the top they are ready to be finally cleansed. This is the most impressive of the falls. The water tumbles about fifteen metres down a series of steps before splashing into a capacious pool with sheer rock on three sides. At

1

2

3

1

2

3

the top of the fall I can see an elderly hippy, all in white, reclining against a rock. He's smoking a pipe, chanting and gently shaking a maraca. The witches stand in a circle, roses are laid out and oil is rubbed on stomachs. Yemanjá has been propitiated and the earth will be blessed. As Tatiana explains, the goddess will evoke in them beauty, prosperity, kindness, motherhood, sensuality, lightness, wisdom, joy and strength. It's a touching, rather beautiful little scene. Basil is less easily moved than I am. 'Desperate Housewives go swimming,' he mutters darkly.

We walk around the town before heading back home. There doesn't seem too much of what I would call normal commerce here. Most of the shops sell crystals of one kind or another and couples with dreadlocks emerge from *pousadas* with names like Camelot and Avalon and amble past signs offering 'Massagem Integrativa'.

I don't see energy. If anything, I see a rather pleasant lack of it.

Day 18 · Brasília

BACK IN THE CAPITAL, I walk out early to beat the tourist crowds, and make for the Praça dos Três Poderes, 'Three Powers Square', where the Legislature, Judiciary and Executive are gathered together. Here, within strolling distance of each other, are all the elements that run the country. If anywhere could be described as the beating heart of Brazil, this is it.

The buildings around the square are all, in their various ways, impressive. Not always because of their size; more often it's because of their delicate, elegant, airy modern lines. The Palace of Congress dominates. Its two tall central towers are flanked by two white hemispheres, one face-up and one face-down, one housing the Senate, the other the Chamber of Deputies. Coming from a country where government buildings are usually neo-classical and rather grand, authority set in stone, I find them fresh and appealing. Power is rarely as restrained as this. Ironic, then, that it took a staunch Communist like Oscar Niemeyer (still alive as I write, at 104) to create a centre of government as modern and light and unintimidating as this. But then Niemeyer is not just a Communist, he's a Brazilian. Somehow these buildings all around me – from the Palace of Congress to the compact Supreme Court with its wide white roof and upswept bird's-wing columns, to the low-slung, airy Planalto Palace from which the President works – could only be Brazilian. In the emphasis on visual pleasure as much as functionality, in their embrace of the sun, and in their informality and lack of pomposity, Niemeyer seems to have found a visual metaphor for the way the Brazilians like to see themselves. And there's a nod to their love of mysticism. On Republic Day the sun rises exactly between the two towers of the Congress building. I'm sure there are all sorts of maintenance issues with this type of architecture but it does seem to put *joie de vivre* first and heritage, tradition, authority and precedent second.

Opposite: ***1*** *· The witches enjoy total immersion.* ***2*** *· They don't take themselves too seriously.* ***3*** *· Most of the shops sell crystals in some shape or form.*
Below: ***4*** *· Brasília. The Palácio do Planalto, the President's office.* ***5*** *· The Supremo Tribunal Federal Building, seat of Brazil's Judiciary.*

I can walk up to any of these buildings. They're not surrounded with tank-traps, ramps, fences and rising bollards. Here at the heart of the Brazilian state there's hardly a policeman to be seen. Two brightly uniformed guards with ceremonial swords are all that would stop me climbing the few steps into the Presidential

4

5

Above · *The Palace of Congress, Brazil's Houses of Parliament.* **Opposite: 1** · *Beside Os Candangos, the memorial to the workers who built Brasília.* **2** · *Flags of the twenty-six states.* **3** · *President Kubitschek, the man who commissioned Brasília, keeps an eye on the cleaners in Three Powers Square.*

Following pages · *The Chamber of Deputies at the Palace of Congress building in Brasília.*

Palace. It's January and Congress is not in session, which might explain the light-touch security, but it is refreshing to see power unadorned by any hint of triumphalism. That, it seems to me, is the success of Brasília. It could only have been like this by starting from scratch, with a clean slate. By starting in the middle of nowhere the creators of the new capital were able to build something unlike anywhere else.

There are criticisms of its vision. Some ask how two men of the people like Niemeyer and Costa could have built a city so dependent on a road network. Public transport is almost entirely confined to buses. Its location, isolated from the rest of Brazil, was heavily criticized by some, though Brazil is so enormous that anywhere you put a capital would be far away from someone. The whole point of the new capital was that it had to appear neutral, unpartisan, far enough away from existing centres of power like Rio and São Paulo to deflect accusations of outside influence. Brasília had to be all things to all Brazilians. This admirable objective is symbolized by a mighty black flagpole at one end of the square. Its shaft is made up of a sheaf of twenty-six separate metal strips, representing the twenty-six states that make up the Republic. The Brazilian flag it carries is the biggest flying flag in the world, measuring seventy by one hundred metres. Such is the strain on this huge area of fabric that it rips regularly and at the end of each month the flag has to be replaced and a new one hoisted. In true federal spirit the bill for the new flag is sent, by rotation, around each of the twenty-six states in turn.

The Three Powers Square was not originally a part of the grand plan. It was designed by Lúcio Costa as a tribute to Tancredo Neves, the first popularly elected

1

2

3

President after the twenty years of the dictatorship came to an end in 1985. Neves was, however, not a well man and he died on the first evening of his Presidency.

The square sends out mixed messages. The Niemeyer pavilions have their own lightness and grace, alongside which the huge likeness of President Kubitschek makes him look rather dour and cross, whereas in reality he was supposed to be humorous and charismatic. And the intention of the square as a whole, lumping together an unholy assortment of buildings, flagpoles and statues to celebrate a kind of grand destiny, defies coherence. The space is just too big. As the sun climbs into a cloudless sky I'm also painfully aware that there is no cover, no shade in Three Powers Square. I turn to go when one of the statues catches my eye. It's striking and rather different. A pair of tall, abstract figures, their arms merged one with the other and both holding long thin staffs.

It's called Os Candangos and it commemorates the thousands of migrant workers who built Brasília. They came predominantly from the traditionally poorest part of Brazil – Nordeste, the North-East. Though no longer the wealth-generating powerhouse it used to be, the North-East of Brazil is a vital supplier of labour for the new and expanding Brazilian economy. There are many rumours about it – that violence is worse there than anywhere else in Brazil, that the beaches are beautiful, that the lifestyle is lazy. Whatever the truth is, there's only one way to find out.

PART 2 | THE NORTH-EAST

ATLANTIC OCEAN
Alcântara
São Luís
Lençóis Maranhenses
Barreirinhas
Parnaíba
Fortaleza
MARANHÃO
CEARÁ
Teresina
Mearim
Serra da Ibiapaba
RIO GRANDE DO NORTE
Natal
Planalto da Borborema
PARAÍBA
João Pessoa
Juazeiro do Norte
Olinda
'Pega de Boi'
Recife
Salgueiro
Parnaíba
PIAUÍ
Piauí
PERNAMBUCO
São Fransisco
ALAGOAS
Maceió
Barragem de Sobradinho
SERGIPE
Aracaju
Chapada Diamantina
BAHIA
Barreiras
Cachoeira
São Félix
Salvador
Contas
São Fransisco
Ilhéus
Jequitinhonha
Planalto do Brasil
MINAS GERAIS
Cardeal Mota
ESPÍRITO SANTO
Belo Horizonte
0 100 200 300 kilometres
0 100 200 miles

Day 19 · São Luís

TO GO NORTH in Brazil you have to go south first. The major airline hubs are in Rio and São Paulo, cities with a combined population of nearly thirty million. So I find myself, three hours out of Guarulhos airport in São Paulo, face pressed tight to the window, as the landscape below me slowly changes from the hard, weathered crust of the interior to the green, thickly forested banks of a river delta. If I have a feeling that I've seen all this before it's understandable. We're almost back at the Equator, and only a couple of hundred kilometres from the mouth of the Amazon.

We're descending towards the coastal city of São Luís. Two wide rivers curl through the dense greenery below. As our path and theirs converge I see small settlements; red-roofed houses surrounded by palm and banana trees, girder bridges carrying roads across the swamp and then suddenly, and almost shockingly, the great bulk of a refinery, a waste pond of red mud catching the last of the sunlight. Then we're out over the Atlantic making our final approach to the capital of Maranhão State, set on an island in between the two river mouths, with bridges connecting it to a populous mainland. São Luís, named by its French founders after their king, Louis XIII, grew rich shipping cotton and sugar from the plantations. Its economy collapsed after slavery was abolished in Brazil in 1888, but there are plenty of signs of twenty-first-century life down there. Despite decades of north-south emigration, there are still almost a million people living in the city below me. Long lines of high-rise blocks run parallel to the sea, and I count a line of seventeen ships waiting to enter port.

This is our introduction to the North-East, that great jut of coastline projecting Brazil into the Atlantic and giving South America the face of its elegant sea-horse outline. From here on, down through Recife to Salvador, Brazil comes to within 3,000 kilometres (1,850 miles) of the African coast, and if ever geography were a key to history it is here. The neat fit between the wedge at the top of South America and the hole on the side of West Africa is exactly what it looks like. The two continents were once joined together. Many million years later, after the landmasses had drifted apart, huge numbers of Africans were brought to Brazil as forced labour. The physical connection may have long gone but, thanks to slavery, a social, cultural and emotional connection has taken its place. The North-East of Brazil still feels very much a part of Africa.

Day 20 · São Luís Barreirinhas

OUR HOTEL is by the beach. Nothing remarkable about this except that Calhau Praia – *praia* being Portuguese for beach – is as clean, comfortable, walkable a stretch of sand as I've ever come across. And it's apparently endless. And it's one minute away. This morning I donned my Havaiana flip-flops, the obligatory,

Above · *There's no easy way to the dunes. Vehicles slither across the sand and plunge through pools two metres deep on the way from the nearest river crossing.* **Opposite** · *It's worth it in the end. The wind and water weave wonderful patterns.*

indeed sole item of footwear across coastal Brazil, crossed the main road, and set out for a walk. Because it's a beach, constantly washed by the tide, there are no footpaths or directions of travel. You can just wander over this vast space any way you want, restricted only by the land on one side and the sea, quite a long way off, on the other. Disappointingly, the Atlantic is not colourful here. The sediment from the Pindaré and the Itapicuru, the two rivers which discharge into the ocean on either side of the island of São Luís, has turned the waves that lap onto the shore a murky brown. The fine line of the horizon is broken by bulk-carriers waiting to collect their loads of iron ore. Despite all this it is a magical and liberating feeling to walk on such a wide and under-populated expanse. Knowing I could run up the beach for an hour in either direction and not come to the end of it is difficult for someone brought up on the shingle and wind-breaks of North Sea summer holidays. For now, the sun is warm and the sand firm and I couldn't wish to be anywhere else. After breakfast – passion fruit, papaya, fresh mango juice, tapioca and coconut cake – we set out for what promises to be an even more spectacular open space.

Around 300 kilometres (200 miles) south-east of São Luís is the Lençóis Maranhenses National Park. Here is sand in its most majestic state. Piled up to fifty metres high by the Atlantic breakers and honed and smoothed by the wind, the dunes spread and billow over roughly 1,600 square kilometres (620 square miles), a landscape which has earned its name by resembling the crumpled sheets on a bed – the literal meaning of the Portuguese word *lenc lençóis óis* is 'white sheets'. So extensive are these sheets of sand that, except for the fact that this is a very wet as well as a very sandy coast, it could be Namibia or the Sahara. After the rainy season, in March, April and May, up to a thousand lagoons appear amongst the dunes. This ecosystem is so rare that by the time our four-wheel drive twists and bounces its way across approach tracks of slippery sand and water-filled trenches, there are seventeen more such vehicles lined up at the edge of the dunes. Brazilian tourists are already out in force. And, being Brazilian, half of them are as close to naked as is permissible. In this land of the uninhibited, the dress code is as elastic as the tiny thongs which cover less than a leaf in the Garden of Eden.

Provided nipples (female only) and genitals are concealed, the rest of the body can be joyfully unencumbered. So my first view of the mighty dunes we've travelled four hours to see is of a skyline silhouetted with men with large stomachs and tiny trunks and women who appear to the naked eye to be exactly that. It shocks me at first. This isn't the beach, it's a National Park, dammit. It's disrespectful. You wouldn't see people in G-strings at Stonehenge. Then, after a few minutes, I cease to notice them. That's largely because, although this water-studded desert stretches for 225 kilometres (140 miles) along the coast, most tourists never venture far from the car park. They meander the few hundred metres to the nearest lake, and sit in it. Which is why this first seductive blue patch of water is called Lazy Lake.

I climb to the top of the first dune, which is so smooth it's like scaling a hill that's been varnished. From its summit I marvel at the abrupt contrast between the green scrub we've driven through to get here and the almost eerily bare white dunes that stretch ahead of me for kilometre after kilometre towards the distant ocean. And the sands are growing, claiming more and more of the land. There are tales of lost cities submerged beneath them by sudden ferocious storms.

I continue on down the far side of the dune, along an elegantly curving ridge, one side of which drops a sheer ninety metres into a dark blue lake. To add to the dreamlike quality of the place, a restless, whispering wind blows, carrying a constantly fluttering veil of sand up and over the dunes. I feel a compulsion to keep walking, and at the same time a primal anxiety that this huge spread of sand

and water is somehow alien, like the surface of the moon. Beautiful indeed, but also mysterious and disorienting. Probably the only National Park in the world which looks different every day. Not a place in which to get lost.

As the sun begins to sink, immense shadows are cast by the dunes and the lakes turn to fire. I'm aware of the heat of the slanting sun, but the sand remains comfortably cool. This sensation is, apparently, caused not only by the ever-present wind, but also by the mangrove swamp beneath the dunes which retains water and keeps the dense-packed sand aerated. Walking barefoot has rarely felt so good.

We head back on the edge of the sunset, not wanting to risk the deeply rutted track after dark. It's only eleven kilometres or so (seven miles) to the ferry across the Preguiça ('Lazy') River, and out of the park, but it takes us almost an hour, in and out of quite deep water, to get there. The ferry is severely functional, nothing much more than a floating steel platform. As we wait for it to come across we buy *empanadas*, made from manioc flour, salt and water and cooked over charcoal in a hut on the riverbank. I choose cheese and coconut filling. Not a familiar combination, but delicious. Out here away from the cities, everything grows quieter after sunset. Sounds are magnified. The laughter of the ladies who are cooking, the plash of a paddle as a dugout slides in from the opposite bank. This tiny glimpse of village life is as magical to me as the extraordinary sand desert we've just seen.

We move on. Across the river and into the town of Barreirinhas, where we spend the night at a vast resort hotel, which only makes me miss the village even more.

Day 21 · São Luís

IT IS MID-WINTER in Brazil and the temperatures are down around 30 degrees Celsius. Which makes a very pleasant climate for the festivities that take place all over the country at this time under the general heading of Festas Juninas. Like so much in a predominantly Catholic country, these celebrations are all linked to saints' days. In São Luís they go under the heading of Bumba Meu Boi, which begins on St Anthony's Day and culminates on St Peter's Day. Most of the communities in the city take part in creating some variation on a 200-year-old tale which originated in the cattle farms of the interior. It involves a slave, Pai Francisco, stealing and killing one of his master's bulls to remove the tongue for which his pregnant wife, Catirina, is desperate. The slave himself is threatened with death. He hides away in the forest where a *cazumbá*, half-man, half animal, comes to his rescue. 'Bumba Meu Boi' – 'Stand up my Bull' – he commands. The bull is miraculously resurrected and everyone at the farm celebrates. It's part-pageant, part-pantomime and comes in all sorts of different styles, known as *sotaques*. Augusto Mendes, an English teacher in his mid-thirties with very black hair, pale olive skin and a great love for his home city, has agreed to take us to see one of the most traditional of the Bumba Meu Boi groups prepare for the big night ahead, the eve of St John's Day.

We drive across the José Sarney Bridge which connects old São Luís with its modern suburbs. The bridge is named after the founder of a local dynasty and one-time President of Brazil who, some think, has done very well for himself and his family, but very little for his home state of Maranhão, which remains one of the worst-off in the country. Twenty-two of the fifty poorest communities in Brazil are in Maranhão State.

Once onto the island we turn off and away from the historic centre of the city with its recently restored mansions and elaborately tiled facades, to an area called Liberdade, which is very different. Most of the people here are descended from *quilombos* – settlements of freed slaves. A national magazine, dubbing it the poorest community in Brazil, revealed that seventy-eight percent of its people depend on government handouts, a mere eight percent have access to the internet and infant mortality is higher here than in Iraq.

101, Rua Tomé de Souza is a hive of activity tonight. It stands in a *bairro* (community) of Liberdade called Floresta (the Forest), and it belongs to a man with the delightfully melodic name of Apolônio Melônio. Apolônio is ninety-two and his wife Nadir is forty-five. Some thirty years ago Apolônio and a local priest, Padre Giovanni Gallo, came up with the idea of organizing a local contribution to the Bumba Meu Boi celebrations that would help raise the spirits and the profile of their downtrodden neighbourhood. It would be based on the performing troupe Floresta – named after their *bairro* – which Apolônio had created a year or two earlier. At about that time a young street kid, Nadir Olga Cruz, by her own admission a 'bad, bad girl', was being helped by Apolônio to break her drug habit

Opposite · *Walking with my companion Augusto along the top of ninety-metre dunes. In another quirk of this extraordinary ecosystem, mangrove swamps, submerged far below, keep the sand wonderfully cool.*

Preceding pages · *Lencóis Maranhenses. A landscape like no other. A desert with lakes. For the lucky few who make it out here there are hundreds of natural swimming pools to choose from. And they're never quite the same from year to year.*

1

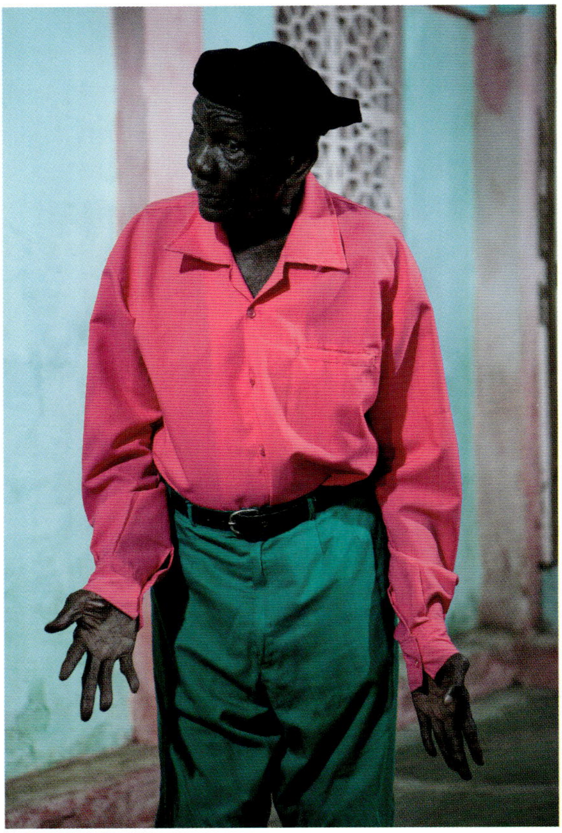
2

3

4

5

6

and get herself an education. She proved to be both motivated and ambitious, and married the redoubtable Apolônio when he was sixty-four and she was seventeen. Nadir bore him two children, which, together with those from his other wives, made nineteen altogether.

I ask her how Bumba Meu Boi differs from Carnival.

'First of all Carnival has no religious attachments. It is a pagan celebration. The religious side is taken very seriously in Bumba Meu Boi. There was a lot of resistance from the authorities in the past. Bumba Meu Boi was considered a dance of drunken people, vagabonds, people with no goals in life. Now the elite understand that it is about art, dance, music, costumes, all in the name of devotion to St John.'

Inspired by Apolônio and Nadir, Floresta has grown from a performing group to an umbrella organization – Projeto Floresta Criativa – for local projects and workshops, and a foundation for helping the deeply disadvantaged local children. All their funds have to be raised. They get nothing from local or national government.

Their house in Rua Tomé, just across the street from the church, looks, like most of those around it, to be a modest single-storey building, but a passageway down the side reveals a labyrinth of rooms leading off it, built into the hill behind the house. In one of these I find Nadir, her slight, girlish figure belying an apparently limitless energy. She's in a big open room, hung with balloons and bunting in the pink and green colours of Floresta. So far it looks as if it might be set for a children's party, but at one end are stacked some enormous headdresses, with beautifully embroidered centrepieces, from which spring the long exotic feathers of the *ema*, the South American emu. Various masks, one with green hair and a carrot nose, hang nearby, waiting for the festivities.

At the other end of the room is a small alcove, framed by pink and green balloons, in which stand plaster figures of various saints. John the Baptist, of course, for it's his day tomorrow, but also St Peter with the keys to Heaven, St Benedict (Benedito), the black saint and patron of the slaves, and various likenesses of the Virgin Mary. In front of this 'altar' of St John is the most important element of today's proceedings, the *boi* – the bull. It's not at all what I expected. It's little

Opposite: 1 · *Bumba Meu Boi. Beneath balloons of green and pink (the colours of Floresta) the crowds squeeze in to watch the blessing of the bull.* ***2*** · *The Godfather. Apolônio Melônio, ninety-two-year-old inspiration behind the Projeto Floresta Criativa.* ***3*** · *At the bull's head, I talk to Nadir Melônio about the creation of the bull.* ***4*** · *Young celebrants in emu-feather outfits.*

Above: 5 · *Wood and goatskin drums are heated to tighten and improve their resonance.* ***6*** · *I bewitch one of the older residents with stories of working with John Cleese.*

1

2

Above: ***1*** *· A boy stands at the door of the local Catholic church. Its one-time priest, Giovanni Gallo, helped Apolônio bring Bumba Meu Boi to Floresta.* ***2*** *· For a poor community, the costumes, worn by young and old, are rich and beautifully made.* ***Opposite*** *· The roots of Bumba Meu Boi are in rural Brazil, hence the preponderance of animal masks.*

more than a headdress, resting on supports in front of the altar, a sheath along its back embroidered in exquisite detail. The way it sits before the pink-swathed 'altar' typifies this confusing – to me anyway – fusion of religion and folklore. I'm not quite sure where one ends and the other begins. Augusto tells me that the story behind Bumba Meu Boi dates back to the late eighteenth, early nineteenth centuries. Though the icons are full of the imagery of Roman Catholicism, the Catholic establishment has turned its back, finding them too unorthodox, too African.

The house is filling up. Costumes are being put on and make-up applied. Those playing indigenous peoples have stripes painted on their faces, the slaves wear bandanas, and the landowners are in sequinned waistcoats. The drummers heat their round, shallow goatskin drums around a fire in the backyard. The man playing Pai Francisco, dressed as a cowboy, laughs blearily and occasionally sends out a blast from what looks and sounds like a vuvuzela. He's had a few.

Nadir gathers them together. Apolônio, a thin but elegant ninety-two-year-old in a green jacket, pink trousers and a beret, exchanges jokes with friends and even has time to talk to me. He tells me he was eight years old when he attended his first Bumba ceremony back in 1926. He started Bumba Meu Boi here in Floresta and has never wanted to move away.

'Until,' he adds matter-of-factly, 'I have to move to the sacred place that everybody needs to go to one day.'

As it draws closer to midnight, when the Feast of Corpus Christi becomes St John's Day, more and more people crowd into the room with the altar to witness the 'baptism' of the bull. A woman in late middle age whose everyday clothes are in marked contrast to all the flamboyant outfits around her is ushered to the front and, standing by the altar, begins to intone prayers. She is the priestess, though she looks more like someone from the accounts department. Behind her is the lead singer, who turns her words into chants which are belted out to the accompaniment of two drums, a saxophone and a trumpet. The crowd chants back. After half an hour of this the jam-packed, windowless room is very hot indeed and I'm aware that there is only one small exit. Emu feather skirts brush dangerously close to lighted candles. To add to the fun, a firecracker is thrown

into the open passageway outside. I flinch, but no one else seems to. Just before midnight a local man who is one of the 'godfathers' of the bull blesses it with burning sticks and flicks it with water. The bull is now baptized and the dancing begins. The various characters in the story move and weave around as best they can in the centre of the crush. The man wearing the bull's head bucks and rears as he chases after sozzled cowboys and children dressed in leopardskin and the relentless rhythm of the music is supplemented by the crack-crack beat of *matracas*, wooden blocks struck together. In the midst of the mayhem, Apolônio Melônio, his drawn, bony face showing quiet satisfaction, sits to one side shaking a diamond-shaped rattle in time with the music.

The chanting becomes more frenetic. A woman grasps my hand, her face suffused with ecstatic suffering, tears spilling from her eyes. Someone is calling out The Lord's Prayer. At midnight there are resounding cries of 'St John be Blessed!' A few minutes later the dancing, chanting, heaving, perspiring throng begins at last to move from this suffocating room, slowly shifting up the steps and out into the street. Rising above them are the magnificent feather headdresses, transforming their mundane, careworn wearers into gods for a night. Free from the confines of the downstairs room the parade joyfully expands to fill the streets outside, defying the pale glare of the sodium lights, and turning an ordinary evening in this run-down corner of town into a night at the theatre.

As we drive home after filming we turn a corner and find ourselves face to face with another Bumba celebration. In the dimly lit street ahead a line of children in white conical headdresses advances towards us along the cobbles. We're waved angrily away by the organizers – and it's very rare to see anyone in Brazil being angry.

Day 22 · São Luís

IT GOES WITHOUT SAYING that Jesus is popular in Brazil, but up here in the state of Maranhão Jesus Christ has competition in the popularity stakes from Jesus Norberto Gomes. Jesus Gomes was a pharmacist who, in 1921, discovered a new formula for a popular soft drink made from *guaraná*, an Amazonian fruit twice as rich in caffeine as coffee itself. The drink was cannily marketed as Guaraná Jesus, and the name can be seen to this day on bottles and billboards right across the state. For some reason it didn't sell well anywhere else in Brazil, and there are stories of Jesus-deprived Maranhãoans having to request family and friends to smuggle supplies south to Rio and São Paulo. This curious situation worked well for the brand at home and Guaraná Jesus came to define Maranhão, where it became the state drink. It was consumed in such amounts that it caught the eye of Brazil's number one fizzy drinks producer. In 2001 Coca-Cola bought the company.

The heavens open this afternoon as we visit the state-of-the-art bottling plant on the outskirts of São Luís where the name of Jesus, a now iconic italic graphic, shares one side of the company sign with Coca-Cola. A special Guaraná Jesus can has been designed for Bumba Meu Boi. Local pride and the drink are intertwined. But despite assurances, and despite production facts – in two-litre bottles alone, the plant produces 200,000 units of Guaraná Jesus every day – I get the feeling

that the local product is seen as very much the junior partner here. The walls by reception are covered in classic Coca-Cola ads, and the crates and delivery trucks are all in Coca-Cola red rather than Guaraná Jesus pink.

We're welcomed and shown around by a smart and publicity-conscious technocrat who is at great pains to point out that Guaraná Jesus is still a very important part of the Coca-Cola family; indeed, recently they have added a touch of Maranhãoan *azulejo* tiling to the label design, following a local competition.

He's coy on the subject of the blend itself, and I'm allowed the merest of glimpses into the laboratory to which the concentrate is delivered from Coca-Cola central to have sugar, water and syrup added. There is less restraint about showing us the production line, which is mightily impressive. I'm fascinated to see that the plastic bottles are made from twelve-centimetre-long templates, delivered here from Manaus. Whizzed into a machine at great heat and velocity, these finger-shaped cylinders reappear seconds later as litre bottles. As an Englishman I'm a little sad to see that the precision-engineered equipment that sends the Jesus on its roller-coaster ride from mixing vat to delivery stack is all made in Germany, Italy or France. Volume, cleanliness, efficiency and a strange beauty too.

Fizzy drinks are hugely popular in Brazil and Coca-Cola has sixty-six similar plants throughout the country. Their presence here in São Luís is a boost for a sluggish economy, but at the possible cost of one of the things that made the state so proud of itself. Guaraná Jesus will no longer exist by right; its future depends on the continuing addiction of the people of Maranhão to this curiously indescribable pink drink.

Despite Coca-Cola's confidence, it's clear the economic rebirth of São Luís still has a long way to go. Give or take a few smart European car showrooms, the arterial road is largely an industrial wasteland, and the roads themselves are a pretty rough ride.

Back at Calhau the families are coming off the beach and the night music is warming up. Brazil is not a quiet country. Volume is a badge of honour. But the beachfront is friendly and most of the restaurants serve good, fresh fish and very cold beers. And you'll never be alone. Hawkers move between the tables offering postcards, beads, jewellery and oysters from polystyrene containers, shucked at your table. A tall, skinny man, swinging a pail of hot coals on which he will grill cheese for you, barely breaks his step as he trawls his way through the outdoor tables. He passes by with grace and style, as if asserting his innate superiority to any potential clients. He's the man. He's doing you a favour. If you want him you have to catch him. This being infinitely accommodating Brazil, land of live and let live, no one either running the restaurants or eating at them would dream of complaining about itinerant oyster-shuckers or cheese-grillers. Unfortunately the same virtuous tolerance also applies to the very bad, volcanically amplified country singer murdering 'Every Breath You Take' at 3.30 in the morning.

Opposite *· A billboard advertises the favourite local soft drink, Guaraná Jesus. The bull shows it's been canned specially for the Bumba Meu Boi festivities.*

Day 23 · São Luís ⛵ Alcântara

IT'S EIGHT O'CLOCK in the morning. I'm standing, a little sleep-deprived, on a spur of sand waiting for a boat to take me across St Mark's Bay, north and west of São Luís, to Alcântara, once upon a time the state capital and one of the most prosperous towns in Brazil. The fact that I have to take my shoes off, roll up my trousers and wade out to a small, run-down catamaran to get there says everything about how times change. There is a road to Alcântara, but it can take many hours to get around the bay, so the town now depends on two ferries a day. They would normally leave from a jetty in the centre of São Luís but it's low tide and there isn't enough draught, so the twenty-odd passengers for the nine o'clock boat wait in line on a strip of beach blasted equally by the sun and the roar of construction from a land reclamation site nearby.

By half past nine we are squeezed aboard, the sail is hoisted and the engine gurgles to life. One of the two-man crew picks up a stack of lifejackets, but instead of giving them out, he stows them under a seat to make more room for people to sit down. Very Brazilian.

As we bounce across the bay I find myself trying out my limited Portuguese on two middle-aged women travelling together. They are in São Luís for a weekend and a visit to historic old Alcântara is a must. They're from the neighbouring

1

2

3

state of Ceará. 'É bonita?' I ask. They turn their noses up. 'Ceará cultura?' Both heads shake in unison 'Não'.

Ninety minutes later there's much gesticulating as our boat slides into a small bay fringed with mangroves. Some are pointing out the twin-towered, white-washed cathedral on the hill but most are looking the other way, at a number of bright red dots on the shoreline. These are scarlet ibis, a bird normally dull grey, but here their plumage has a vivid blush owing to their diet of crustaceans. The engine dies and we pull alongside a jetty. In the murky weed-strewn water beside it the wooden skeleton of an old sailing ship lies beached and slowly rotting. It seems such an apt symbol of Alcântara's fortunes that I wonder if it's been left there deliberately. But the place isn't dead yet. As we walk across a bridge and onto the shore, we're greeted by Brazil at full volume. A thumping blast of reggae shakes the air from the Lanchonete (snack-bar) Ponto Sagrado. It's very hot and humid, so before climbing up the hill into the heart of the town we seek out a nearby *pousada* where a big Afro-Brazilian lady prepares coffee and toasted ham and cheese sandwiches. She's assisted by two daughters, the prettier of whom serves at table whilst the other, I notice, is confined to the kitchen. A dog lies stretched out blocking the doorway and across the street two men sit on a low wall in the shade of a mango tree. One of them rolls his sweatshirt up to air a large, round belly, which he rubs reflectively as he talks.

Opposite *· Low tide forces us to board the catamaran from the beach.* ***Above: 1*** *· Packed together on the morning catamaran. Believe it or not there aren't many quicker ways to get to Alcântara.* ***2-3*** *· On Calçada do Jacaré – Alligator Street.*

1

2

Above: 1-2 · Houses of the rich and poor in Alcântara; the poor houses still lived in, the rich now just a shell.
Opposite · In Alcântara's once-grand Praça da Matriz, flags flutter for the festivities to come. Among the many colonial buildings is a ruined stone church on the right and in front of it the limestone pelourinho, the pillory, where slaves were bought and sold.

The road up to the town is called Calçada do Jacaré – Alligator Street, because of the grey and white overlapping pattern of its paving blocks. On either side are a range of fine old houses, some painted and with attractive wrought-iron balconies, others fallen into ruin. At the top of the hill the road forks on either side of a little church and runs along the ridge, past once-grand houses with *azulejo*-tiled facades until it opens out onto a spacious grassy plaza dominated by the mottled, coffee-coloured remains of a church. In the shadow of its high, dismembered wall stands a white limestone post, its surface chipped and weathered. It's been here a long time. This is the *pelourinho*, the whipping-post, where slaves came to be bought, sold and punished. Its proximity to the cross and bell-tower behind it says much about the relationship between the Church and the slave trade.

And yet there's no denying this is an idyllic spot. A breeze disperses the sticky humidity of the shoreline, and blows the flags and bunting set up for Festas Juninas celebrations. And the views are spectacular. On one side of the promontory a ragged banana plantation fringes a secluded, seductively empty beach and on the other side out across the bay can be seen the Miami-like skyline being constructed for the affluent of the new São Luís.

There were once some rich people here too. Plantation owners who would come to Alcântara in the winter to escape the hardships of the interior. The French proprietor of La Maison du Baron, where we have lunch, shows us around the Portuguese house he has carefully restored. It's beautiful inside, with cool, well-shaded rooms which still smell of the rich, dark timber from which they were constructed.

For Alcântara, the golden days of European comforts came to an abrupt halt with the abolition of slavery in 1888. The sugar plantations, deprived of their mass bonded labour, could no longer survive the international competition. The lunatics took over the asylum as the freed slaves moved in and Alcântara became a *quilombo*. On all sides there are remnants of fine old buildings either pulled down or left to rot. A convent beside the cathedral must have been very beautiful. Now it's in pieces, razed to the ground in anger at the old monarchy when Brazil became a Republic in the year following abolition.

The demise of Alcântara mirrors the predicament of Portuguese Brazil. The subjugation of a huge slave workforce to a relatively small number of Europeans couldn't last. A nation which has the whipping-post as a symbol of its power is never going to enjoy consensual rule. Slavery continued in Brazil for much longer than most countries, so it's hardly surprising that when it went it left a correspondingly deeper power vacuum. Alcântara must once have been a fine place to live. A ruler's town. Now the best they can do is to gather the old stones and leave them for the tourists to wonder at what went right and what went wrong.

However there is a postscript. And it came from the proprietor of the Maison du Baron. He's booked out for the foreseeable future. Not by a flood of tourists but by executives of a French/Ukrainian construction combine building a rocket launch site a few kilometres up the coast, which will employ some 2,500 people. Alcântara could yet become a rich man's town again.

On our return we're landed at the Estacão Maritima, the port of Old Town São Luís. From here it's a short walk up into in the Centro Histórico, the colonial core of the city, known as the Zona. It's an hour before sunset and the glaze on the tiles in the narrow streets catches the sharp intensity of the sunlight, making the houses glow and sparkle. Though they look handsome, there were strictly functional reasons for the widespread use of glazed tiling. The tiles provided vital protection for walls vulnerable to the hot and humid climate of the tropics. They also made useful ballast for lightly laden ships coming out from Portugal to collect the riches of their new colony.

They certainly contribute a decorative panache to the attractive, colourful UNESCO-listed heart of São Luís. The Old Town is slowly benefiting from a big

1

3

2

4

***Above:** 1 · Impromptu party in Old Town São Luís outside the Café da Casa das Ferragens - Ironmongers' House. 2 · The blue-glaze tiling that often came out from Portugal as ballast for ships. It looks lively and offers better protection to heat and rain than stone or wood. 3 · Learning soccer skills, barefoot on the flagstones. 4 · Catching the sunset on a colonial balcony. Brazilians behind me seem less interested in the dying light.*

restoration scheme called Projeto Reviver, but many of the houses still show the wear and tear of heat, moisture and general tropical decay. Balconies are broken and greenery sprouts out of holes in the walls. But the area is full of life. A group of young boys play football barefoot in a small, paved square. They are fast and skilful, as keeping the ball in play in such a confined space the passes have to be quick, short and accurate. In these São Luís backstreets I have a glimpse of what makes Brazilian football such a joy to watch.

In those streets that have been made-over there are shops, bars, internet cafés and restaurants. Brazilians like their music and there's a good crowd outside the Café da Casa das Ferragens, which has the date 1861 inscribed in the filigree ironwork of its arched doorway, and coat of arms above it. It's only tea-time but a live band plays and a few people samba joyfully and a little unsteadily beside it. Others sit beneath the cosseting shade of the mango trees and drink cold beers. A small group of young men lie sprawled on their backs, completely out of it, an empty bottle of *cachaca*, the sugar-cane spirit that comes closest to Brazil's national drink, at their feet. This is urban regeneration in its infancy, as yet devoid of shopping malls and international brands. This is still São Luís, capital of the poorest state in Brazil. And perhaps that's why I find it so appealing. It just couldn't be anywhere else.

We stand on the terrace beside the pristine white, recently restored governor's mansion, the Palácio de Leões, and watch the sun turn red and gold behind the tower blocks of the smart beachfront neighbourhoods. Now they *could* be anywhere else.

Day 24 · São Luís

IT'S SUNDAY – Domingo – and my friend Augusto wants to show me what happens to the north-eastern beaches on a day off. He drives me south and east of Calhau down the road to Araçagi Beach. And to my embarrassment he doesn't stop there. He drives off the road and onto the beach, weaving in and out of people doing exactly the same thing. As far as the eye can see the golden sands are full of cars, usually parked up beside a little gazebo, a *barraca* as they call them, which offers a postage stamp of shade for the plastic table and four chairs beneath. And those who can't afford a car come in by bus. By mid-morning the beach resembles a vast replica of suburban life. Long rows of cars and tents stretch side by side into the distance. Trolleys, either pedalled or pushed, keep the *barracas* topped up with pastries, juices, ice-creams, coconut milk and Guaraná Jesuses, whilst fishing boats bob around in the waves offshore waiting to supply this beach city with fresh crab, shrimp and prawns. Football and volleyball pitches have been improvised. Pick-up trucks with customized disco in the back thud, thump and blare their way up the beach, and nobody bats an eyelid. Sunday is a family day, and any family that can, goes to the beach. Fathers read the Sunday papers. Children kick a ball, fly a kite or splash in the muddy surf. Teenage girls in the tightest and skimpiest of bikinis display themselves with carefully posed nonchalance, whilst saggy grannies and grandpas, often equally skimpily dressed, walk quite unselfconsciously up and down the beach, soaking up the sun.

Below *· The beaches of São Luís are so big you can drive a car along them. Not that I'd recommend it. Except for the view.*

1

2

I learn from Augusto that girl-watching, rather like train-spotting, is an activity engaged in largely by adolescent boys. I'd seen some of them at one of the cafés up by the road, passing round a pair of binoculars as they scanned the beach like naval officers looking for U-boats. Augusto, a little bashfully, for he's thirty-six now, reveals that girl-watching has its own vocabulary of fruity metaphors. On Brazilian beaches the buttocks are the most admired parts of the female form and they're referred to as *melões* – melons.

'If the girl has a big bum we call her melon-woman. Watermelon-woman if she has big hips, and if she has a good shape, pear-woman.'

Beauty criteria are always interesting and I'm fascinated to hear from Augusto that it is the strap marks from a bikini that drive Brazilian boys wild.

'All the girls in São Luís like working out to wear bikinis and to go out at night to the reggae and show the "shadow".'

The more marks on a shoulder the more desirable is the bearer considered. Equally curious are the number of women to be seen on the beach applying a white, soapy solution to their arms and legs. This is, apparently, a form of bleach which will turn the hairs blonde.

Taking all this in at the end of the day over prawn *empanadas*, a plate of *carne de sol* – dry-cured beef – and a couple of *caipirinhas*, I reflect on English versus Brazilian attitudes to the beach. For us it's a luxury, for them it's a necessity.

Day 25 · São Luís

THIS IS our last day in São Luís and it's also the last big day of Festas Juninas and the climax of the Bumba Meu Boi festivities. Which is why we find ourselves, just after sunset, back in the streets of Floresta, waiting to travel with Nadir and her performers to one of the specially built stages in the Old Town where every group from all over the city is given its forty minutes in the spotlight.

The Florestans have been rehearsing for almost two months, but Nadir is still not sure how many of them will turn out on the night. They arrive slowly, slipping out of the dimly lit streets and down the passageway into Apolônio's house, which once again acts as rehearsal room, costume store, make-up and music room.

3

4

Nadir, slight and fragile in jeans and a T-shirt, runs the whole show, organizing, directing, cajoling as young and old arrive to take part. The magnificent headdresses of emu feathers and palm leaves are loaded onto two pick-up trucks together with a selection of hand-made masks. Old men, children, mothers (one wearing an 'I Love Shopping' T-Shirt under her sequinned red waistcoat) put finishing touches to their make-up. Under the glare of the lamp outside number 101, Rua Tomé de Souza, a man in green trousers and a pink shirt runs through some dance steps. Apolônio isn't coming into the town. It's too much for him now, but I see him through the iron-grilled window, holding court in a room with a red sofa and a television. With a grinding of gears and a rasping roar of old engines, two chunky school buses lumber up the hill and heave to a halt in the narrow street beside the church.

One by one people climb aboard, most of them carrying the costumes they'll change into when they reach the centre of town. Such has been the turnout that it's clear that not everyone will be able to get aboard. But somehow they do, almost 160 of them. It's an impressive endorsement of Bumba Meu Boi, especially for somewhere so bereft of resources. Wedged ever closer to each other, we wait for the buses to fill up to bursting point, but no one complains and there's always room found somewhere.

The drive from the *favela* into the Old Town is mercifully short. A couple of kilometres at most. The streets are heaving with people, and the Florestans are only one of a score of other groups from round the city come to show themselves off. Costumes are put on in the bus or in the car park, and within a few minutes the participants are transformed. Tiny Nadir has turned into a tree, with bands of feathers round her neck, waist and ankles. We all trail into the town, past various stages set up for performers who will keep on dancing till daybreak. The first performance of Floresta's show is at the end of one of the prettiest streets in the city, the Rua Portugal. The elegant, tiled facades of these arched colonial houses could not be more different from the ill-lit, shabby streets from which the Florestans have come, and yet their costumes and masks, led by the towering emu feathers, look so fine here that the dispossessed of Floresta find themselves being photographed by the rich white girls from the other side of town. They and

Opposite: 1 *· With the car park in the background, a seller of pretty much everything you need demonstrates children's kites.*
2 *· Boys and a football. The irresistible Brazilian combination.*
Above: 3 *· The Florestans come to town; headdresses are unloaded from the bus.*
4 *· Nadir (left) doesn't just organize, she joins in.*

The Rua Portugal in Old Town São Luís and the Bumba Meu Boi festivities, part of a larger religious festival devoted to St John, are in full swing. Dressed in home-made costumes of emu feathers and palm leaves, performers from Floresta, a poor community in the suburbs, are acting out a two-hundred-year-old story.

their friends and boyfriends are clearly impressed by the parade from the *favela* and they trail along after the Florestans, moving slowly up the Rua Portugal in the company of trees, cowboys, men dressed as pregnant women and all the other characters of Bumba Meu Boi.

When the Florestans are called forward there are too many of them to fit on the stage so their performance takes place on the cobbles. The caller starts it all off and keeps the action going as the music and the singing and dancing begin. They're allowed forty minutes and they don't let up for one second. This is a continuous powerhouse of energy and enthusiasm. Their moment of glory. The night that makes it all worthwhile.

From here on we lose touch with Nadir and her co-celebrants. They're just having too much of a good time. As I watch them move on to the next stage I admire not only their spirit but also the quality of their particular performance. There are many groups here who use Bumba Meu Boi as an excuse for some advertising, or merely to emulate the dancers in one of the glossy TV shows. Not so Nadir and Apolônio's group. Their presentation is defiantly traditional and local. It owes nothing to glamour girls or rock stars. It tells the original story of Bumba Meu Boi with conscientiously embroidered, home-made costumes, original, inventive masks and a real feeling of a community creating something out of nothing. And something wonderful too.

The clocks strike, announcing St Peter's Day is here. It's midnight and in São Luís things are just beginning to get going.

Day 26 · Olinda

IN THE GARDEN of our hotel there's a very tropical sign. Nailed to one of a cluster of tall shady trees is a wooden board on which is written in large white lettering 'Cuidado Frutas' – 'Beware Fruit'! This provokes some discussion amongst us as to what the dangers of being struck by fruit might be. Mangoes fall only when ripe so it might be nothing worse than a wet surprise. Coconuts, on the other hand, especially given the height of some of these trees, could well crack your head open. Decide to avoid the garden for now and opt for the relative safety of the streets.

Above *· One of Olinda's many fine, old Portuguese churches. For a while the city was the state capital.* ***Opposite*** *· Looking out over the attractive and colourful centre of Old Town Olinda to the skyline of Recife, the city that grew to eclipse its neighbour.*

Olinda, over 1,000 kilometres (620 miles) down the coast from São Luís, has a split personality. There is a colonial town of some beauty, stretching up and over the hills, and there is Nova Olinda, a big, bland, modern accretion which the guide books tend to ignore. It was once the capital of Pernambuco, the richest state in Brazil, and the colonial heart of the town still resonates with the style and affluence of those days of glory, back in the seventeenth and eighteenth centuries when plantation owners grew fat and monastic orders counted in the money. There are even more churches here than up north, and there is an itinerary, in English, which will guide you round what is called the Circuit of Churches. The first one I come to, up the hill from the hotel, is the Church and Convent of St Francis. Begun in 1580, it's the oldest convent in Brazil and according to my guide book 'among the finest in South America'. I wander in and pay a couple of pounds to look around. Very ornate, barely a surface unattended to, and the sacristy is particularly splendid, with a massive cabinet carved most delicately from hard, dark jacaranda wood and an elaborate coffered ceiling with clusters of painstakingly carved green leaves surrounding the painted panels. There are all sorts of visual surprises here, including a soaring arch at the entrance to a side chapel, every inch of which is covered with intricately worked wood carvings that seem to hang there with no visible means of support, defying gravity. But it's the cloister that dazzles. Its cool and serene arcades are richly decorated with a mural of the life and work of St Francis, picked out in blue *azulejo* tiles, and off to the side a doorway leads into a secluded garden with a panorama of the Atlantic Ocean spread out below. And, unlike the sediment-stained waters off São Luís, it is a beguiling blue.

I walk on up the hill, passing two more fine baroque churches in the space of a few hundred metres. But there was a time when Olinda could have looked very different. The Portuguese founded the town in 1535 when no one in Europe knew much about Brazil, but the success of Brazilwood and sugar exports changed the situation and almost a hundred years later tempted the formidably mercantile Dutch to turn their attention from east to west. Under the leadership of Maurice

of Nassau they attacked Olinda and set up a capital of Dutch Brazil on the river delta land which they drained south of the town. The reclaimed land is now called Recife, after the long offshore reefs that protect it, but for twenty years it was Mauritzstadt, a Protestant town in a Catholic empire. Maurice was a tolerant man and allowed freedom of religion. A synagogue, established in Recife, exists to this day. But the men who ran the Dutch West India Company were hardline Calvinists, as severe in their architecture as they were in their taxation. Catholic churches were threatened and all building stopped. In frustration Maurice returned to Holland, leaving them to impose their own zealous Protestantism in Brazil. Not surprisingly, the Brazilians rebelled against their repressors, defeating the Dutch in a big naval battle at Guarapes in 1649. The Dutch West India Company finally abandoned Brazil in 1654, as had the French, who founded São Luís in 1612 only to abandon it three years later. For the next two centuries, Brazil was left to the Portuguese.

A last steep climb brings me out in front of the Alto da Sé Cathedral and to a breathtaking view over the city and across the water to the vast spread of tower blocks that is the skyline of Recife, incomparably more huge than Olinda.

There are enjoyments to be found in a small town and one of these is an early evening stroll through largely traffic-free streets to watch an unhurried world coming together at the end of the day. I discover the modest charms of the Bodega de Véio, a local pub, corner café and general store combined. There isn't much room inside, but what there is is packed with everything you could ever want. And customers are treated like family, and encouraged to stay and chat.

1

2

Above:* 1** *· Evening in Olinda. Everyone's out on the street or in* **2** *· the Bodega de Véio, the shop, bar and café that music promoter Paulo André has introduced me to.* ***Opposite *· Looking out over the 'Venice of Brazil' from the apartment blocks they call the Hollywood of Recife. The Capibaribe River sweeps out to sea passing some of Recife's finest old buildings, including the white-domed Palace of Justice.*

As well as selling brooms and batteries and babies' nappies, the staff behind the counter dispense beer, *cachaca* or whisky, whilst cutting up cheese and slicing ham and sausage snacks to eat with them. As you eat and drink you can ruminate on shelves stacked to the ceiling with rulers, biros, pet food, tampons, cans of Red Bull, bathroom mirrors, cigarette lighters, postcards, stamps, umbrellas, shovels, school notebooks and hairbrushes. And somehow there is still space for photos of the family who have owned and run the shop for generations. The Bodega de Véio is a place to meet and gossip and very few people who go inside seem to want to come out.

Day 27 · Recife

LYING at the far eastern tip of Brazil, Recife has the advantage of being just about the closest the continent comes to Europe or Africa. With better port facilities than Olinda, Recife grew to be the outlet for the huge wealth, mainly of sugar and cotton, from the state of Pernambuco. The export hub has now moved sixteen kilometres down the coast to the burgeoning modern port of Suape, but Recife remains the fourth-largest city in Brazil.

Like São Luís it's another city built where rivers reach the sea. In this case across the point where the mouth of the Tejipió, the Jordão (Jordan) and the Pina empty into the wide Bacia do Pina. There are so many secondary waterways in this river system that Recife has been dubbed, wholly optimistically, the 'Venice of Brazil'.

This morning, I'm looking down on the Venice of Brazil from the twentieth floor of one of a group of four tower blocks known as the Hollywood of Recife. Though outwardly undistinguished, these hefty waterside apartment blocks on the Rua da Aurora are home to some of the creative talent that is reviving this once-unambitious city. In recent years Recife, a city which grew rich on sugar cane, has become the scene of new and adventurous cultural work, especially in music.

I've been brought here by Paulo André, a tall, bearded music promoter in his late thirties, who has done as much as anybody to put the Recife and Pernambuco

sound on the map. Not only in Brazil but internationally, at world music festivals in Central Park New York and Womad in London.

We're in the apartment of a slim, unostentatious young man called Helder Aragão de Melo, who under the deliberately provocative nickname of 'dj dolores' has become famous across Brazil for his fusion of the trombones, *rabeca* fiddles, drums and guitars of local music with electronic sampling.

'Music is the invention of the slaves,' dolores explains. 'In all America the music base is African, from samba to blues to reggae.' And Recife, where the bossa nova originated, now has some of the best of the emerging national talent.

He and his band Santa Massa are playing Brasília this evening before going on to São Paulo. He says that, unlike the UK, there no outlets on the radio for experimental work like his. Television plays soap operas all day long, so if he wants to be heard he's no alternative but to take his band round the country. With typical Brazilian generosity he makes time before he leaves for the airport to show me how he creates his music, simply by opening his laptop.

'The laptop,' he enthuses, 'is like the new drum for this generation. The bass in the music, the beat. They are creating their own musical identity using this. You can have it with you all the time and you can make music everywhere.'

His apartment may have a fantastic view over the old city and out to the long reef which gives the city its name, but inside it's defiantly geeky. Apart from a punchbag which hangs in front of the window, a poster or two and a stack of vinyl albums by the likes of Tom Waits and Bob Marley, the only furnishings are strictly functional. Cables, batteries, disk drives and other bits of wiring lie around. He sits beside me and feeds in and mixes various samples. What is interesting is how much of this hi-tech approach depends on traditional sources. He points out the Arabic and Turkish sounds in there. dolores calls it a Balkan harmony.

1

2

3

4

5

'We love Balkan music, sometimes the rhythms are very similar to Brazilian rhythms.'

These, he says, are part of the Portuguese heritage. Portugal, like Spain, was part of the Moorish empire for several centuries, and absorbed North African and Mediterranean influences to which was then added the music from sub-Saharan Africa that the slaves brought over with them. Yet another element comes from *baião* and *forró* – the country music of the North-East, as popularized by Luiz Gonzaga, a Brazilian national hero who died in 1989. The international influence stretches even farther here as Gonzaga was brought up on polka from Russia.

We leave dj to pack for Brasília and walk outside. Across the busy road, along the embankment and opposite a filling station is an eye-catching statue of a naked coiled figure bound up in a ball and hanging from a single steel post below a wall of metal sheeting. It commemorates the victims of the dictatorship and military government which ran Brazil for more than twenty years, from 1964 until 1985.

Paulo looks up at it. His own uncle was one of those arrested and imprisoned.

'That's the position they used to torture people.' It was called the *pau de arara*. The parrot's perch.

Though the repression was nowhere near as brutal as it was in Argentina and Chile, those who opposed the government, especially Communists or other left-wingers, were tortured and some exiled. As part of this Torture Memorial are sixty stones in the ground, each of which represents someone who was tortured for their beliefs. I notice a few of the brass plaques are missing. Paulo, with some embarrassment, explains that they have been stolen. Stolen for the metal on which the names were inscribed.

He shakes his head and says candidly:

'We are a poor country. People take whatever they can.'

Further along the road is another dramatic structure. A huge crab, made from scrap metal, rises some three metres above the grass, its legs and body vividly painted and heavily graffitied. Paulo is more cheerful as he explains this one. The shoreline around Recife was once thick with mangrove beds. During the bad years of political stagnation much of this was destroyed for indiscriminate development. The recent halting of the mangrove destruction is seen as a sign of hope. A new respect for the environment and a new era for the city. As the mangrove beds are the natural habitat of the crab, so the crab has been adopted as a symbol of a new era for Recife, politically, environmentally and artistically.

We lunch at the Pernambuco Yacht Club, out by the sea wall. It's certainly not Cowes, but the food is glorious. A tumbler of *caldinho*, a fish soup, loosens the taste buds, which are further indulged by a fine *moqueca* of fresh shrimp, red mullet and beans, washed down with the deliciously aromatic mango-like juice of the *caju*.

Recife is the only place I've seen which has posters warning of shark attacks. In any other country these might be dismissed as exaggeration by the health and safety-conscious, but Brazil is not big on warnings so it must be something serious. And it is. A helicopter flying low overhead as we walk out along the sea wall is from a local news channel following up a shark attack that took place only yesterday. A young surfer was quite badly mauled. It's a bit of a cause célèbre here as surfing anywhere near the reef is illegal. Some think he got what he deserved. Meanwhile the cheery victim has already announced that he will be back on his board as soon as he's out of hospital.

There is a kind of craziness in the air here. In the nicest possible way. It shows itself in a teasing of conformity, a duty of self-expression, whatever shape or form it takes. This afternoon I met a film director who declared himself a big Monty

***Opposite:* 1** *· The tortured figure commemorates those arrested and imprisoned during the years of dictatorship from 1964 to 1985.* **2** *· With Paulo André, paying musical homage at the statue of the great Luiz Gonzaga, king of north-east Brazilian country music.* **3** *· Street art by the river. The crab that is the symbol of the resurgent cultural life of Recife.* **4** *· With dj dolores. He and his band, the hugely popular Santa Massa, play a rich and complex mix of traditional and electronic music.* **5** *· Cycling to work.*

Python fan. He gave me a copy of his latest film, called *Recife Frio,* a sort of meteorological horror story, examining what might happen to Brazilians if it ever got cold here. He shook his head incredulously.

'I mean, it's like, what would happen if we had to put *coats* on.'

Another example of artistic audacity is the Sculpture Park located at the very end of the great pile of granite stones that shelter the harbour. To reach it you have to run a gauntlet of spray from Atlantic rollers smashing into the wall. The sculptures are all the work of a celebrated local artist, Francisco Brennand, and the park was opened in 2000 to commemorate the 500th anniversary of the first European footfall in Brazil. There are various fantastical figures – birds with huge feet, green eggs, women's heads, mouths agape as if screaming – but the centrepiece is the Coluna de Cristal, the Crystal Column, which rises over thirty metres above the sea. There are metal bands around it with holes in and ceramic tiling on the shaft. At the top is what looks like a flower in bud. When it was completed the wife of the then Mayor was quoted in a newspaper saying that she thought it resembled a huge penis. The Mayor was so incensed at this that he visited the newspaper's office armed with a gun, vowing to shoot dead the journalist who'd written the story.

Paulo tells this with some relish. The Mayor never recovered credibility after this incident and is now out of power. A good result, as far as Paulo is concerned.

'He was one of those friends of the sugar barons.'

Day 28 · Olinda and Recife

BASIL LOOKS a bit hollow-eyed at breakfast. Encouraged by my account of my first morning's walk, he got up very early to take some pictures on the Circuit of Churches. Seeing a column of nuns processing into the Cathedral, he set up his camera to catch the shot of a lifetime when they re-emerged. Everything was right – the light, the location, the white walls of the Cathedral. He waited over an hour before tentatively taking a look inside to try and estimate how long they might be. He found the Cathedral empty and a door at the back faintly ajar.

Street art is all over the place in Brazil. It's unselfconscious, expressive and seemingly tolerated however obscure it might be. Opposite an immaculately painted Baptist church in the tidy streets of Olinda is a wall covered with a mass of graphic images created by a twenty-four-year-old artist called Derlon Almeida, known, as most celebrities are in Brazil, only by his Christian name. Derlon is not an angry graffiti artist. He sees his work as urban art, using walls instead of canvases. His surreal images remind me of Brennand, he of the Crystal Column, or Picasso with a sense of humour. There's a striking image of a fish with a man's body sitting on a chair holding a huge bottle of Pitú, the popular local brand of *cachaca*. Drinking like a fish is what it's all about. Fish is a big thing in Olinda/ Recife, as is drinking; so, he says, he's just put the two together. Derlon is almost mainstream now. He has a studio, and takes on commissions, but at the weekends he still likes to get on his bike with his paints and look for some walls.

Derlon's inspiration comes from the legends of Pernambuco, which spark off his own fertile imagination; but in everyday life Brazil delivers all sorts of odd, surreal and striking images. On the way into Recife, I noticed a line of six people waiting for a bus, all standing in a perfect diagonal one behind the other, and occasionally shifting an inch or two to the right. Then I realized they were all sharing the thin column of shade cast by the bus stop. A little way further along a busy, fairly anonymous road, I was brought up short by a magnificent pair of wrought-iron gates, set in high walls above which I could just make out strange shapes of cracked and bulging stonework. I asked Paulo and he told me that this

Opposite · *The Sculpture Park, dominated by the thirty-metre-high Coluna de Cristal, was opened in 2000 to mark 500 years of a European presence in Brazil.*

Below: 1 · *Nuns outside the rain-stained Cathedral in Olinda.*

2 · *Drinking like a fish. With graffiti artist Derlon Almeida beside a fine example of his work.*

1

2

was the British Cemetery. Evidently a lot of British came out to Brazil at the end of the nineteenth century to help build the railways which, after the abolition of slave labour, became the most efficient way of bringing the coffee, cotton and sugar out from the interior.

Another eye-catching sight is a fine station in the heart of Recife. It was built 150 years ago for the EFCP – the Estrada de Ferro Central de Pernambuco – with British steel and French style. The railway network, up here in the North-East particularly, has been superseded by road transport and there's no longer any traffic into the station. But a team is now at work making a very good job of restoring the dashing exterior, with busts of the engineers who built the railway, heraldic company emblems, and a magnificent semicircular window with a pattern of wrought ironwork fanning out across it. Inside, under the original Victorian canopy, are a few chunky steam engines bearing the letters GWBR – the Great Western of Brazil Railway Company. In recreating the station industrial archaeologists came across steel beams with the name of 'Dorman Long, Middlesbrough' stamped on them. The man who showed me the work at the station seemed surprised I knew the name.

'You know them?'

'Oh yes,' I said, with a touch of Yorkshire pride. 'They built the Sydney Harbour Bridge.'

The Venice of Brazil might be pushing it a bit, but I like Recife. Its buildings are a mix of old and new with little of distinction in either. Many of them, especially the modern ones, are in a shabby state, with concrete mildewed and peeling. But it stands out, this prow of Brazil, head onto the ocean, going about its business, sustained by the rich hinterland behind it, and by a creative energy within it. In some ways it reminds me of my home city of Sheffield. Robust, unstylish and indomitable. Adapting itself to a present very different from its past. We end the day back in Old Olinda, Recife's predecessor as capital of a prosperous state. It delivers everything that Recife doesn't: small-scale good taste, an homogeneous architectural style, a soft, fragrant prettiness and a feeling of being close to, indeed barely out of, the past.

I'm rather glad that my last memories of Olinda are quite the opposite of theme-parked colonial cosiness. In search of a last taste of the music scene I find myself at a club called the Xinxim do Baíana, *xinxim* being a classic Bahian dish of spiced chicken braised in palm oil. Though technically in Olinda, it's well off the toy-train circuit, being just one of a number of small crowded clubs beside the main road. Right next door is the Paramedics Union Social Club, where they're already dancing. The music that unites both places is called *forró* (from *forrobodó*, meaning 'to party') and it's Brazilian country music, big in the sertão, the hard, cattle-raising interior of the north-eastern states. It was originally played on accordion and percussion with the triangle featured. Now it's become fashionable with a young crowd and young bands which remain true to the style but experiment with the accompaniment. At eleven at night the band is still setting up. Paulo, who describes *forró* as 'the soundtrack of the North-East', looms above the crowds gathering outside. Most of them are drinking, but not aggressively so.

Forró may be a traditional style of music, but it's a very young and quite affluent crowd milling around outside Xinxim. Basil says they look like librarians. Paulo checks his watch, something Brazilians rarely do, and smiles at my English concern about getting to bed before travelling again tomorrow.

'Brazilians are night people. They're in no hurry,' he says, and my heart sinks.

But the music, when it does come, is worth waiting up for. Fresh, fast and lively, it's provided by a line-up that includes two percussionists sharing a variety of drums, shakers, a triangle and tom-tom, a fiddle player on a *rabeca*, with a hand-made bow, and an electric guitarist. The *forró* dance steps, done well, are amazing to watch. The couples dance close and the movement seems to come

Opposite · *The railways may have gone but Recife looks after its historic station. The magnificent old window dates back a 150 years. French-designed and built with British steel.*
Below: 1-2 · *Clubbers gather outside and inside the Ximxim in Olinda for* forró *night.*

1

2

Above · In Brazil, everybody dances. Band in the background. Englishman learns forró *in the foreground.*

almost entirely from below the waist, feet moving in a rapid pattern, whilst hips gyrate rhythmically in a loose and sinuous, constantly rolling movement. This is extrovert, sexy stuff and the best dancers are marvellously agile. Paulo bellows through the wall of noise to point out that this is not a dance you sit and watch, and the next thing I know, I'm invited into the mêlée by two young girls and the standard goes way, way down. Despite all my reservations there is something so infectious about dancing the *forró* that I completely forget about tomorrow. Which is now here.

Day 29 · Recife 🚌 Salgueiro

A FEW HUNDRED kilometres to the west of Recife is the land where the *forró* was born. It's called the *sertão*, and it's famously hot and dry. We leave Recife in pouring rain as another depression moves in off the Atlantic, but by the time our plane puts down at Juazeiro do Norte, over 500 kilometres (310 miles) inland, there is not a drop of rain to be seen. Nor has there been any for quite a while. Away from the coast the heat is less humid but more intense. Juazeiro is a pilgrimage city, the home, from the 1870s to the 1930s, of the legendary Padre Cícero who devoted his life to the poor and dispossessed. But what turned Cícero from a good priest to a legend was that he was believed to have miraculous powers. During a Mass, a Communion wafer, blessed by Padre Cícero, is said to have bled in the mouth of a woman he passed it to. This and other perceived examples of his powers (there were those who suddenly won the lottery after praying to Padre C) resulted in an enduring popularity. There are six annual pilgrimages to Juazeiro do Norte every year.

We head south from Juazeiro, hoping to find cowboys. There aren't many of the traditional *vaqueiros* left but their values are still practised and upheld in the remote outback area on the border between the states of Ceará and Pernambuco. At first the road runs through green and cultivated land where the prevailing *caatinga* scrub has been cut back. There are farms with large ponds, and crops as well as cattle. The small town of Jardim, literally 'Garden', announces itself as 'Capital do Milho' – 'Corn Capital'. The cafés are rough and ready. Most have a brazier outside with hot coals always on the go, for this is meat country and a snack nearly always involves something from the barbecue. We sit and have coffee, without meat, in a small establishment whose walls are plastered with emblems and posters of the Rio football club Vasco da Gama. The team motifs hark back to the early Portuguese explorers: galleons and Maltese crosses. The only other table is occupied by a large contingent of black-clad policemen, bristling with weapons and bearing the words 'Força Táctica' on their backs. Now they *are* eating meat.

As we continue south the farms get smaller and fewer and the *caatinga*, with its mix of low thorn trees and cactus, closes in around us. We're almost at Salgueiro, where we're to spend the night, when we come across heavy equipment, construction sites and road diversions. Below us a long deep cut in the hard red rock stretches into the distance in both directions. It's the bed of a brand-new railway. Not a passenger railway, even though Brazil is desperately short of them, but a freight line to transport iron ore and other minerals from the interior to the coast, and from there, almost certainly, to China, now one of Brazil's major trading partners. It's known as Lula's railway, as the ex-President is from these parts, and it will provide thousands of jobs in a pretty poor area.

Maybe this mini railway boom explains the unlikely presence of a modern steel and glass hotel just outside Salgueiro. The only problem is that the hotel isn't finished. Reception is a building site, with cement splashes everywhere, bare breeze-block walls and light fittings on the end of wires hanging from the wall. The staff sit at trestle tables with computer wires trailing around them. The staircase is still wrapped up and not fully attached to the wall. My room, however, is spacious and comfortable, but I have to make my own bed.

A new road, perpetually busy with construction traffic, runs past the hotel. Apart from the noise, it also involves a dice with death to get to the only restaurant in the area. It's a *churrascaria*, a grill, typical of Brazil, especially here in the interior. 'Sabor do Sertão', it announces. 'Taste of the Sertão'. This turns out, surprise, surprise, to involve lots of meat, fresh off the fire, and brought to the table on long skewers from which you slice off your own requirements. The skewer keeps returning with fresh cuts of beef, so beautifully tender that after ten days of fish, I'm a raving carnivore again. Good preparation for the cowboys.

Day 30 · West of Serrita

***Above** · Christ the Redeemer looms over the streets of Serrita – 'The Cowboy Capital'.*
***Opposite:** 1 · 3 · Weathered from the constant exposure to the sun, cowboys arrive for the Pega de Boi – 'Catch my Bull'. 2 · A celebration of their skills.*

A HALF-HOUR DRIVE from the Grand Hotel Inacabado – *inacabado* means 'unfinished' – is a small town with a steel arch across the road bearing the sign 'Bem Vindo à Serrita. A Capital do Vaqueiro' – 'Welcome to Serrita, the Cowboy Capital'. Which is about as exciting as it gets. There are rows of identical tiny houses, not much bigger than hutches, running in straight lines up the low hillside to one side of the town. At the centre is a crossroads, around which are grouped an Evangelical church run by the Assembly of God, a store and filling station, and a tall stepped plinth at the top of which is a small statue of Padre Cícero, absurdly out of proportion to its pedestal. There's a certain listlessness to the place. A few people sit by the roadside, their faces more Indian than African, eyes following the occasional well-worn pick-up truck as it clatters past. Eventually a car draws up and a tall, good-looking young man gets out and hails us. His name is Tiago Câncio. His father was João Câncio, another legendary padre. Padre João loved the cowboy way of life and was so deeply concerned that it was in danger of dying out that he devised an event called the *Missa do Vaqueiro*, the Cowboy Mass, which would bring together all the *vaqueiros* scattered about the region to worship together. He won support from no less a figure than Luiz Gonzaga – the hugely respected man of the *sertão* who'd become a nationally famous singer and musician. The Mass was so successful that it is now a regular institution. Meanwhile Tiago's father had fallen in love with one of those who was helping him and he left the Church to marry a much younger woman called Helena, who became Tiago's mother and who is sitting next to him in the car. She, like her son, has handsome, regular features. Golden hair spills out from beneath a wide-brimmed hat.

The success of the annual Mass spawned a number of other initiatives including a monthly get-together of cowboys called Pega de Boi, 'Catch my Bull'. It's a celebration of cowboy skills, a chance to win some money and an excuse for a party. This is what Tiago and Helena are taking us to today.

As we drive north and west from Serrita the farms become fewer and the scenery more monotonous. The heart of Brazil is a plateau of very old, hard rock and apart from the odd dramatic sweep of an escarpment, the landscape of the *sertão* consists of kilometre after kilometre of low undulating hills, covered with a mix of small thorn trees, cactus and scrubby bush. The switchback roads, following the old cattle trails, stretch ahead, long and straight. They're in pretty poor shape, pitted and potholed.

After almost an hour we turn off the road, through gates marked with the name 'Fazenda Angico'. We follow a sandy track past fields of withered maze until

1

2

3

we come to a red-tiled, whitewashed farm cottage with a large tree outside and beside it a makeshift tent, with a covering stretched across four tree trunks. This is where the Pega de Boi gathering will take place. Though the high point of the day's activities is the capture of the bulls, this is also a family get-together, and already there are young men drinking in the tent and women in the house preparing food. A few real cowboys are arriving, galloping in on horses, some of which look pretty threadbare and some of the riders much older than I had expected, men with tired eyes and deeply lined faces. The organizer of the cowboy side of things is a whippet-thin seventy-year-old called Julio. His eyes are anything but tired. They dart around with a restless energy, in a face dominated by a fine beak of a nose and a defiantly jutting jaw. Like most of the cowboys his skin is leathered and weathered and drawn tight across his cheekbones. It's also bruised and dotted with scabs of dried blood. I ask if he might have been chasing too many bulls but he explains with much laughter that he was nursing a cow's wound and had forgotten to tie its legs together first.

He is the archetypal *vaqueiro*. He learnt the skills of the cowboy from his father, who in turn learnt them from his father. I ask if he'd ever wanted to do anything else and he shook his head vigorously.

'Once a cowboy, always a cowboy!'

I wonder about the next generation. In a world of mobile phones and motorbikes, do boys still want to be cowboys? He chuckles.

'Oh yes. Every single child. When they come to age the parents send them to school and they say that they don't want to. They want to be cowboys.'

Julio is also a successful farmer, which puts him in a stronger position than some of the desperate-looking men who are riding in today to try and pick up some prize money in the bull chase. He, like Tiago Câncio and Helena, is also very much aware of the need to assert the relevance of the profession to modern life, to foster a sense of community amongst men who often don't see each other for weeks on end, to support the families and to keep alive the skills of the *vaqueiro*.

This morning, as the cowboys, their families and other hangers-on are appearing out of the bush, Julio takes the younger boys off to a paddock to teach some of the techniques of bull-catching for which he is renowned. Like Julio, Tiago Câncio is equally committed to the cowboy way of life.

'They risk their lives to earn the bread to survive,' he tells me.

Tiago is wearing the conical leather cap that belonged to his father and which many *vaqueiros* still regard as the best defence against the spikes and thorns they ride through.

'In this way, he's always with me.'

Tiago has no ambitions to be a cowboy himself but as a local politician he champions their cause and, with his mother, has opened a centre in Serrita where the history of the *vaqueiro* is told and skills like leather-cutting and decoration are kept alive.

I ask him if cowboys are naturally religious people and he nods vigorously.

'Very religious. They go to church. They pray when they wake up and before going to bed and before meals. But mainly when they go after the bulls, then they always ask for God's protection.'

As the place fills up I must say I can't see strong signs of spirituality. The young men just here for a drink are gathered in tight groups drinking beer and *cachaca* chasers. The mothers are preparing lunch, and their daughters are climbing out of cars in high heels and party dresses, their hair long and glossy and faces thick with make-up. Even more incongruous in this environment is a squad of half a dozen well-armed policemen, who stand together looking hot and a little self-conscious. They're accompanied by a small ambulance, attended by a nurse in a long white coat, huge shades and a floppy straw hat with a purple flower attached. And of course no event in Brazil is complete without a sound-system and sure enough, even here in the middle of the bush, speakers the size of small power stations are being prepared for the dancing that will come later.

Despite this elaborate equipment there is a marked lack of basic facilities. With the bar at full tilt and goat stew and beans being generously dispensed, there is a steady stream of punters, defying the thorns as they dash in and out of the surrounding undergrowth.

It's early afternoon before attention turns to the Pega de Boi, and the cowboys get their chance to show their skills. Five bulls are secured in a corral a little way up the track. They will be released and after a fifteen-minute interval the cowboys can begin their pursuit. The first thing that strikes me is how small the bulls are. These are not the fearsome brutes of Hemingway's world but apparently mild-mannered specimens about the size of a small cow. To protect themselves from the viciousness of the spiky scrub, the cowboys don the leather equivalent of a suit of armour. It's sturdy bull's leather, and some of it is as ornately fashioned and elaborately decorated as a medieval knight's. The legs are protected by a pair of chaps, some of such thick leather that they stand up on their own. An apron is worn from the neck to the groin to protect the chest and stomach and on top of that is a bulbous leather jacket, the *jibão*, curved at the back like a tortoise's shell. Leather gauntlets are worn over the back of their hands and on their heads are the distinctive conical caps with drawstrings secured beneath the chin. I'm told that despite this comprehensive protection some of the cowboys will deliberately leave a strap untied or a hand revealed, as drops of blood are seen as a badge of courage.

Above · *Cowboys' families and admirers arrive for the party. Not exactly dressed for catching a bull. Or are they?*

As the time of release approaches Julio looks pleased. There is a good turnout. Some 160 riders are lining up along the path. They look timeless. They could be any army, anywhere in the world, anytime in the last 2,000 years. And the horses stand waiting, with their inscrutable, patient eyes.

1

2

3

4

5 

 6

Then comes a shout and a muffled cheer as the gates of the corral are opened and the bulls, surprisingly unhurriedly in some cases, make their way out. Once loose, they accelerate enthusiastically into the undergrowth and are soon out of sight.

The fifteen minutes allowed for them to get well clear seems to last for ever. It's growing hotter by the hour and must be almost unbearable inside the heavy leathers. Lips are licked, eyes rubbed, flies flicked from faces. Some of the young riders look around cockily, exchanging a joke or two. Some have taken too much drink and look ill-prepared for what's ahead. The old hands narrow their eyes and wait. This, after all, is what they do for a living, and have done for a long, long time. Music drifts up from the nearby encampment. The jolly, upbeat strains of an accordion, carrying the sound of *forró* in the wind. Probably a Luiz Gonzaga song. Appropriate really, considering he was one of those who helped put the *vaqueiro* back on the map.

'Ao boi!' the shout goes up, and with cheers and shouts of encouragement from the spectators, the army charges off into the thick scrub, leaving behind a cloud of dust that takes a while to settle.

There are no leader-boards for Pega de Boi, or helicopters or cameras to enable us to follow the action. Instead we rely on the frequent and consistently unreliable shouts of boys who've climbed up the trees to try and be the first to spot a winner. Almost forty-five minutes have passed before one is sighted and the bull is led out of the fields and down the hill. There are four or five riders around it, but the capture has been claimed by one of the younger men who has the tail of the bull held firmly against his saddle. His face shines with pride and perspiration, and from the look in his eyes as he struggles to steer the bull back into the corral you'd think he'd just killed the Minotaur.

Once the celebrations have died down there's quite a long period of nothing much happening. After an hour there is still no sign of a second or third bull, and people are beginning to drift away, back to the party. In a sense it's an image of what today has been all about. The determination to preserve a proud, ancient and immensely tough way of life in a world that's moving on.

Opposite:* *1 *· The bulls are let out.* ***2*** *· The cowboys give chase.* ***3-4*** *· The first bull is brought back and into the corral.* ***Above: 5*** *· With Tiago Câncio, wearing his father's traditional leather hat, and his mother Helena. Behind us, the lethal cactus scrub the cowboys have to ride through.* ***6*** *· A hug from Julio, the inspirational cowboy.*

Day 31 · Salvador

Above · *A young Salvadorean paints the brightly coloured facades of the old town.* *Opposite* · *Walking the cobbled streets of the Pelourinho, named after the pillory that stood here and where slaves were traded. Newly restored, the colonial buildings glow with fresh paint, and African drums beckon the tourists.*

BAHIA IS the fifth-largest of Brazil's twenty-six states, with a land area just about the size of France. In terms of Brazilian history it is one of the most significant. It was on its long and pristine coastline that the first European set foot in Brazil – by accident, as it turned out. A Portuguese expedition headed by one Pedro Alvares Cabral was blown off-course whilst trying to sail round Africa. Somewhat confused, they stepped ashore on 22 April 1500 near what is now Porto Seguro, in southern Bahia State. They discovered thick forest along the shore. A later, and this time deliberate, Portuguese expedition found this to be an abundant source of a wood they called *pau-brasil*, which produced a valuable red dye which glowed like hot coals (*brasa* in Latin). So the new-found land took its name from its chief product. Brazil.

They also discovered an indigenous people called the Tupinambá, who had in all probability been Brazilians for at least 10,000 years. Once the Europeans landed they set about converting them to Christianity, or if it suited them better, slavery. It's been estimated that there were then five million indigenous people in Brazil. The number now is around 350,000.

The Portuguese soon discovered that an enormous natural harbour lay a couple of hundred kilometres up the coast from where they had first accidentally stumbled on Brazil. It offered shelter and abundant safe havens and in their devoutly thankful way they christened it the Baía de Todos os Santos – All Saints' Bay – as it was discovered on All Saints' Day in 1506. At over 180,000 square kilometres (7,000 square miles), it is believed to be the second-largest in the world after Hudson Bay. In 1549 Tomé de Souza set up the first capital of Portuguese Brazil on the eastern headland of the bay and called it Salvador da Baía de Todos os Santos. The state became Bahia and Salvador the name of the capital. It remained the capital of Brazil for over two hundred years. Sugar and cotton production made Bahia rich but, like all the other unlocked wealth of Brazil, that could never have been achieved without the millions of slaves brought over from Africa. This potent mix of a relatively small number of Portuguese, a much greater number of indigenous tribes and a huge number of slaves created modern Brazil. The city of Salvador may have ceded its capital status, first to Rio and then to Brasília, but it remains the third-biggest city in Brazil, with a population of over three million, eighty-two percent of whom are black. Salvador is the biggest African city outside Africa.

As our flight from Recife descends through scudding clouds I can see the spread of All Saints' Bay below me, an enormous body of water contained by the island of Itaparica on the west and the peninsula of Salvador to the east, with its bristling

crest of skyscrapers clustered between the bay and the Atlantic, dazzling in the sun.

It's a given that there are weird and wonderful things to see in Brazil, and Salvador is no exception. It's partly a lightness of touch, but also a lightness of taste. So the road snakes out of the airport through a long bamboo tunnel, which at night is lit up in blue and green, like a grotto. Halfway into the city, on the central reservation of a six-lane highway, there rises a huge cross made from the compressed bodies of crashed cars. A divine warning to drivers. Even higher than the cross is the long, elegantly curving shape of a newly built Metro line. It runs above us for a few kilometres, offering tantalizing but unfulfilled hope for all those stuck in jams below. Finished five years ago, it has yet to run a single public train. A disaster, I'm told, cheerfully. Trains ordered proved wider than the tunnels and it doesn't connect anywhere that people want to go to. The magic and the madness continue, as we drive through underpasses whose walls are decorated with hundreds of white-tiled seagulls, and rumble up the steep cobbled streets to a hotel called the Redfish, painted green of course, in a half-smart, half-run-down neighbourhood of colonial-style houses. A tall baroque church stands opposite my balcony, uncomfortably big for the narrow streets it overlooks. From my third-floor terraceI can see the waters of the bay over which a new-ish moon hangs decoratively, on its back, like a man in a hammock.

Intoxicated by the unfamiliar feel of the city, I walk the twenty minutes or so from the Pousada Redfish down towards the Pelourinho, the centre of the Old Town. Having seen a *pelourinho* in Alcântara, I know that the word means a whipping-post and marked the place where slaves were bought and sold and beaten, so I'm surprised the name should still be used in such a black city. Not

only used, but used with some pride, for much money has been spent in restoring the steeply angled square and the buildings around it, and the Pelourinho is now a magnet for visitors.

This brings its disappointments. Tourist attractions are somehow predictable wherever they are in the world, and even in Brazil they can't defy the trend. So there are a lot of big smiling ladies about, made even bigger by their wide Bahian skirts. They wear brightly coloured bandanas and stand around in front of shops managing to look both maternal and seductive at the same time. The tourist cameras obligingly record them. But up the side streets there is still plenty of unstaged life to catch the eye. Men playing draughts with beer caps, a barber's shop

with football posters from the 1950s and grass growing out of one wall, a group of very black men all dressed in white, sitting on chairs beside a grubby old wall, phone booths in the shape of two enormous ears, a white poodle with red shoes on. And there is music everywhere, one band overlapping another, sounds from the street mixing with a thudding beat from somewhere inside.

All of a sudden the street opens out into a long rectangle of cobbles with houses and grand municipal buildings on either side, and at each end mighty double-towered churches, one Franciscan, the other Jesuit, face each other. The little breath I have left to be taken away is shed inside the Church of St Francis, an overwhelmingly powerful interior with gold-encrusted walls rising all around, profusely decorated and carved in copious detail. Flowers, foliage, fruit, cherubic faces all lead the eye towards the dominant image of Christ, with St Francis clinging to him, that soars above the altar. I walk up to the Jesuit church, on a square called the Terreiro de Jesus, and am just standing there, marvelling at this amazing city, when a big black four-wheel drive draws up nearby. Four or five people get out and open the tailgate, revealing a white polystyrene icebox of beers and a honeycomb of speakers. At the flick of a switch the music crashes out, and they start to dance. Intuitively I look in their direction, registering toxic disapproval. Their reaction is to smile, wave and invite me over for a beer. My anger withers and I join them. I'm slowly learning not to worry that Brazilians don't worry about the things we worry about.

Opposite · *Salvador, the biggest African city outside Africa. On the streets the women wear big smiles and even bigger Bahian dresses. Everyone's out to sell you something, in the nicest possible way.*

Above · *The breath-taking, gilded interior of the eighteenth-century Church of St Francis in Salvador.*

Day 32 · Salvador

A SHORT WALK through the streets near our hotel with Charles Butler, an artist who created the Pousada Redfish from a shell of a house which he bought for something like $10,000 back in 1998. It's now worth well over a million. We walk in the opposite direction from the touristy Pelourinho. This area, called Santo Antônio, is much less comprehensively restored. I'm surprised to hear that even the most picturesque houses we pass are not nearly as old as they look. Most only date from the 1920s, when Brazil had been independent for forty years, so they can't be described as 'colonial'. They look older, says Charles, because the European styles took a long time to get out to Brazil. And, what with the heat and the rain and the termites, the fabric of the buildings deteriorates fast. Their preservation is largely in the hands of foreigners, with French, German and Italian money leading the conservation investment. According to Charles the Brazilians don't really have an idea of 'old'. When they want a house they want something new. And there's a marked lack of modernity in these streets. A wiry old man comes by, pushing a wheelbarrow piled high with fruit and vegetables. Every now and then he'll be asked for something, or he'll stop at a house and ring the bell. Charles has been living here for almost thirty years. He likes the fact that this neighbourhood still has room for rich and poor. He says it's a good place for an artist, and much of his work reflects the strong, vibrant colours of the neighbourhood. His only real criticism is reserved for state education. He has two children by a Brazilian from whom he's separated and though he'd far rather have them publicly educated, he says the system is so bad that he has no option but to go private.

At the end of the road is a square, the Largo de Santo Antônio, from which comes the sound of clapping and chanting. On a wrought-iron bandstand in the middle of the square four women in white robes, white tunics and white shoes are singing to a small congregation, members of which stand in line to have healing hands laid upon them. One of them has her eyes tight shut, as hands are moved over her stomach. A small distance away a massive body-builder is working out on a set of exercise bars. His muscles spread like sails on a ship as he hoists himself into the air, his grunts of effort a counterpoint to the chanting of the Evangelicals. Do the Brazilians have a word for self-conscious? I can't think when they'd ever use it.

There are extremes of wealth and poverty here in Salvador, as anywhere else in Brazil, and there are many young people from the *favelas*, the shanty towns, who leave home and live on the street, dealing drugs and getting into prostitution to earn some money. Over recent years there have been a number of inventive initiatives aimed at these lost children. Among the most successful is Olodum – the name is African, short for Oludumare, the god of gods of the Yorubá people of Nigeria. Through the Escola Olodum the organizers aim to bring some dignity and achievement back into the lives of these street children by teaching them the

1

2

3

art of African drumming. At the same time, and a little more controversially, they have the political agenda of reminding them of their African heritage. Olodum was dreamt up in 1979 by a charismatic figure called João Jorge, born and brought up here in the Pelourinho. He has political aspirations and is running as a Socialist candidate in the next mayoral elections. A confident and energetic man in his mid-fifties, thick-set, dreadlocked and bespectacled, he says he was brought up on Bob Marley, James Brown and, less predictably, the Beatles and Elvis. He talks to me in the Nelson Mandela Auditorium, a rather grand name for an upstairs room, but Mandela has once been to visit and it's clear that the whole issue of African pride is very important to him. João insists I sit directly opposite him at the table as he punches out figures about Olodum's success. Famous on five continents. Taking 360 poor children, black and white, from the *favelas* to their summer school each year. Their drummers chosen to accompany Michael Jackson and to back Paul Simon in his *Rhythm of the Saints* album. And below the Nelson Mandela Auditorium they have a shop selling Olodum-related merchandise.

I ask him why the drum is so important in Brazilian music.

'Because of the African heritage. The presence of Angolans and Nigerians and slaves from Benin and Ghana and Fanti-Ashanti brought the percussion. Through the drums we express our feelings, our love for the culture and heritage.'

'Are the children growing up now losing their attachment to African culture?' I ask.

João is emphatic.

***Above:* 1** · *Churches are everywhere in old Salvador. This one is right outside my window.* **2** · *The Pousada Redfish is disconcertingly green.* **3** · *Inside the Pousada the sturdy grille on the front door shows security remains a big issue in these poor inner-city areas.*

Above · *Drum master Pacote whips up a terrific morning of dance and percussion as students of the Escola Olodum fill the streets of old Salvador with seemingly inexhaustible noise and energy.*

'They are gaining an Afro-Brazilian identity. They don't want to be Africans, but they are proud to be from an African background and have a consciousness that this is a positive thing; being black, being strong, being beautiful.'

Oddly enough, Brazilian interest in Africa doesn't seem to have been reciprocated. A recent air service between Rio and Dakar in Senegal had to be abandoned for lack of interest.

The theory is one thing, but the practical display of the Olodum sound, given by thirty children from the school, ranging in age from five to eighteen, is quite another. They perform in the streets of the Pelourinho, without warning the locals in advance. It's a stirring thing to watch. The drummers are in floridly designed T-shirts and uniform white cotton trousers and the half-dozen girl dancers are in loose, swinging dresses in Rainbow Nation colours. All are expertly and enthusiastically marshalled by their tall, gangling, drum-master Pacote, in blue baseball cap, 'Escola Olodum' black T-shirt and long red shorts. He starts it all off with a resounding cry.

'Let's wake up the Pelourinho!'

As they drum away, Pacote listens to each of them and gives advice and instruction, none of it more inspiring than his own example of joyful driving energy. For an hour the streets vibrate with the sound and by the end even those they've woken up are applauding. As they disband I walk down the street to take a wide-shot of them all. Beside where I'm standing a pile of uncollected garbage is stacked against the wall. I look again and see that there's a young man sprawled asleep in the middle of it. Initiatives like Olodum will never solve everything.

In the afternoon we go to see an example of how the other half of Salvador lives. In the fashionable area of Garibaldi, close to the zoo, we turn off the freeway onto a green and pleasant lane which takes us up a hill, through security gates and into a neighbourhood of large, comfortable detached houses set back from the road and surrounded by gardens. We're in the company of Suzana Glogowski, an architect from a smart São Paulo practice called Studio MK27, which has designed one of these state-of-the-art houses for a rich Salvadorean who made his money in the restaurant business. Susan is slim and pale and physically about as far from the Bahian stereotype as you could imagine. She calls it the Bahia House, because their brief was to reproduce the essential characteristics of Bahian life, which boil down to the architectural equivalent of 'laid-back'. She smiles at this. Paulistas, she agrees, do have a stereotypical view of the Bahian.

'In São Paulo, where everyone's always busy all the time' – she does a busy-busy mime here – 'there is a feeling that Bahians are all lazy. In fact they're not. They are slow, in the best way you can be slow. They speak slowly and they just enjoy life.'

In the garden stand three large mango trees, classic symbols of the tropics, which feel like guardians of the house. And the design responds accordingly, making use of natural ingredients wherever possible. Instead of conventional air-conditioning the house is aligned to make the most of the cooling breezes that blow up from the ocean and across the peninsula. There is a respect for the Portuguese tradition as well. Lattice-work Mozarabic grille screens can be drawn across to adjust the air flow. The interior is finished throughout with Freijó wood and the roof is of traditional red pantiles. From the 1950s onwards, Suzana thinks, modern design has been something Brazilians have been particularly good at, and apart from the house itself the stylish recycled wood armchairs of Carlos Motta

Below · *The other side of the Bahian dream. A state-of-the-art eco-house in one of Salvador's smartest neighbourhoods. Nature's own air-conditioning comes from the breeze that flows through the retractable walls and the sliding Arabic screens.*

1

2

3

and the benches of Sérgio Rodrigues show what a flair they have for the original and expressive. The lamps, by Tom Dixon, are British.

What Suzana and her partners from chilly, grey São Paulo have achieved is a satisfying balance of light and air. Every one of the many rooms feels as if you are indoors and outdoors at the same time. In the Bahian lifestyle, she says, the word 'varanda' has become a verb as well as a noun. This is the consummate house for people who like to veranda.

We drive back into the city in time to catch the sunset at the Barra lighthouse. It's on a promontory where All Saints' Bay meets the Atlantic Ocean. Apart from the lighthouse it's also occupied by the Forte de Santo Antônio (even military installations are called after saints), built in 1605 and solid as a rock. Clustered around the old walls is a crowd of sunset celebrants, mostly white, I notice. White-faced clowns, pipe players and the usual groups of the stoned and in love. A couple stare out at the ocean, hand in hand. Her T-shirt reads 'True Love', his 'The War Is On'. On one side, surfers ride in perilously, joyfully close to the rocks. On the other side, the powerboats of the young and rich slap and bounce their way across the waves. The sun sinks and disappears to a chorus of applause.

Day 33 · Salvador

THE VALE DAS PEDRINHAS, the 'Valley of Small Stones', is an appropriate name, perhaps, for one of the poorer neighbourhoods of Salvador. It's an untidy mess of buildings in various stages of construction, stacked together in narrow streets at the bottom of a hill. In a rooftop room on one of the grander houses, I'm being introduced to something Bahia has given to the rest of Brazil, to South America, and to the world. It's another legacy of the African connection, a fighting style developed by slaves in self-defence, now reborn as a dance of fast, swirling intensity that has become the second-biggest participation sport in Salvador. It's called *capoeira*. If you're very good at it you become a Master, or *Mestre*, and the trim sixty-six-year-old who is taking today's class is very good at it. Mestre Boa Gente was born south of Salvador at a town called Ilhéus, where he first saw Angolan-style *capoeira* being practised. He came to Salvador, took up wrestling in the school of the Brazilian champion, the Black Leopard, and at the age of eighteen became wrestling champion of Bahia. He eventually gave up the wrestling and now runs his own Capoeira Academy.

Despite being in his mid-sixties, he has remained taut and fit and can still do the moves fluently. The respect on the faces of his pupils today, from young ones of five or six to men in their twenties, is unequivocal. And that's important to him. He's been living and working in this *favela* for many years now and knows the importance of order and discipline in lives all too often lacking either. Everyone in the class is dressed in clean white T-shirts and well-pressed trousers. No one looks poor. No one looks rich. First off, the Mestre takes the youngest ones, both girls and boys, and prowls, lithe as a tiger, talking gently but persuasively as he does so, asking them questions and smiling reassuringly as they give their answers. His aim is to get them loose and relaxed. He encourages them to imitate the movement of animals, alert and wary.

On the walls of this rooftop space are trophies he and his school have won, and a poster of a *capoeira* high-kick with the caption, in English, 'A dance-like fight, a fight-like dance. A song. A way of life.'

Mestre Boa Gente is now ready for some *capoeira* moves. He takes up his *berimbau*, a gawky-looking instrument comprising a curved bamboo bow just over a metre long with a gourd attached at one end, which acts as the sound box. It has one wire, recycled from the lining of reinforced tyres, a stone which acts as a bridge and a thin stick with which to produce the sound from the wire. At the same time he clasps in one hand a small basket of beads which he shakes as he plays. One of his helpers taps away at a tom-tom, and the children begin the dance moves. It's one to one and the idea is to be as aggressive as possible without making contact. Hitting each other would be easy, but it's not hitting each other that makes *capoeira* such a skill. Later in the afternoon the Mestre has laid on a public display by his best Academicians but for now he dismisses the children,

***Opposite:* 1** *· Sunset at Santo Antonio Fort. The walls I'm leaning against are over four hundred years old. When it was built, in 1605, Salvador was the capital of Brazil and its flourishing trade in sugar, cotton and slaves had to be protected.* **2** *· The rich kids in their powerboats race the sun down.* **3** *· The headland soon fills up. There is a long tradition of sunset-worship here.*

1

2

Above: ***1*** · *Mestre Boa Gente, king of capoeira, with the berimbau, the instrument they fight to.* ***2*** · *Highland dancing seems to go down well with his class at the Capoeira Academy.* ***Opposite:*** ***3*** · *Agility and poise are taught at the Academy on the top floor of the Mestre's house.* ***4*** · *In Brazil, the sound-system is on your car, not in your car.* ***5*** · *Taking a breather at the window of the radio station – Voice of the Valley of Small Stones – after a gruelling interview with the Mestre.*

climbs back down into his house on a precarious ladder with one rung missing, and crosses the street to his day job, as a presenter for Vale das Pedrinhas Radio.

'A Voz do Vale das Pedrinhas' – 'The Voice of Vale das Pedrinhas' – is housed in a small, white building with a wooden shutter on the front which opens upwards as in an old cricket score box. The Mestre, who has travelled the world with his *capoeira* school, invites me on his show as a visiting celebrity. The audience, as far as I can tell, is confined to this *favela* – indeed largely consists of those within direct earshot of the building we're in. I can hear my voice booming out into the hot and dusty streets below. This is fine when we're talking about Elvis and world peace but is a little alarming when the Mestre turns serious.

'Michael Palin, you have travelled all over the world. You are a famous man. What do you think of gay marriage?'

This is so out of left field that for a moment my lower jaw goes into free-fall. As I phrase my reply I think of whom I shall offend most, Catholics or Brazilian-Africans of a superstitious bent to whom homosexuality is an abomination. I hear myself clear my throat and then launch into my reply. The Mestre, to his credit, shows neither shock nor approval as I speak of love being the important thing between human beings, and if the two human beings involved are both men, well, there's nothing wrong with that. The Mestre nods, and I feel to my relief that I've got away with it. Now can we please talk about Elvis again?

'And abortion?'

Is it me or is it suddenly very hot in this little studio?

Again I express the classic liberal position and can sense his disappointment. Reasonableness is the last thing he wanted. So un-Brazilian. But the Mestre is moving on, flicking down his computer screen, and I've never been so happy for an ad break.

Discussing this afterwards with our Brazilian translator Dulce, I likened what I'd been through to verbal *capoeira*. But she assures me that there was no aggressive intent. This is the way Brazilians are. They will leap from Elvis to gay marriage because they're plain-speaking people. And apparently gay marriage and reform of the abortion law are two very hot topics in Brazil at the moment.

3

4

5

Mestre Boa Gente is irrepressible. No sooner has he finished his afternoon show than he is out on the streets mobilizing the participants for the evening's *capoeira* fest. It's still hot and I can understand that, without someone like the Mestre to galvanize people, inertia and apathy could easily claim the day. As it is, it takes him a while to get people together. His students from this morning, free from the hawk-eyed discipline of the class, are much less obedient. The older brethren take time to gather. A few women stand looking on, unimpressed. And when the procession is finally assembled, and the *berimbaus* are raised and the drums start to beat, no one seems to notice the large, neatly dressed, elderly man who lies asleep in the gutter, legs outstretched, a ring of keys in the crook of his arm.

For all this, there's a relaxed feeling to the crowd as it moves slowly down the street to an open area a few hundred metres away, with shops and houses on three sides and a very smelly creek on the fourth. They spread out around a cracked concrete circle on which the performance will take place. Boa Gente, always aware of including everyone in the community, starts with the children, who show their skills, before gradually narrowing down the *capoeiristas* until you have only the smartest and the fastest in there, weaving, circling, feinting, teasing, swinging, kicking, turning and swinging away as the remorseless thudding of the tom-toms and the hypnotic skirl of the three *berimbaus* plays them on. People come out onto their balconies or appear on top of half-built breeze-block walls

1

2

3

4

to watch what's going on. A man, quite unconcerned, pushes a wheelbarrow with an air-con unit, two women walk by with babies. A freshly shorn customer comes out of the Barbearia Ebenezer and stops briefly before walking back up the street.

Inside the circle the tempo rises. Mestre leads chants, cracks jokes and urges on the dancers. One of the older men, missing most of his teeth and unsteady with drink a little earlier, is transformed into a whirling dervish once in the ring. He taunts his opponent with tumbles and cartwheels and fierce flicks, all at dazzling speed, at one point appearing to spin round on a single buttock. Two tall and unbelievably agile younger men stalk each other deliberately slowly, their arms and legs moving as if in slow motion. The crowd love it, clapping and cheering them on until they break loose into a whirr of flailing limbs. And still they don't touch each other.

Then there is dancing in which everybody joins, including me. The shanty buildings around, the roar of a nearby highway and the smell of the stagnant stream are all forgotten. And in the middle of it all is the shining, sweating white-toothed-grinning Mestre. His work is known across Brazil and in many other countries. In his worldwide advocacy of *capoeira* as a teaching tool for children, he has lectured in Europe, the US and Australia. Yet home for the remarkable Mestre Boa Gente remains the Valley of Small Stones.

__Opposite: 1__ · Mestre leads the Capoeira Academy, and hanger-on in background, through the favela *to the big public demonstration.*
__2__ · Hanger-on has moment of glory.
__3-4__ · Capoeira *as it should be. The combination of speed and balance is breathtaking to watch. And this being Brazil, they smile as they spar.*

Day 34 · Salvador

THE AFRICAN-NESS of Bahia is nowhere more evident than in the influence and beliefs of Candomblé, which permeates so many areas of life in Salvador and beyond. Its roots are in Africa, amongst the Yorubá, and yet it has become quintessentially Brazilian. When the slaves were brought over to work on the plantations they were deliberately discouraged from practising their own religion, in case it became a rallying point for resistance to the landowners. So instead of one all-pervasive belief system, different elements of African tradition became interwoven, both with each other and then with the prevailing Catholicism of the Portuguese. Candomblé is a syncretic religion, faith-based and animist at the same time, a melding of Europe and Africa, of gods and saints.

To try and understand what all this means I'm taken by Sophia O'Sullivan, daughter of Irish-Brazilian parents, currently studying architecture here, to a remarkable church, the Igreja de Nosso Senhor do Bonfim – literally 'the Church of Our Lord of a Good End' – a reference to its foundation as thanks for safe delivery from the sea. It's a large white, twin-towered church built in the rococo style in 1772, standing in a prominent position on a hill in a north-west suburb of the city. At one time slaves were required to scrub the steps of the church and even after they were granted freedom they not only continued to do so but brought hundreds of other volunteers with them. Now the annual washing of the steps, the Lavagem do Bonfim, has become a major fixture on Salvador's calendar.

1

3

2

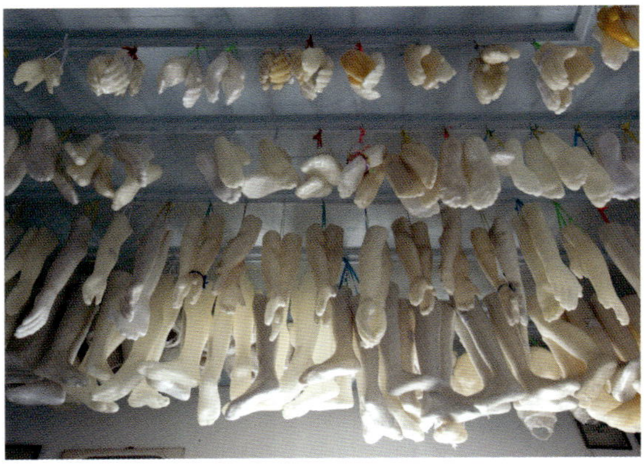

4

*Above: **1-2** · The 240-year-old Church of Nosso Senhor do Bonfim, endowed by a thankful, and rich, Portuguese sea captain for surviving a fierce Atlantic storm. **3** · Fita ribbons, representing a mix of superstition and faith, are bought and hung on the church railings.*

Every third Sunday in January as many as a million pilgrims make the nearly ten-kilometre (six-mile) walk from the downtown port area through the streets to the church. When they arrive they ritually wash the steps with lavender water. This annual celebration, which honours the Creator god of Candomblé as well as Christ, is a fascinating example of the fusion of African animism and faith-based Catholicism. And there are other areas where faith and superstition merge. Sophia shows me strips of ribbon entwined round the railings of the church. They're called *fitas*. Their function is entirely superstitious yet their origin is Catholic. Sophia explains that above the altar in the church is an image of Christ on the cross, a replica of one in Setubal in Portugal, endowed by a Portuguese sea captain as thanks for safe passage through Atlantic storms. What makes it so special is that Our Lord is seen to be dead. It is the only image of a dead Christ on the cross anywhere in Brazil. This, together with its donor being saved from drowning, is believed to have given it miraculous powers. The length of the *fita* is equivalent to the distance from the stigmata on Christ's hand to his heart. The ribbon is tied around the wrist and three knots in it indicate three wishes made, which will only be granted when the ribbon falls apart. Which, in some cases, can take months, even years. They are immensely popular and there is a specially appointed team of young men in blue polo shirts giving them out on the church steps.

Inside the church is another remarkable demonstration of the power of Our

Lord of Bonfim. A small side room off the exuberantly ornate interior is full of quite extraordinary votive tributes to his healing powers. From the ceiling hang wax and plaster models of arms, legs, heads, hearts, breasts, penises, lungs and tiny babies. An artificial limb hangs next to a tennis racket. On the walls are photographs of those who have been cured by Our Lord's intervention. There are portraits of women with babies, proud students with degree scrolls, patients in hospital beds with heart-rate monitors, a man displaying the before and after of a hernia operation, and one or two body-scan images. I ask Sophia if the young generation still believe in all this. She nods very firmly. In Brazil almost everyone believes in some kind of religion or some kind of superstition. Atheism is considered profoundly weird.

Sophia takes me to an ornamental lake called the Dique do Tororo, dammed by the Dutch in the middle of the seventeenth century when they were a force to be reckoned with in this part of South America. It's close to the centre of town, right beside the site of the Fonte Nova Football stadium being built for the World Cup in 2014. As we pass it I see a countdown board. It reads, '1070 Dias Para a Copa 2014' – '1070 days to World Cup 2014'. Beside it is a big red hole in the ground.

Rising from the waters of the lake are a series of distinctive bronze figures representing the *orixás*, the Candomblé deities. Each one has their natural property and their distinctive colour. Xango, in red and gold, is the male god of Fire, Oxum, in gold and white, the goddess of Calm Water (rivers and lakes), Oxóssi, green god of the Forest and the Hunt, Iemanjá, turquoise-blue and gold goddess of the Ocean, Iansã, red and gold, goddess of the Wind and Storms, Ogum, the Warrior god, blue and gold. All attempts to suppress Candomblé and impose Catholicism on the slaves failed.

'The slaves would go to Mass and would be praying for a saint but behind it they were praying for their *orixás*,' Sophia explains. Which is why the *orixás* have their equivalents amongst the Christian hierarchy – Ogum with St Anthony, Iansã with St Barbara, Oxóssi with St George, Iemanjá with the Virgin Mary and so on. But it was only in the 1960s that the religious establishment admitted

Opposite: 4 · *Waxwork offerings hang from the ceiling of a side chapel. Arms, legs, hands, hearts – the equivalent of the part of the body that people believe has been healed by the miraculous powers of this church.*

Below · *Set in an ornamental lake, images of the* orixás, *the gods and goddesses of the African-Brazilian Candomblé religion.*

1

2

Above: ***1*** *· Children play in the street near the* terreiro, *the temple where the Candomblé ceremony will take place. It is a religion that thrives in poorer neighbourhoods.* ***2*** *· Leaves and water are scattered across the entrance to the* terreiro *to propitiate the gods.* ***Opposite: 3*** *· The ceremony begins.* ***4*** *· Participants gather in the kitchen.* ***5*** *· I'm shown to a throne of honour next to the aunt of João, the priest or* Pai de Santo. ***6*** *· The drums start and the rhythmic dancing begins.*

defeat and people were finally allowed to practise Candomblé without fear of being arrested.

'Candomblé basically worships the forces of nature,' says Sophia. 'It's a very ecological religion.'

It's still not that easy for outsiders to watch a traditional Candomblé ceremony, which is why I'm returning this afternoon to the Vale das Pedrinhas. My friend the Mestre Boa Gente has put in a good word for me with his local *terreiro*, or temple. Dressed in white, as instructed, I turn up at Ile Axé Omim Ogunja, as the temple is called, to find myself in a modest house a few streets away from the Mestre's radio station. I had expected something mysterious and unfamiliar, but all seems rather mundane and domestic. A room opening onto the street is decorated with a lot of pink, glittery fabric and white ribbons intertwined with greenery. This is Oxalá's Day – Oxalá being the god of Creation – and a column in the centre of the room is painted to represent a tree trunk and adorned with branches, whilst leaves are scattered across the floor. Before the ceremony proper I'm shown into a tiny cubicle off the main room where I am to have my *búzios* – cowrie shells – read for me by the local Candomblé priest, the *Pai de Santo*, Father of the Saints. His name is Pai João. He's a big man and a tight fit in the confined space. He squeezes a large round belly into an armchair above which is an arrangement of feathers and an African mask. Between us is a low table with a white cloth over it on which are a ring of beads, some cowrie shells, two dice and a glass with some brown thing inside it. He asks me questions, then gathers up the cowrie shells in his big hands, summons up the gods in an African dialect, shakes the shells and scatters them on the table. Each time one of them flies off and I have to retrieve it from the floor. This doesn't seem to bother him much, which suggests to me that this will not be revealing. The replies from the gods are anodyne. I'm healthy but must watch my blood pressure. I have lived a happy, successful life. His credibility is somewhat restored when, after consulting the shells, he quite correctly states that I have three children, and he gets their sexes right (I only discover later that Mestre Boa Gente had disclosed this to him the day before).

When it comes to my turn to ask the gods something, Pai João does display a sense of humour. The comic timing of his reply to my question as to whether England will ever win the football World Cup again is spot on. The gods are invoked, the shells are thrown and he looks at them for some time, occasionally rearranging them in front of him. After much study he takes a deep breath, exhales slowly and looks up at me.

'No.'

Having been given a relatively clean bill of health by the gods, I'm taken back into the main room, which to my eyes is looking more and more like a boudoir and less and less like a temple. I'm shown to a heavily varnished wooden armchair, facing the door and next to where the drummers stand. João's mother was a much respected *Mãe de Santo* who had died only recently. Her photograph is on the wall and her sister sits beside me, impassive behind a pair of thick-rimmed glasses which, together with her age and status, make her look awfully like the Queen. Meanwhile the various participants in the ceremony gather in the doorway of the kitchen. I catch one young man quickly lifting up his tunic and applying a furtive squirt of deodorant.

Then the drum beats begin, loud and fast and insistent, their rhythm pounding off the low ceiling. The twenty celebrants begin circling the column and summoning up the *orixás*, moving ever faster, spurred on by chants from Pai João. After a few exhausting minutes the rhythm changes and a new dance

3

4

5

6

begins, each one reflecting the different part of Africa from which it originates. After almost an hour of sustained frenetic movement, one or two of the dancers show signs of falling into something between trance and hysteria. A young man shakes and shudders as if possessed. Through the open door I can see children playing football in the street.

The *orixás* are now deemed to have been summoned, and in the second part of the ceremony individual dancers reappear dressed as gods in elaborate and complex costumes. They remind me of the similarly ornate, and vigorous, African-inspired ceremony of Bumba Meu Boi up in São Luís. A man is dressed to represent the forest, another wears the swirling red robes and headdress that I'd seen on the figures in the lake. After two hours everyone needs a break and quite suddenly this highly charged ritual turns into a pleasant late-afternoon party.

The Candomblé ceremony is at times powerful and at times mystifying, but the complexity and richness of quite a commonplace event struck me as another instance of the passion and vitality with which black Brazilians approach their religion. The act of worship has to move and involve the participants in something special. What impresses me is that it also has to be fresh each time. In Candomblé no one quite knows exactly what will happen when the drums begin.

Opposite · *The Candomblé ceremony in full swing. A participant dances himself into an apparent hypnotic state, rolling around on the floor as if possessed.*

Above · *The dancers take on the costumes and characters of the* orixás *– gods that they have previously summoned. The small room is hot, yet they gyrate for an hour or more.*

Day 35 · Salvador

Above · With Dadá, the doyenne of Bahian cuisine, selecting fruit for the meal she's making today. ***Opposite: 1*** *· Dadá's daughter and grandson Bernardino.* ***2-4*** *· Produce can be bought at street stalls all over the city. Dadá always buys fresh.*

BAHIAN COOKING is, like Candomblé, a hybrid of African, Portuguese and indigenous influences. Based largely on the abundance of seafood, it has a reputation for being a lot more interesting than the meaty fare that predominates in much of the rest of Brazil. If there is one woman who can claim to personify Bahian cooking it's Aldaci dos Santos, loved, envied, criticized, but known to all as 'Dadá'. From selling snacks on the beach she rose to become a restaurant owner and chef to the famous, including the musician-turned-Culture Minister Gilberto Gil, the hugely popular Salvadorean writer Jorge Amado and Hillary Clinton. Now she has not only opened a second restaurant in Salvador, but is branching out beyond Bahia. There are already some intimations of collateral damage. Two guides both mention her flagship restaurant, Sorriso da Dadá, but one grumbles that 'all has sadly fallen somewhat from grace' and the other warns that 'Dadá has taken her eye off the ball'. None of this seems to have affected Dadá's naturally sunny disposition when we meet up outside the fish market, the Mercado do Peixe, early this morning. Dadá is in her fifties, generously proportioned but not statuesque, dressed in a leopardskin dress with her hair bunched up in a knotted white headscarf. She beams broadly as she introduces me to her daughter Daniela and her grandson Bernardino, about the same age as my two-year-old grandson Wilbur, so we have things beside food to talk about.

Introductions done, Dadá takes me off into the fish market for the first stage of my crash course in Bahian cuisine. She draws admiring glances from the porters. As we go by one of them does an improvised samba for her, and pretty nimble it is too for a man in rubber boots. She's going to show me how to make *moqueca*, the classic dish of the North-East which I first tried in São Luís. Its origin is thought to be from the Tupinambá, one of the indigenous tribes who were here long before the Europeans and Africans arrived. It's basically a fish stew, so Dadá is on the lookout for a good fleshy redfish – what we would probably call red snapper – and after some careful weighing up and turning over in her hands she selects the ones she wants, and we then go on to audition the prawns. She forensically examines the various grey bucketfuls that are presented to her and, having made her choice, indicates to me that the time has come for my co-operation. She points at the bulging bags of prawns, and though she doesn't speak much English, the body language says it all.

'You carry those two.'

There's something about Dadá that discourages argument, so I pick up the bags – how can prawns be this heavy? – and make off after her to a stall on the other side of the white-enamelled hall, where she's casting a critical eye over the

1

3

2

4

caranguejo, crabs. Not the pink and red, freshly dressed crab that were such a treat on my summer holidays in Norfolk, but a string of crabs all covered in thick black mud as if just pulled from a riverbed.

'We cook them in boiling water. It's a tradition in Salvador. In a lot of bars they serve them with beer.'

Pausing only to add mussels, *lambretas*, to the ingredients, Dadá, running a gauntlet of lustful glances, sails serenely out of the fish market with her prawn- and crab- carrying assistant in hot pursuit. Our next stop is the main food market of Salvador, called after a saint of course. The Mercado de São Joaquim.

This is a big, wonderful rambling mess of a place populated by all humanity. Dadá, fearful of losing me in the crowd, takes me by the hand and weaves me through the narrow alleyways, dodging loads of potatoes, men with parts of pig across their shoulders, and the odd motorbike. There are no shopping trolleys in São Joaquim. Instead they have sharp-edged steel trailers dragged around by porters whom you can hire by the hour. There's clearly a skill to manoeuvring through this clattering, noisy throng, and despite all the various obstacles, everyone just manages to get out of everyone else's way.

Dadá's celebrity follows her around, and there's much smiling and joking with the people she meets. A man shaving fur off a calf's leg breaks off for a word, the purveyor of dried shrimps lets her dig around. There is, as far as I can see, nothing

1

2

ready-wrapped here; every ingredient can be tasted and tested. Dadá is after some particularly strong pepper, and once she finds it, she asks me if I'll grind it whilst she checks out the chillies.

Then she gives me a short treatise on the apparently infinite varieties of manioc flour – white, yellow, a thicker greyer variety, one that looks almost purple. And they all have their own names. Entirely predictably, one is St Anthony, another St Philip and, well, you get the picture. There are beans of all shades from white to jet-black, all in huge open sacks, and a huge choice of herbs and spices. Coriander is the staple for *moqueca*, but Dadá introduces me to a powerfully flavoured African version called *cilantro*.

'Bull's coriander,' she explains, with a wink. 'The slaves brought it over. It grows wild.'

Then there's dried shrimp and banana leaf and peppermint and spring onions and cassava and of course various meats – smoked pork ribs, dry salted beef, spicy sausages called *calabresa* – so we have to trawl through the piles of liver and sweetmeats and the pigs' faces lying there on the slab like ghoulish party masks. By the time we're finished I'm completely wrung out and more than a little peevish when, squashed up between a delivery of custard apples and a man with a box full of football shirts, I find someone at my feet. I think he might have dropped something but he brings out brushes and polish and starts to clean my shoes. He does a wonderful job and I add an extra *real* or two for being such a sourpuss.

I'm quite relieved when this shopping assault course is over, but if you enjoy people-watching there can be few sites on earth to rival the Mercado São Joaquim. Sad then to be told that its days are numbered, and in a year or so the market will move into new clean, tidy, sweet-smelling, non-leaking, air-conditioned premises nearby. I feel about the Mercado São Joaquim as people feel about Cuba – see it now before it all changes.

Having gathered the ingredients we repair to Sabores da Dadá, the restaurant she has recently opened on the sea front. The decoration has Candomblé overtones. The front is decorated with a colourful swirl of *fitas*, the ubiquitous good-luck wristbands. Inside there are images of the *orixás*, looking like figures out of fairy

3 

 4

tales, and on the wall a figure of St George/Oxóssi and a small shrine to John the Baptist, portrayed as a young boy with a mass of black curls, a halo and a fleece wrapped around him. Once in the tiny kitchen Dadá exchanges her long white scarf for one in vivid yellow, which she ties around her head, before setting to work. She begins by marinating the redfish in lime, salt and ice whilst giving me the task of slicing onions and chopping chillies. As we work she tells me a little more of her history. Her mother worked in the fields for a big landowner, and as a menial in the kitchens Dadá's first acquaintance with good food came from eating the leftovers of the pots and pans before washing them up. She came to Salvador at the age of fourteen to be a housemaid and, except for some time in São Paulo, has been here ever since. Her mother died of cancer and more recently her brother died too. As she tells me this she blinks back tears and I don't think it's just from slicing onions. These losses strengthened her resolve to work even harder. Her tenacity and ambition paid off with the opening of her first restaurant some twenty years ago. When I ask her if she is bored with cooking after all this time she stuffs the sauce of onions, tomatoes, green and red peppers and coconut milk into the fish's underbelly and shakes her head dismissively.

'Each day that goes by I like it more, much more,' she declares adamantly. 'Cooking for me is like having sex. I feel complete, as if I was having a great orgasm.'

'It must be exhausting every time you make a meal.'

She considers this for a moment, then chuckles.

'No. Making love is more exhausting.'

As a series of fierce downpours whip in off the bay, buffeting the little restaurant, Dadá efficiently but unhurriedly puts together a banquet. Apart from the *moqueca*, there are mussels with coriander, and redfish stuffed and served with coriander, the kidney bean and shrimp dumplings known as *acareje*, and *farofa*, the yellow manioc flour fried in oil with bacon and onion to which I'm rapidly becoming addicted. Then passion fruit and mango to cleanse the palate. Dadá leans across the table when I ask her what makes Bahian food so special, so envied in Brazil.

'Bahian cooking is like the Bahian people. It's very colourful, it smells good, is full of flavour and has a soul.'

***Opposite:* 1-2** · *At the Mercado São Joaquim. Soon to be redeveloped, it's a hustling, bustling place where you can get fresh chickens, a surprise shoe shine, and just about anything else.*

***Above:* 3** · *In the kitchen at Dada's seafront restaurant. 'Cooking for me is like having sex.'*

4 · *Enjoying the rewards of our morning together. Superb* moqueca *and a lot of laughs. Very Bahian.*

When we come out there's a patch of sun amongst the downpours. Whatever the guide books may think about her restaurant, Dadá has been responsible for the best meal I've yet had in the North-East. She's a remarkable, ambitious and determined woman who you feel can do anything she sets herself to. Except, perhaps, for the one thing she really needs to be able to do. Clone herself.

Day 36 · Salvador

APPARENTLY the Baía de Todos os Santos, of which I catch tantalizing glimpses from my balcony, is not quite as perfect as it looks. Shining bright and stretching away to the horizon, it would seem to be the perfect getaway from a busy city. The reality is that Bahia and the bay from which it took its name are insidiously intertwined. Eighty percent of all the state's sewage drains into the waters of the Baía, and it is all untreated, as is most of the industrial effluent from the plants and refineries around the bay. There have been crisis meetings between the environmentalists and the water board, but I read that, for now, the pollution continues.

Today, of all days, I wish I hadn't read that, for we're being taken out onto the bay for a sail. And not in any ordinary sailing boat, but in one of the increasingly rare *saveiros*, the big, thick, timber-built barges which were once the workhorses of the inshore cargo trade.

Yesterday's rain has blown through leaving a perfect morning of high blue skies and deep blue seas. We make our way down to the Cidade Baixa, the Lower City, to the port area where the ferries leave for Itaparica Island on the opposite side of the bay. This once-busy, now down-at-heel port area is dominated by the seventy-two-metre-high shaft of one of the city's most remarkable landmarks, the Elevador Lacerda. This great vertical tube has provided pedestrian access between the Higher and Lower cities since 1874. The present monumental construction was built in the 1930s, with an Art Deco finish, and its four separate lifts take about a minute to rise and fall. A ticket costs around 3p. On working days it's busy, for apart from the ferry terminal, there's a big tourist market down here, and promised investment in a new hotel, as well as the recently opened Museum of Black Music, should regenerate this seedy strip by the time Salvador hosts the World Cup.

The two men who are to be our hosts today are, for various reasons, passionate about the old boats. One is Bel Borba, a trim, dapper artist who's just had his first child at the age of fifty-four. He looks like an artist. An Impressionist maybe, all in white with a straw hat and a sharp black moustache. He's bright, expressive and famously prolific, producing portraits and lithographs and ink-point sketches and, most spectacularly, a lot of street art. They were his white seagulls that decorated the underpass as we first drove into the city, and since then I've seen another Bel Borba-decorated embankment, this one covered in orange fish. His fellow director of Viva Saveiro, the trust that is trying to save and restore these old

1

2

sailing boats, could hardly be more different. He's a very large man called Malaca, an engineer by trade, wearing shorts and a voluminous yellow T-shirt with a picture of a *saveiro* printed large on the front. He seems to talk entirely in jokes, and is loving the fact that our sound recordist Seb can't find a microphone harness long enough to fit round his waist. If the Brazilians have a word for extrovert, Malaca would be its embodiment. But I'm sure they don't. Brazilian means extrovert.

The boat lies moored up at the end of a long wooden jetty, the yellow, red and green stripes of its wide wooden hull conspicuous amongst the monochrome fibreglass yachts around it. Malaca hails the crew, an older man called Jorge who's the skipper, and a much younger mate who is immediately despatched to collect supplies of beer and food for the barbecue lunch. Malaca looks up at the sky with approval and shouts something to Bel, which makes him smile.

'He says São Pedro won't take a piss today,' Bel translates, adding helpfully, 'São Pedro is the patron saint of the weather.'

When eventually we're ready and the supplies are on board, the mighty sail is raised, reminding me of the high-masted wherries of the Norfolk Broads or the Thames Estuary, and we move majestically out towards an old fortress that guards the harbour. Having no engines, we're at the whim of the wind, and until we can get up some speed the trans-bay ferries glide effortlessly past us. All of them are named after famous women. I note the *Anita Garibaldi* heading out, as the *Vittoria Regia* makes her way in.

In the 1950s there were over a thousand *saveiros* plying All Saints' Bay. Malaca remembers first going aboard one of them when he was on holiday at the age of five. Once on it, he never wanted to get off, and, in a sense, never has. New roads and the rise of truck transport superseded the *saveiro* and today there are only twenty left, of which only a handful are seaworthy. Malaca is determined not to let them die. Though his energy and ebullience, along with the involvement of local cultural icons like Bel Borba, have gone a long way to raising awareness of Salvador's maritime heritage, they have two big problems facing them. One is finding craftsmen with the traditional skills to work on these big, curved timber frames. They only have two or three full-time restorers, and one of them is

***Above:* 1** · *Three men and a boat. With artist Bel Borba, centre, Malaca, and behind us the brightly coloured hull of a* saveiro, *one of the old wooden sailing boats they're trying to save.*
2 · *Aboard* Sombra da Lua, *'Shadow of the Moon'.*

Above · Sombra da Lua *in full sail on All Saints' Bay. Salvador's skyline in the distance. Rich tower blocks to the right, Liberdade, settled by freed slaves, to the left.*

eighty-four. The other problem is that, thanks to rules imposed by IBAMA, the government's environmental protection agency, the hardwoods from which the boats were built are protected, making it often impossible to get permission for replacement timbers. So they have to cannibalize materials from other *saveiros*.

Once out on the bay the wind picks up and the sun beats down and beers are called for. There's much macho banter between Malaca and his crew, as they cook sausages and make up a salad of onions, tomatoes and coriander with a dish of *farofa* on the side. Over lunch Bel talks of his first experience of travelling in the hold of a *saveiro*. It was like being in a barrel, he remembers, with the smell of cognac, *cachaca*, tobacco and whatever else they'd carried permeating the timbers.

One of the benefits of being out at sea is being able to look at Salvador from a new perspective. The wide panorama of the city skyline runs from the high-income skyscrapers clustered at its southern end, through the Financial District and the Old Town with its landmark church towers, to the long spread of Liberdade which, like its namesake in São Luís, was the area settled by the slaves freed after 1888. Here, also, it is the poorest part of town.

Our return journey, tacking slowly against the wind, is slow, and it's late afternoon before *Sombra da Lua* is finally back at the port. On our way back to the Redfish Bel invites us to see one of his workshops, in a row of old houses in one of the steep streets leading from the Pelourinho to Santo Antônio.

The studio is up on the first floor, with his work on sale downstairs. It's all a bit of a clutter and makes for easy browsing. I ask him his inspirations and he shrugs. Just people, he says, people in the street.

His public work is entirely self-generated. The city doesn't pay him, but it more or less lets him decorate where he wants, which to an Englishman sounds almost unbelievably liberating. And it all began because, as he admits, his free-style work wasn't accepted by the established art colleges so he thought he'd just do it himself. 'What moves my creativity is intuition, spontaneity, and even moments of rage. I have to have fun to create,' says Bel.

Hence the seagulls and the orange fish decorating highway embankments. He's currently using some of the old *saveiro* wood to make new installations and sculptures around the city. There's one in the street outside, a chunky, playfully colourful wooden horse. I can't help but admire the way Bel has remained working at the heart of the city. It certainly isn't the usual genteel art quarter. Only a few yards up from his studio I pass a man slowly sorting through a pile of rubbish, stowing what he selects into different plastic bags before hitching them up onto his shoulder and moving off down the hill, past Bel Borba's shop. Different levels of achievement, maybe, but both men share the same spirit. Waste nothing.

Day 37 · The Recôncavo

THE MANY RIVERS that drain into All Saints' Bay may bring modern pollution problems, but they are also the reason why Salvador and its surrounding towns became so rich. The muddy deposits they brought down with them from the *sertão* made for a fertile shoreline where almost anything would grow. They call this area the Recôncavo (the closest translation in English would be the 'Bight'), and it's some of the most productive land in the country. To try and find out more of where the wealth of old Bahia came from we take the road north and west towards Cachoeira and São Félix, the prosperous twin towns at the heart of the Recôncavo.

Once off the six-lane highway and away from the car dealerships and the shiny, new residential towers of expanding Salvador we're into green rolling hills and a landscape which at first glance could have come straight from the Welsh Borders. Then you look closer and pick out the palms and banana trees tucked away in the folds of the hills. The first sign of the industry that once made so many so rich is a tall brick chimney and beside it the high, grey-smeared walls of an old pitched roof building. It's a sugar factory. In the heyday of world demand, there were over 800 sugar plantations around Salvador. They depended heavily and complacently on their slave workforce, and once that was disbanded their lack of investment in modern production left them hopelessly ill-prepared for open-market competition. There are now a mere handful of sugar producers left.

Evidence of the good times past can be seen in the narrow-gauge railway lines running through the countryside from small towns like Santo Amaro. They're

1

2

rusting now and used as pathways by streams of people, coloured umbrellas raised against the sun, making their way to and from the market.

Thanks to the richness of the soil, there is plenty that grows here besides sugar. Fruits are abundant. Pomegranate, breadfruit, mangoes, custard apples, cashew and cacao, papaya and passion fruit are stacked up for sale by the roadside or loaded into trucks to be shipped into Salvador. In the late sixteenth century the first cattle were introduced here and as the road climbs high over a ridge healthy-looking tan and white cows with great, swinging dewlaps graze the verges beside us.

Signs direct us to eco-resorts, *fazenda* (farm) hotels, roadside stalls with 'Honey for Sale' and other indications that tourism is becoming the new income for farmers capitalizing on the jaded urbanite's appetite for wooded escarpments and undulating meadows. And it's amongst scenery like this that we come upon the town of Cachoeira, set in a protective cluster of hills that run down to the limpid Paraguaçu River.

Cachoeira, the highest navigable point on the river, grew prosperous as the main trading port for the produce of the Recôncavo. As much of this was tobacco and sugar cane from the slave plantations, there was, and still is, a big African influence on the town. Religion is fervently popular, both Candomblé and the newer tide of Evangelical Christianity which is sweeping across Brazil. I see premises belonging to the Foundation of Jesus, the Temple of the Adoration of the Living God and the Assembly of Jesus. On a lamp-post a sign reads 'Confess your Sins to Jesus' and gives a phone number. Strident voices boom out from loudspeakers selling the latest car or the latest religion. I think again of my guide Sophia's observation that in Brazil everyone wants to believe in something.

An old girder bridge, which once carried a railway, leads over the wide, slow-moving Paraguaçu River to São Félix. The river, draining down from the highlands of the Chapada Diamantina, was once a force to be reckoned with, frequently flooding the towns. Now it's been dammed a few kilometres upstream for a big hydroelectric scheme and is a shadow of its former self. São Félix, like Cachoeira, is full of relics of former days, remaindered buildings like the fine, stuccoed station, and some neo-classical warehouse facades. It also boasts a relic that's very much

alive. By the riverside is the Dannemann cigar factory, first established in 1883, and not only still producing cigars, but also hosting the Centro Cultural Dannemann, a gallery for modern art which is the venue for the internationally recognized Recôncavo Art Biennale.

The freshly painted white and straw-brown exterior of the old factory, with two immaculately restored pediments, arched blue doorways and wrought-iron fanlights, gives no indication of what lies inside. It's like stepping forward a hundred years, into an uncluttered, mid-town gallery. Artfully spot-lit, open-plan and with the most modern paintings, collages and installations elegantly displayed. Much of the credit for this must go to an enterprising and charismatic Dutchman called Hans Leusen, President of Dannemann and Dutch Consul in Salvador. Mr Leusen strides out to meet us wearing a well-pressed pair of chinos and an open-necked shirt. He's seventy-four years old and first came out to Brazil in 1962. Tall, with silver-grey hair, he stands very straight, head held high and a proud but steely look in the eye, like a craggy old eagle. In his right hand is a cigar. As he shows us through from the light, airy gallery area to the cigar-making operation at the back of the building, I ask him if, as a gallery owner, he feels at all cut off from the cultural mainstream in the South. He shakes his head. He thinks far too much is made of the North-South divide.

'São Paulo [in the South] is fifty percent people from the North. When I first came here there was no Carnival in São Paulo. That came from the North.'

Opposite: 1 *· The railway terminal in São Félix.* ***2*** *· At the Dannemann cigar factory an expert test-smokes a cigar she's just made.* ***Above*** *· I talk to the head of the company, Hans Leusen, on the factory floor.*

As, of course, did the tobacco industry, though it's much reduced from the old days. Dannemann survives as a small, high-end operation. A sign, 'Welcome to the Circle of Connoisseurs', sets the tone. And the dozen women who are making the cigars in a clean, cool room with plenty of natural light sit at old rolling machinery looking as if they might be an artwork themselves. Hans points out what it is that makes a Dannemann cigar so special. The workforce has strong traditional skills handed down from mothers and grandmothers who worked here. They roll the cigar in paper, by hand, and not in a press. Then it's left in a humidor for a minimum of two weeks before being cut and labelled. Hans himself is a fine advert for the product. He has a cigar on the go all the time and quietly but firmly rebuts any suggestion that it might be less than good for him.

'Cigarette is for the kick,' he says. 'Cigar for the taste.'

Not that Hans Leusen seems to need a kick. He's a restless soul.

'I'm good at setting things up, but then I get bored.'

Deeply aware of the responsibilities of the tobacco producers towards the people they employ and the environment, he provides educational facilities, like computers and tractor lessons for the farmers. He's worked hard to re-forest the Dannemann tobacco farms, and initiated a highly effective adopt-a-tree project which has helped restore over 100,000 trees in the dwindling Mata Atlântica rainforest, which once ran the length of the Brazilian coast. But Hans has interests way beyond the tobacco business. He sometimes stays in a *favela* to remind himself what life is like for the underdogs, and he's a regular visitor to the Amazon forests, extolling *ayahuasca*, a traditional herbal brew with purgative properties, as eloquently as he does cigar-smoking.

'A wonderful way to clean out the system.'

His insatiable curiosity about the world around him makes Indiana Jones look like an assistant librarian. He extols a tribe on the Peruvian border called the

Huni Kuin. For Hans they embody the spirit of self-sufficiency that he so admires, living from the produce of the forest and from what they themselves hunt, fish and plant. On a recent visit to them he was quite seriously bitten and, twelve hours away by boat from any help, nearly lost a leg. With his cigar hand he gestures to his upper bicep.

'And I still have an insect in my arm.'

To help his recovery he does gymnastics training seven days a week.

Hans has lived in Brazil for fifty years and what he likes about the Brazilians is that they're flexible, they adapt and move on. What he also admires is their sense of a unifying national identity. His wife, now dead, was Lebanese.

'But she was a hundred percent Brazilian. In Brazil everyone wants to be Brazilian.'

He contrasts this with his home country. The Dutch, by acknowledging and encouraging the cultures of all the different immigrant communities, have lost sight of what it means to be Dutch. He's very happy to stay here, at least until his consulship is up in 2013.

'What attracts me to Brazil is when I wake up in the morning, I don't know how the evening will be and that is a big challenge for you! Cigar?'

We have a late lunch up in one of the farms that have become guest houses. The Pousada Santa Cruz has a fine view out over St Felix, Cachoeira and the Paraguaçu dam and hydroelectric station gouged out of the verdant hills. Once a sugar farm, it could hardly be more different from the jostling *favelas* of Salvador. Here there is light, air and space in abundance. The trees in the garden have labels. Lunch is served out on a veranda, as eagles and kites ride the thermals and flies worry away at the fresh-fallen mangoes.

It's a glimpse of what plantation life must have been like for the lucky few.

Opposite · *In the heart of the Recôncavo, the rich alluvial hinterland of All Saints' Bay, lie the twin towns of Cachoeira, in background, and São Félix. Their position at the lowest bridging point of the Paraguaçu made them prosperous.*

Following pages · *Docks in foreground and the skyline of bell-towers on the hill hark back to Salvador's golden years as a trading city.*

Day 38 · Salvador

TODAY we bid farewell to Salvador, a most remarkable city.

Breathtaking architectural beauty sits side by side with corrosive poverty and decay. A non-stop music track animates and deafens, and a life ethic rather than a work ethic dominates. The Old Town has been our home for almost a week. I have at times felt trapped, as locals warned us against some of the surrounding streets after dark, and I noticed taxi drivers didn't stop at red lights after a certain time of night, but I prefer this edginess to being in a city tamed for the tourist. Then I think of the number of hotels and *pousadas* opened in the streets of Santo Antônio since the Redfish and others showed the way, and I think of the economic boom and the luxurious Bahia House and someone telling me that air travel inside Brazil was expanding by ten percent every year, and I wonder if Salvador will be able to resist being tamed.

What is indisputable is that here in the North-East the story of modern Brazil can be read most clearly. This is where Brazil was born.

5
4

PART 3 | MINAS & RIO

GOIÁS
Paranaiba
MINAS GERAIS
Planalto do Brasil
Serra do Cipó
Cardeal Mota
ESPÍRITO SANTO
ATLANTIC OCEAN
Grande
Belo Horizonte
Mina Alegria
Ouro Preto
Vitória
SÃO PAULO
Tietê
Serra da Mantiqueira
Campos
RIO DE JANEIRO
São José dos Campos
Rio de Janeiro
São Paulo
Santos
0 100 200 300 kilometres
0 100 200 miles

Galeão International Airport
Guanabara Bay
Favela Complexo da Maré
Ilha da Cidade Universitária
Complexo do Alemão
Bonsucesso Railway Station
NITERÓI BRIDGE
Rio de Janeiro
Ilha das Cobras
0 1 2 3 kilometres
0 1 2 miles
Central Station
Santos Dumont Airport
Metropolitan Cathedral
Maracanã Stadium
Arcos da Lapa
SANTA TERESA
Santa Barbara Tunnel
Laranjeiras
Pico da Tijuca
Fluminense Football Club
State Governor's Office
Tijuca Forest
Rebouças Tunnel
URCA
Corcovocado
Sugar Loaf Mountain
BOTAFOGO
Christ the Redeemer Statue
Tijuca Forest
Favela Tabajaras
LEME
Lagoa Rodrigo de Freitas
COPACABANA
Favela Morro do Cantagalo
GÁVEA
IPANEMA
ARPOADOR
Favela Vidigal

Day 39 · Cardeal Mota, Serra do Cipó National Park

FOR 200 YEARS after the first European strayed by chance onto the coast of Brazil, the wealth of the country was largely generated by the world demand for sugar. This was serviced from the huge slave-worked plantations in the North-East of the country. Then, in 1693, something happened to change all that. Reports came into São Paulo of an adventurer who had returned from the mountains with traces of gold in small dark nuggets of rock. This was what the Portuguese settlers had been waiting for. They knew there was gold in the continent – their Spanish counterparts had struck it rich in the Andes 170 years earlier – and they knew that one day God would guide them to their own El Dorado.

The *bandeirantes* (flag-bearers), privately financed bands of freebooters, had long been penetrating the Brazilian hinterland looking for slaves. It was one of them, Antônio Dias, who led an expedition into the area where the *ouro preto* (black gold) had been found. It wasn't easy to locate the source. All they had to go on was a particular rock formation – a big rock with a smaller rock beside it, jutting out like a thumb. Eventually, in 1698, in a range known as the Serra do Espinhaco (the 'Spiny Mountains') some 320 kilometres (200 miles) north of Rio, they found what they were looking for. The gold rush that ensued revealed that the mountains were also rich in diamonds and other precious stones as well as apparently inexhaustible reserves of bauxite, manganese and iron ore. God had rewarded them beyond their wildest dreams. Churches were built and profusely decorated. A new state was created under the blandly functional name of Minas Gerais ('General Mines'). Agriculturally blessed, as well as minerally rich, it became the new commercial epicentre of Brazil. The capital moved from Salvador to Rio de Janeiro in 1763. The transfer of power from the North to the South of Brazil was complete. It has never been reversed.

Our first night in Minas is spent at an attractive, artistically furnished *pousada* at one end of a long, thin tourist town called Cardeal Mota. The owner has created an attractive garden with bendy trees rather like the ones you see on Willow Pattern china, in which noisy, yellow-breasted birds dart about and hummingbirds, which the Brazilians call *beija flores* ('flower kissers'), gyrate among the blossoms. Comfortable chairs are scattered around in which you can recline and watch the sun set on the mountains behind the house. Contentment.

Day 40 · Cardeal Mota, Serra do Cipó National Park

A FIERCE WIND smacks at the shutters of my room and, for the first time in almost seven weeks of travelling in Brazil, I'm aware of having to add bedclothes rather than shed them. We're in the mountains for the first time, though probably at not much more than 750 metres. Difficult to find out exact details as the Brazilians aren't terribly good on maps. Ordnance Survey could clean up here. All

1   2

Above: **1** *· Serra do Cipó National Park. Pedro Sales remembers how it used to be out here when everything came in by horseback.* **2** *· Horses, less needed these days, graze the lake shore.* **Opposite** *· Pedro Country. The restless inventor and engineer Pedro Sales has virtually taken over this picturesque headland to build and design his highly individual properties. All for his children, he says.*

I know is that despite being the fifth-largest country in the world, Brazil has no peaks higher than 3,000 metres and this corner of Minas is exceptional in having anything that looks like a real mountain range. It's a diverse and fragile ecosystem, with over two thousand species of plants, many of which are unique to the Minas Mountains. This is typical *cerrado* country, dry and high, and plants, and rare birds, need to be tough to survive. The Serra do Cipó National Park was created to protect a habitat over 30,000 square kilometres (11,600 square miles) in size.

By mid-morning we're about fifty-five kilometres (thirty-five miles) to the north-west, in Lapinha, taking a closer look at this fine highland scenery from a cabin overlooking a long strip of lake in a lonely stretch of the Park. A terrific wind screams around us but the man I'm talking to is quite unperturbed. Pedro Machado Sales is in his mid-fifties, lean and fit with close-cropped white hair. Unlike most Brazilians I've met, he's not one for the expressive, expansive gesture. He has a contained, defensive air and talks softly, barely moving his lips. As there's a force 8 gale blowing outside this is not a good combination. I have to lean close to hear his story. He was once a hippie. 'I had big hair,' he says, with a half-smile. Since those days, his hair has got smaller and he's become a very rich man, having invented a process for crushing rocks which is now widely used in the mining industry. This has allowed him to combine his love of the outdoors with his other passion, building houses. He points out at least half a dozen constructions of his which dot the slope running down to the lake. Pedro, a born innovator and a restless experimenter, simply cannot stop building houses, though his ambition seems confined to their design and construction. He seems less interested in what goes on inside them.

In the teeth of the gale, he takes us on a tour of his various properties, one for each of his five children, whether they like it or not. Pedro has elevated Do-It-Yourself to an art form. From the design to physically pouring the concrete, bolting the steel frame together, putting on a roof or laying down a deck, Pedro is the man. They're quite spartan houses, appropriate for this spare but beautiful environment. He loves the challenge of these lonely lakes and mountains but he's not sentimental about the country life. There is some fishing to be had, but the land isn't that fertile out here and what agricultural work there is, is done almost

entirely by the women. When I ask what the men do, Pedro shrugs. 'They sit around getting drunk.'

By the time we've reached the marshy reed beds by the lakeshore we're protected from the worst of the wind. Egrets, heron and crowned plovers flit and skitter about. A few skinny horses graze on the water-meadow. They're immediately rounded up by Pedro's constant companion, a hyperactive German Shepherd dog which just loves rounding things up. Animals or humans, he likes them to be in a group, where he can keep an eye on them. The talk turns to mining and, though he's a keen environmentalist, Pedro defends the business he's been involved in for so much of his life. The miners, he claims, no longer have it all their own way and are in constant dialogue with conservationists. And their work is much less obtrusive than the cattle ranches up north. 'When *they* want to clear the land they just drag chains through the forest.'

He shakes his head and, brightening up, turns away from the lake to show us his most recent acquisition, a patch of land he calls his ranch. He's already started building on it, though the house, at the moment, seems to consist only of a toilet.

Pedro appreciates the beauty around him and yet he has helped create technology to crush mountains into dust. Maybe it's as well that Brazil is such an enormous country and that, for now, the two sides of Pedro Sales can exist side by side.

In an even more remote part of the mountains we meet someone at the other end of the economic scale. José Branco is a subsistence farmer. He has chickens and cows, one of which has five legs and is called Surprise. He also grows mango, papaya and oranges and makes his own biscuits, jam and coffee. The house he was born and brought up in, sixty-five years ago, is now one side of a muddy cowshed

and he and his wife have moved into a modern extension where they serve food. The kitchen has few mod cons. The pots and pans hiss and spit over a fire which is fed by sticks and branches pushed in beneath it. It's the familiar meat-led diet of the Brazilian interior. Beef and chicken, spare ribs and beans, spring onions and pork crackling, followed by their own home-made cheese, jam and *doce de leite*, a sweet and smooth Minas delicacy. José hovers. He's no *maître d'* and seems much happier out and about on the farm. A wiry little black dog, looking up expectantly at his owner, accompanies him everywhere. José, short, slim and straight-backed, with a neat grey moustache and a patient, weathered face, is a Minas man through and through. He's descended from German and English diamond hunters. They say that his English great-grandfather had eighty-two children, so if anyone did get rich there can't have been much left after sharing it out.

He expresses no regret at having to live on what he produces. He left school early.

'Five years I spent there. I didn't learn much, and what I did learn I forgot,' he tells me proudly. The recollection makes him smile, and reveals two fine gold-capped canines. He's worked on this same farm since the age of eight. When I ask if he has ever wanted to travel, to see more of the country, he shakes his head, more reflectively than regretfully. 'It's difficult for us. We don't know how to travel.'

It's begun to rain and low clouds are closing down the spectacular views. But

1

2

3

I can't go without checking out Surprise, the five-legged cow. And there she is, in the yard, an extra leg hanging down from her backside as if in the process of giving birth. Apparently the vet didn't arrive in time to tidy up the deformity and Surprise has lived with her added appendage ever since. And that's not all. When I ask him what it's like for the cow he looks towards her. 'She also has two places to shit and two places to pee-pee!'

At which he dissolves into laughter for quite some time. And he's still chuckling a half-hour later when we bid our farewells and set off down to the valley.

__Opposite__ · José Branco, a farmer in these mountains all his life.

__Above: 1-3__ · 'We don't know how to travel.' José politely dismisses any suggestion of ever leaving his farm.

Day 41 · Cardeal Mota, Serra do Cipó National Park

STEADY RAIN in the night and, around four o'clock, something more sinister. It sounds as if someone in a nearby room is packing. Things roll around and there is a noise of crunching and crackling as if something is being wrapped and unwrapped. But as my mind slowly focuses I realize that it's not coming through the walls at all. It's coming from above me. Someone or something is moving about overhead.

I'm relieved to hear at breakfast that I'm not the only one who heard noises in the night. Roberto the proprietor is initially sceptical, but eventually comes clean and admits that what we probably heard was a skunk, driven indoors by the wet

1

2

3

weather. Becca, our location manager, says that her sister had two of them in her flat in Rio. They had to be removed by masked firemen. All I can think of, as I look out of the window at the solid sheet of rain, is that my visitor may be joined by a few friends tonight.

Ironically, we are off to see someone whose home in the nearby mountains was recently close to being destroyed by a massive forest fire. Today, slipping and sliding along an ochre mud track to her house, with ash-strewn soil and the blackened stumps of trees glimpsed through the mist, the Brazilian mountain landscape resembles a First World War battlefield.

Felicity 'Flick' Taylor is a New Zealander who lives in the forest up near Morro do Pilar. Once married to a Brazilian whom she met as an exchange student, and by whom she had two children, she returned home to New Zealand when the marriage ended. When her parents died fourteen years ago she felt drawn back to Brazil. She bought a house deep in the National Park and filled it full of her parents' furniture. Considering the rain and the cold, she welcomes us in most cheerfully. But then she had been up since dawn listening to New Zealand's 7-6 victory over France in the final of the rugby World Cup.

The forest fire that had so recently threatened her spectacularly situated house sounded horrific. It had burnt on and off for the best part of a week, practically dying away at night then surging up again in the heat and dryness of the day. She tried to keep it at bay with her garden hose but on the fourth day firemen arrived to escort her from the house. Flick had other ideas.

'I told them I'm not leaving, and neither are you guys!'

That night she put up the fire-fighters in her house and next day, though the flames advanced to within twenty metres of her back window, they at last put them out.

If the house had surrendered to the fire it would have been a terrible loss, because not only is it in a fine location but it also contains all sorts of good furniture and an eclectic collection of glass and ceramics. The architecture is based on the traditional *ranchinho* – the 'little ranch' style of the early pioneers, the *bandeirantes*, who rode their mules out to these mountains in search of diamonds.

The materials are wood and palm thatch and the big, wide roof is open-sided. There's a huge kitchen on whose smoky wood fires a Sunday lunch is being prepared. Meanwhile, there's tea and coffee and local cheese-bread snacks. Flick, an engaging, entertaining, independent woman, sees herself, I feel, as inheriting the mantle of the pioneers she so much admires. Like Richard Burton, better known for his African exploits, who came this way with his wife in the mid nineteenth century, when he was briefly the British Consul in Rio. They travelled up the São Francisco River to see the mining concessions he'd acquired in the area. Or Margaret Mee, a diminutive English botanist, explorer and superb illustrator who fought the miners who she felt were destroying much of Brazil's natural habitat, and for whom Flick doesn't conceal her admiration.

'She was the first person to make people aware of the deforestation of the Amazon, back in the 1950s,' she says, then adds 'and she was only little.'

Flick and her friends are still fighting the same battle. She tells me, with great consternation, of a huge pipeline, the biggest of its kind in the world, being built at a small historical town nearby, down which iron ore will be sluiced 600 kilometres (370 miles) to a new terminal complex at Vitória. Nine thousand construction workers will be invading the area and vast amounts of water will have to be diverted from the ecologically important Santo Antônio River to flush the ore down to the coast. Old colonial farms will be destroyed to make way for this leviathan of pipelines and the four new mines that will feed it.

'It'll change the whole structure of the area – social, economic and cultural – overnight,' she warns.

Opposite: 1 *· A rainstorm lashes the forest that was burning only a week before.* ***2*** *· Filming a vehicle trying to extricate itself from a sea of mud.* ***3*** *· In a fire-ravaged forest, a palm frond shows the only sign of resistance.*

1

3

2

4

Flick's indignation comes from a great respect for the traditional way of life in the Serra. With a passion that perhaps only an outsider can bring, she celebrates the land and the people amongst whom she's chosen to live, from the diversity of the plant life to the cautious nature of the inhabitants, which marks them out from the more extrovert national stereotype. *Mineiros* (as they call those from Minas State) are, she says, shrewd, discreet, unflamboyant and, until they get to know you, wary of outsiders.

'You never know what they're thinking.'

This latter quality is, she considers, why they make good politicians. The current President, Dilma Rousseff and President Juscelino Kubitschek, who built Brasília, were both mineiros.

It's not surprising that the food she sets on the table for a Sunday lunch is typical *comida mineira* – miner's food. The ingredients are basically what was portable, what the *bandeirantes* and the *mineiros* could carry with them and that wouldn't go off; hence a staple of rice, beans, cheese and pork that could be salted and kept. As the chill wind blows out of the forest and across the wide timber deck the local product we most appreciate is a locally brewed *cachaca* of oaky taste, cherry hue, and quite outstanding smoothness.

Tonight I hear the scratchings and shufflings above me, but now I know that it's only a skunk and not the ghost of some thwarted gold prospector I just turn over, pull up the bedclothes and go back to sleep.

Day 42 · Belo Horizonte

AN HOUR AND A HALF'S drive south of Cardeal Mota a huge city springs up, almost out of nowhere. The winding roads of the mountains are transformed into a network of sweeping, swirling, criss-crossing highways and the natural forest into a man-made forest of thousands upon thousands of tower blocks. The rain and cloud of the Serra do Cipó have been swept away, and on this bright sunny morning Belo Horizonte, capital of Minas Gerais and one of Brazil's fastest growing cities, is, as its name suggests, like some shining city on the hill. A hundred years ago it was a small provincial town; now it has two airports and upwards of five million people living in and around the city limits.

Though mining is the primary source of the city's wealth, it's also the centre of a rich agricultural area and Minas Gerais is the heartland of one particular product which Brazil has an awful lot of. Coffee. It's an industry that is worth some seven billion dollars a year and it's not surprising to find that in the centre of Belo Horizonte there is a place dedicated entirely to the preparation, consumption and dispensation of Brazilian coffee. The Academia do Café (the Academy of Coffee) is a two-storey town house overshadowed by twenty-storey tower blocks on a corner of the Avenida do Contorno, the ring road. The owner, Bruno Souza, boiling and simmering like one of his own machines, exudes information and enthusiasm at a breathless pace, and it doesn't altogether surprise me to learn that in an average day he will drink a litre and a half of brewed coffee and two or three espressos. Of the two main species of coffee, Arabica and Robusta, it is clear which is his favourite. At a sampling table, laid with bowls to test the consistency

Opposite: ***1*** · *A wide deck for watching forest life.* ***2*** · *'Flick' Taylor brews up coffee for the crew.* ***3*** · *A lot to write about. The magical house in the forest is full of Flick's family furniture, shipped all the way from New Zealand.* ***4*** · Comida mineira. *Traditional food of the miners cooking over a wood fire. Sausage, beans, rice and cheese – food they could carry with them as they travelled.*

Left · *The new Minas Gerais government complex on the outskirts of Belo Horizonte. Designed by Oscar Niemeyer, the architect of Brasília.*

1

2

Above:* 1 · *At a sampling table, laid with bowls to test the consistency of the flavour, we both sip, hiss the air into our mouths and spit out. Of the two main species of coffee, Arabica and Robusta, it is clear which is Bruno's favourite.* 2 · *Bruno puts a trainee barista through his paces at the Academy of Coffee.

Opposite:* 3 · *Praça da Liberdade, Belo Horizonte. Modern glass box constrasts with neo-classical square.* 4-5 · *Niemeyer school and apartment block in Belo Horizonte.

of the flavour, we both sip, hiss the air into our mouths and spit out. The level of exactitude is way beyond me, but the pure Arabica beans, grown on his father's farm, give a much more fruity taste than I expect from coffee. That, says Bruno, is because I'm used to Robusta beans which contain more caffeine and are preferred by the big coffee-shop chains. Arabica has less caffeine, so delivers more of a taste than a buzz. Despite his massive daily intake he still sips it as if it were a fine malt whisky. And, like whisky or good wine, the location of the plantations is all-important. One of the best local coffees is grown inside a volcano.

It is a great source of pride to him that forty percent of all the Arabica coffee in the world comes from Brazil, and he talks, mouth-wateringly, of the prospects opening up as China and Korea and other Asian countries begin to get a taste for it.

For more than half an hour Bruno and I have been sipping, slurping, spitting and generally analysing some of the finest coffee beans in Brazil and all I want now is a decent cup of coffee. But there is a catch here. I have to make it. Bruno, eyes gleaming, says he can give me a specially abbreviated version of his barista training course. Six minutes instead of six months. All I can say is that I do get to make coffee on the fabulous La Marzocco, doyenne of espresso machines, handmade in Florence and retailing at a touch over £6,000. I can almost hear it wince as I try, unsuccessfully and embarrassingly clumsily, to click the portafilter into place. With a little help from Bruno the coffee I've ground and tamped down does eventually appear as a liquid, and it's a deep, dark colour – and, I have to say, rather delicious. Bruno produces some high-grade *cachaca* which complements it perfectly. There can be few more pleasant ways to greet a new city.

Day 43 · Belo Horizonte 🚌 Ouro Preto

OUR HOTEL is in a part of town called Lourdes, but the only pilgrims here are pretty well-heeled. I'm told that it's the new hip quarter for smart clubs and trendy restaurants, though I must have got the wrong time of day as I set out for an orienting walk this morning. The streets seem quite devoid of personality. Curiously neutral high-rise corridors, stripped of any historical or cultural

3

4

5

context. I'm glad that before we move on south to Ouro Preto I have the chance to see the few memorable parts of Belo Horizonte. The graceful rectangular Praça da Liberdade is an open green space laid with gravel paths like a Parisian park. A majestic avenue of palms runs the length of it and reminds us we're in the tropics. Around the square is an esoteric collection of good-looking buildings ranging from the Governor's Palace at one end, all grand flourishes embellished with Art Nouveau, to an Edwardian wrought-iron bandstand and an eye-catchingly original multi-storey apartment block designed by Oscar Niemeyer in the 1950s. With its bold curves and swirls it looks like the way cities of the future were depicted in the science fiction stories of my childhood. The rest of Belo Horizonte, alas, looks like the way the cities of the future actually turned out.

On many of the signs on the road south to Ouro Preto I see the words Estrada Real – the Royal Road. Constructed in the early eighteenth century, this was the route along which the new-found bonanza of gold and diamonds was transported from Minas Gerais to the port of Rio de Janeiro, to be shipped out to Portugal or, more often than not, to London, to pay off the debts that the Portuguese had built up there. Some say that it was Brazilian gold and diamonds that financed Britain's Industrial Revolution. So important was this road that the Crown took especial care of it. It was planned and built by royal surveyors and protected from ambush by crack troops of the King's army.

The gold may have run out, but the iron ore, the 'black' in which the 'gold' was first found, has now far superseded it in earning power. As we pass close to where it's mined, the grass, the road, the cars, the trees and houses, even the grazing cattle, are all coated with a layer of red dust. The Estrada Real becomes a worksite as trucks race up and down carrying material from mines to crushing plants. After a while it clears and the landscape left unscarred can be appreciated in all its glory. Mountain ranges, their forest cover still intact, catch the afternoon sunlight, rolling alongside us until we descend into Ouro Preto. This was the capital of Minas Gerais before power was transferred to Belo Horizonte just over a hundred years ago, and like Belo, it is set in a bowl, or perhaps more accurately, several bowls, among the surrounding mountains. And there the similarity ends. Much of Ouro Preto can barely have changed since the eighteenth century. The only remotely tall buildings are all churches. They stand on conspicuous bluffs around the town, like precious objects set on shelves. Some with one tower, others with two, and all with white-rendered walls and ochre-painted borders and the sweep and curl of the Baroque.

The stoutly cobbled streets at the heart of the city radiate out from the spacious Praça Tiradentes, named after a leader of a rebellion against the Portuguese crown who is commemorated with a bronze and granite statue and a fountain. Fine period buildings are everywhere, the most significant being the

1

2

Governor's Palace of 1740 and, facing it at the other end of the square, the monumental classical facade of the old City Chamber and Jail House, built forty years later. If Belo Horizonte represented the promise of the future, then Ouro Preto dazzles with the prosperity of the past. It's a cradle of Brazil's history, a showpiece, as the buses drawn up in the square and the crowds of schoolchildren being photographed on Tiradentes' statue testify. But it's on a human scale. And thanks to its thriving university, it doesn't go to sleep at sundown.

This is a theme reiterated by the Mayor of Ouro Preto, Angelo Oswaldo de Araújo Santos, as he shows me the town. The students keep it lively, and noisy, he adds, with a slightly apologetic smile, but there are also many conferences held in the city.

'Conservation policy here is a model for the rest of Brazil,' he declares proudly. Unlike most people I've met in Brazil the Mayor is passionate about what history, as represented by his city, means to the rest of the country. 'It is our patrimony, our personality, our roots, our spirit, our soul. Nothing less.'

Angelo is neat, dressed in jacket and tie, and has a law degree but works as a journalist. He's been elected and re-elected Mayor three times, has held various high offices in the cultural world and is a friend of another *mineiro*, the current Brazilian President, Dilma Rousseff, who used to help him with his maths when they were at school together. He's good on the history, as you'd expect, but also has a journalist's ear for little things you might not know. For instance, that the word *caipirinha*, one of Brazil's great gifts to the throats of the world, actually means 'a country girl'. So this is what I've been ordering every night in the bar.

We look out over the town as the sun sets. Handsome colonial churches, built in grateful thanks for the gift of gold, dominate its skyline. There are thirteen of them in a town of 45,000 people. Angelo points out the rich and convoluted shapes of the summits and valleys that rise behind them and then indicates the outline of the facades.

'To understand the churches you have to understand the landscape. The mountains are baroque, don't you think?'

I'd never thought of it like that.

Opposite *· The main square of Ouro Preto. The central statue is of Tiradentes ('the tooth-puller'), a national hero for leading an uprising against the Portuguese.*

Above: 1 *· The three-term Mayor explains the rich cultural history.* ***2*** *· The old City Chamber and Jail House, now a museum of the Inconfidência rebellion.*

Almost everywhere you want to go in Ouro Preto involves a steep climb and that includes the restaurant in which we eat tonight. Halfway through the meal a girl comes round selling jewellery that she's made herself. Everyone a bit sniffy until we start to look and such is the quality of the work that she's virtually bought out by our table alone. She's from Peru and works in silver. Which is the one thing Brazil has always lacked.

Day 44 · Ouro Preto

HEAVY RAIN and thunderous wind in the night. In the semi-darkness of dawn I can see the cars coming down the hill into the town, weaving their way in between the baroque churches, headlights twinkling like another layer of decoration. Rush hour in Ouro Preto.

Yesterday, when I asked the Mayor if gold-mining was still a part of the local economy, he'd told me that these days it was cheaper and easier to extract gold from Amazônia, and the last mine here had closed down twenty-five years ago. But, in keeping with Ouro Preto's spirit of conservation, it has been kept open as a mining museum. As the rain spattered against the windows it seemed the perfect day for going underground.

To be honest, the Mina da Passagem looks as if it might have closed down a lot more than twenty-five years ago. The outbuildings are grubby and the mine itself is accessed by a cable-hauled trolley driven by a clanking, wheezing piston engine which first entered service in 1825. It was made in England, as was much of the gear on show at the museum. Perhaps not surprisingly, as the British owned and ran the mine for much of the nineteenth century before selling it on to the French.

I'm bent almost double on a hard seat in a very old, low-slung rail trolley when a hooter goes and the ancient winding gear propels me, quite rapidly, down through a hole in the hillside and along a cavernous tunnel chipped out by thousands of miners over a period of 277 years.

When we come to a rest some 120 metres below the surface, I'm only too glad to get off the trolley and follow my chirpy young guide Ícaro into a network of subsidiary tunnels that lead to an underground lake which divers come to explore at weekends. On the way he pauses and traces a band of quartz on the rock face, until it meets tourmaline, iron oxide and calcite. Where all these materials come together is where gold would have been found. Always in dust form here, never in nuggets. The tunnels are extensive and easily wide enough to stand up in, but when you consider that mining went on here more or less continuously from 1719 to 1985, it's perhaps not surprising. Extraction was labour-intensive. For every six grammes of gold, 1,000 kilograms of rock had to be removed. For much of its existence Mina da Passagem was dug out by slaves, who would often secrete gold dust in their hair or their clothing in the hope of using it to buy their freedom. For reasons like this, accurate production figures are hard to come by, but in the final fifty years of its life, when it was in Brazilian government hands, the mine produced thirty-five tonnes of gold.

This being Brazil, religion is ever present, even below the ground, and we pass a sizeable shrine to Santa Bárbara, patron saint of miners. Beside her is her African Candomblé counterpart, an *orixá* particularly known for her vanity, so she has been propitiated by a row of lipsticks. Some of them have been used to daub names and messages on the rock face. This turns young Ícaro into a bit of a Colonel Blimp.

__Opposite__ · Eighteenth-century churches dominate the hills of Ouro Preto.
__Below: 1__ · The Mina da Passagem. The railway line, and the tunnel entrance beyond. __2__ · The steam-driven winding gear, almost two hundred years old.

1

2

1

2

3

‘These are not good people!’ he says, shaking his head in disapproval. ‘They are, how you say, vandals!’

Ícaro, who has never been out of Minas Gerais, let alone out of Brazil, loves being a guide. He’s taught himself French, English and German, so he can do it better. When we reach the clear, cool water of the underground lake, he tells me that it is nearly seventy-five metres deep and conceals thirteen square kilometres (five square miles) of caves and tunnels beneath it. Then he adds, ‘Take a glass for your mother-in-law. It contains arsenic.’

This joke, he confides, works in every language.

When we’re hauled back up to the surface the sun is struggling out and back in Ouro Preto the domed church towers and the red rooftops are sparkling after the overnight rain. The crowds are queuing up the long impressive steps of the old Chamber House and Jail, which is now one of the country’s most significant historic monuments and a shrine to Brazilian independence. At the end of the eighteenth century the ideals that inspired the French Revolution were taken up by a group of leading citizens of Ouro Preto, or – to give it its full name at the time – Vila Rica de Nossa Senhora do Pilar do Ouro Preto, who were angry at having to pay taxes to Portugal for the wealth they themselves had produced. Their grievances became lumped together in a protest called the Inconfidência Mineira. Their leader was Joaquim Xavier, a dentist. In Brazil everyone has a nickname and his was Tiradentes (tooth-puller). The uprising he led was a failure but the Portuguese took it seriously enough to sentence all those who took part to death or exile in Africa. The death sentences were revoked at the last minute, but it was too late to prevent Tiradentes from being hanged, on 21 April 1792, at the exact spot where his statue now stands. His body was cut up and parts sent round to other mining towns as a warning.

Their leaders were dead or dispersed but their actions had set people thinking. The Portuguese crown's right to the *quinto*, its fifth-share of all the mineral wealth, and its tight control of local industries continued to be questioned. With Tiradentes the martyr as a figurehead the movement for change grew; and thirty years later Brazil at last won independence.

In 1942, the Vargas government, anxious to foster a spirit of national pride, gave the political equivalent of canonization to the Inconfidência, and now the tooth-puller and his fellow rebels – physicians, carpenters, soldiers, poets and lawyers – are remembered in rows of austere grey tombstones, beneath a solemnly lowered national flag, at the back of the museum that is dedicated to them.

And 21 April is now officially designated Tiradentes Day.

Opposite: 1 · With my excellent guide Ícaro beside the shrine to Santa Bárbara. 2 · Tunnels dug out over 277 years of gold-mining. 3 · The underground lake. Divers come here at weekends to explore the network of tunnels submerged beneath.

Day 45 · Ouro Preto

THE GOLD MINERS had to crawl under the mountain to dig out the precious dust. The iron ore producers of today simply take the mountains apart. As I saw from the air as I first flew into Belo Horizonte, there is no discreet way to extract iron ore. The mines stand out from the lush mountain landscape as a series of gaping wounds.

On the ground, however, they're easy to miss. An hour's drive east of Ouro Preto is a complex of huge open-cast mines operated by Vale, the world's second-largest iron ore producer. In 1942, in the same mood of nationalistic optimism that enshrined Tiradentes in his Pantheon, a publicly owned company was set up to exploit the reserves of what became known as Minas's Iron Quadrangle. The company, rather endearingly christened Companhia Vale do Rio Doce (the Sweetwater River Company), now produces fifteen percent of the world's total production. A quarter of a million tonnes of iron ore and pellets a year. Despite strong opposition the company was sold off to the private sector in 1997 and renamed simply Vale.

As the road passes through a series of small towns there's little evidence of the scale of Vale's work, except in the scattered *favelas,* the shanty town settlements created by the demand for work at the mines. Otherwise everything is normal. Huge billboards by the roadside depict thick, creamy chocolate cakes and dripping gateaux with a carefree relish that you just don't see back home any more. Cows munch contentedly in sun-dappled meadows, and jacaranda blossom colours thickly wooded slopes. Not until a conveyor belt curves out of the woods and over the road do we have any inkling that there is anything but natural beauty all around us. Then we glimpse a lake through the trees. But there's something not quite right. The water lacks any movement or sparkle. It lies there, thick, viscous and inert. Islands of brown sludge break its torpid surface. Then the trees close around it and as we're swept along wide, well-kept roads to the gates of Vale's Mina Alegria complex, you begin to wonder if you really did see what you thought you saw. Apart from the ubiquitous presence of red dust there still isn't much at the mine entrance to suggest heavy operations, and this unreality continues as we find ourselves being led across the site to an immaculately restored stone and timber period farmhouse with a neat garden and a big reception room with coffee, juice and pastries laid out beside comfortable chairs. A full-size snooker table stands in the background.

__Opposite__ · At the Vale mine. __1__ · Rather disconcertingly, our tour of the vast iron ore mine begins at a beautifully preserved period farmhouse. __2__ · A train, laden with 6,500 tonnes of iron ore, leaves for the coast. __3__ · A silicon-based spray keeps the ore from blowing off the train on its 154-kilometre (96-mile) journey.

We're shown around the house, which is almost two hundred years old and was built, as our sweet guide Fabiana tells us, by a Captain Manuel. 'He was a miner, he was a farmer and he was a slave businessman.'

It's quite beautifully preserved with well-polished timber floors, elegant dining rooms and very tall, arched pale blue doors, which Fabiana tells us were an indication of social status. 'The taller the door, the more power you had.'

After refreshment we're given a briefing about the mine and particularly Vale's interest and enthusiasm in minimizing the environmental impact of their work. Then we're helmeted, jacketed and, preceded by a Vale escort vehicle with a flag flying to make sure it's visible at all times, we leave this delightful *fazenda* for the real world of mining. Ten million tonnes of ore were produced here last year. This means digging out roughly twenty million tonnes of rock and earth, which is then crushed, processed and shipped by rail to the new deepwater port at Vitória. Bulk carriers then shift twenty-five percent of this production halfway round the world, to China. Such is the world demand that operations here go on twenty-four hours a day, every day of the year. I ask one of our escorts if they stop for Christmas.

'Only if something is wrong,' he assures me.

We're shown one of the trains leaving for Vitória on what they call the Estrada de Ferro, the Iron Road. An enormous diesel engine, in freshly painted company livery of turquoise and yellow, pulls eighty-four trucks, each one filled to the brim and beyond. This train alone is carrying around 6,500 tonnes of ore. As it leaves, every wagonload is sprayed with a mixture of polymer and water. What used to happen was that during the 154-kilometre (96-mile) journey to Vitória, a lot of

1

2

3

the black dust would blow off the truck and into people's houses. This spray treatment is shown as evidence of the new caring face of the company, which we see again as we're taken to the canteen for lunch. Everyone, from top management to the lowliest sweeper, has the same food under the same roof as everyone else. As there are 1,100 people working at Alegria at any one time, this means a very big floor and a very big roof. The workforce is dressed identically in green shirts and black trousers, and outside as we eat there is a band playing to a small crowd as part of Safety Week. Throughout the day and night a fleet of buses shuttles shift-workers between their homes and the plant. The sheer numbers involved make one realize just how vital the company is to the local economy.

And all the time I hear echoes of a conversation I had with Flick in her mountain cabin in the Serra do Cipó. The man who was the head of Vale before it was privatized was a man called Eliezer Batista. His son Eike became fabulously wealthy and now heads the EXB group, a big energy and mining conglomerate which owns, among many other things, the new port at Vitória and the projected pipeline through which the iron ore from Minas will be flushed. Eike Batista is now said to be the richest man in Brazil.

I'm not sure if our hosts at Vale are being deliberately evasive or just saving the best for last, but it is not until the afternoon that we are finally taken to see what we really came to see – an iron ore mine at work. It's another half-hour drive through slumbering countryside. Up and over the hills until we burst out onto the rim of a massive, gaping hole. Where there was once a mountain there is now a monstrous gash in the earth, thousands of metres across. It has been mined in concentric terraces. I count fifteen of them, tapering down to a murky white lake nearly 300 metres below me. Long-armed diggers, little more than Dinky Toys from up here, are at work, scraping away the rock and tipping it into equally tiny yellow dump trucks. The whole thing is timed to precision so that a digger is never left without a truck to fill. As the tiny trucks climb laboriously up towards us we can see that they are enormous. The wheels alone are three metres high and the driver's cab is a full six metres off the ground. And the load each one has hauled up from the depths is close to 150 tonnes.

The sliced mountain is rather beautiful. The revealed stone surfaces reflect every nuance of the changing light. From black to deep burgundy to terracotta, ochre, white and blue. The work may be little less than demolition of a landscape but the new landscape it has created is not without its own beauty.

I'm allowed up into the cab of one of the big Caterpillar dump trucks. I imagine the driver will be some macho redneck, but he's a quiet, rather slight

young man called Dagmar. Once we're up there, over six metres above the people below, I feel as if I'm on the bridge of a ship. The cab is set to one side, with the offside wing mirror over two metres away. Air exhaust pipes mushroom out beside me. There are two computer screens in the cab, one controlling load levels and the other scanning for obstructions that it might be difficult to see from these Olympian heights. It all combines to create a sense of sublime detachment. I feel that Dagmar and I are in a world of our own, and not for the first time I curse my inability to master Portuguese. Like so many Brazilians I have met, he's absolutely dying to talk, I feel. And I'm dying to know what it's like driving one of the biggest trucks in the world.

I get a short ride and Nigel, our cameraman, gets to join Dagmar right down into the bowels of the earth and back again. Then it's time to go. As we hand back our helmets and high-visibility jackets I notice a work gang in a long line up near the top of a gently sloping hill. I'm told they're landscaping what we in Sheffield used to call slag heaps, and which here they call 'tailings' – the huge amount of material rejected during the processing of iron ore. A little further down the hill and closer to us, a horse is quietly grazing on the newly laid turf. Our hosts at Vale have been helpful and attentive, but as we shake hands for the last time, beside the mountain they've half destroyed, I can't help wondering if the horse was put there just for us.

Opposite · *A big wheel in Minas. These Caterpillar dump trucks bring the earth to the surface, 150 tonnes at a time.*

Above & Following pages · *The price of iron ore. Mini Grand Canyons like this stud the rolling green landscape of Minas Gerais as trucks and diggers push hundreds of metres into the earth. The colours they reveal have their own beauty.*

Day 46 · Rio de Janeiro

FROM MY HOTEL window twenty-five floors up, I look down onto the long golden curve of Copacabana. The waves breaking on the shore have their counterpoint in the undulating pattern of black and white mosaic tiling which swirls across Copacabana's pavement. It was commissioned from the landscape artist Roberto Burle Marx in 1970, a reminder that this is no ordinary beach. It is perhaps the most famous beach in the world. And not always for the right reasons. I spent a night here in 1996, whilst changing planes from Cape Town to Chile on my way to the South Pole, and I can remember it being a threatening place. Stories of muggings were constantly exchanged. This time it looks and feels much better. Money has been spent on the beachside cafés and bars and last night when I walked out there seemed far less aggression than I remembered.

Right now it's early on a Sunday morning and already the great industry that is Brazilian beach life is moving into action. Trucks have shipped in their loads of green coconuts which are being stacked up at beachside cafés and bars. Red sunshades are mushrooming right along the four-kilometre sweep of sand, and the purveyors of chairs and towels and refreshments are trolleying their wares across the Avenida Atlântica, the six-lane highway which runs between the crescent of hotels and apartment blocks and the beach itself. One of the carriageways is closed today and a mix of joggers, walkers and cyclists have already taken possession. They are people of all ages, shapes and sizes. Grey-haired ladies in bikinis, tight-buttocked roller-bladers, large men with breasts and bellies swinging out over a minuscule pair of Speedos, nearly naked eighty-four-year-olds hand in hand, bodybuilders flicking their heads as they go. All embodying one of Brazil's most delightful characteristics – a complete absence of embarrassment.

I've been out early, running in and out of the breaking waves, and I've had a *coco gelado* to refresh myself. I enjoy watching the ritual as the green husk is slashed open, then putting in the straw and drinking the sweet cold contents. I'm told they're rich in potassium, which makes them very good for hangovers. Not that I've been here long enough to get one.

I have breakfast at the top of the hotel with the 360-degree view that takes in not just the golden beaches but the mass of apartment blocks that makes Copacabana one of the most densely populated urban areas in the world. And up on the hills behind, where surely the most expensive real estate should be, are the famous, or infamous, *favelas*, the unplanned, unregulated settlements where the poor of Rio live with the best view of the sea. And now I can see crowds beginning to gather just below us. Rainbow-coloured streamers and clusters of pink balloons herald what is expected to be the biggest Gay Pride march of the year. And one in which I am to take part.

Opposite · *The world's most famous beach. Copacabana at the weekend. The uniform red parasols are an important part of its style.*

It is remarkable that when such an event was first mooted in Rio twenty-one years ago, only twenty-eight people attended, and they were abused and pelted with oranges. Today the organizers are expecting a million people to turn out, and I have been invited as the guest of the President of the Association of Transvestites and Transsexuals of Rio de Janeiro State. Thus fast have things moved.

My host is a man who calls himself Marjorie. Her official title is President of the Transvestites and Transsexuals Department of Rio State. Marjorie Marchi has had no surgical alterations so is not a transsexual, but lives with a male partner and refers to himself as a woman. She has campaigned strongly for greater recognition for all sexual minorities and earlier this year was rewarded by the passing of a government decree allowing transvestites and transsexuals to use their adopted name in public and on official documents. She's also one of the organizers of today's parade, which I'm told is on the theme of Peace, so white clothes would be appreciated. This takes care of any fashion choices on my part as all I have that's remotely white is a T-shirt and a pair of faded khaki shorts.

Marjorie turns up to meet us wearing an off-the-shoulder cream dress and high heels.

'White is not my colour!' she says decisively.

She is struggling a bit with a long black wig and, with friends and fellow organizers assailing her from all sides, she looks a little frazzled. But she is someone I instantly warm to, and have faith that she will get us through this increasingly manic event. She leads us out towards an assembly point, across the other side of the Avenida Atlântica which by now is just a sea of faces. There are twenty floats in the parade but they are almost submerged by the huge and growing

throng and I'm not sure we shall ever get there. Marjorie is forever greeting people with kisses and wildly gesticulating conversations. Despite the alarming crush of people the air is one of celebration rather than confrontation. The police presence is minimal. I see two men, arm in arm, posing as if drunk across the bonnet of a police car without any opposition. People pass by in all sorts of outfits, from a group of girls in scanty Scottish kilts to a frighteningly good Obama lookalike. There are knights with helmets and chest armour but very little else, and Marilyn Monroe impersonators and motorcycle punks dressed by Tom of Finland. In amongst them are people selling food and drinks and handing out anti-hepatitis leaflets. From somewhere above me a man dressed as Superman screams above the din and thumps the air.

'Are you all bisexual?' he screams.

'Ye… ssss!' the crowd shouts back.

I ask Marjorie who he is.

'He's one of the organizers!'

I'm really quite relieved when we reach the relative safety of the float for transvestites, or *travestis* as they call them, rather unfortunately, in Portuguese. It's hung with red fabric all the way round and adorned back and front with public health posters and slogans like 'Rio Sem Homophobia' ('Rio Without Homophobia'). The sides are decorated with a blizzard of red lips on a shiny

Opposite · *Gay Pride takes over on Copacabana; the big march attracts all sorts.*
Left · *Talking with Marjorie, my Gay Pride guide, and one of the organizers, and the celebrants in party mood on the transsexuals' float.*

background. A prow-like superstructure is built out over the driver's cab and gaggles of transsexuals stand at the rails waving at friends and showing off their breasts. As a sixty-eight-year-old British heterosexual in khaki shorts I feel, to quote an old Eric Idle line, like a lost lamb in an abattoir.

When at last we move off, our on-board disco kicks in. The whole truck starts to vibrate and the decibel level is unmerciful. Everyone is shouting but no one can hear a word. I push my way to the rail and, squeezing between a pair of transsexual twins, look out at the crowd below. Once we're on the move, albeit at the pace of an arthritic tortoise, the spirit of celebration becomes irresistible. Shyly at first, I exchange a few waves with people in sequinned G-strings and nuns in feather headdresses and motor-racing goggles. They could be men, they could be women. It doesn't seem to matter anymore. I just go with the flow, carried along Copacabana on a warm and wonderful tide of alternative sexuality. Below us, a rainbow banner has been unfurled. It must be nearly 500 metres long and it's borne, like a rippling river, on the ecstatic shoulders of the crowd.

It seems to me that what motivates this multitude is more than just a good day out. It is an affirmation of freedoms and liberties which we might take for granted, but which were unthinkable in Brazil a few years ago, and which are still bitterly resisted and resented. Last year in Rio alone 250 people were murdered because of their sexual preferences. Marjorie, with her unsteady wig and her

SOMOS TODOS IGUAIS PERANTE A PAZ

too-tight cream dress, may at times cut an odd, even pathetic figure, but there's no denying that her courage and her commitment to the cause has made lives better for many people. The battle isn't yet won, which, I suspect, is what gives today's parade something beyond celebration. A purpose. A spectacular collective cry for tolerance.

After a few hours we've completed our filming and are about to leave the bus, when I take one last look out at the spectators, ten deep on the sidewalks of the Avenida Atlântica. There at the front of the crowd, on the very edge of the packed pavement, is an old, frail, white-haired lady in a wheelchair, with her carer in a white coat beside her. And as our float goes by, full of men dressed as women and men who have had themselves turned into women, the lady in the wheelchair looks up and smiles and waves. And she keeps on waving.

Opposite · *Rainbow-coloured streamers and the longest flag I've ever seen mark the loud and lively progress of the procession. In 1990, only twenty-eight people were brave enough to march for Gay Pride. Today they estimate nearly a million have turned out.*

Day 47 · Rio de Janeiro

A PORTUGUESE EXPEDITION, blown off course in 1500, brought the first Europeans to Brazil. Two years later, another Portuguese expedition, this time with cartographic intent, came nosing down the coast. In early 1502 they found themselves at the mouth of what they thought was a great river, flowing out between two headlands, one of them with a most striking rock formation (which later settlers were to christen Pão de Açucar, Sugar Loaf Mountain). It was January, the hottest part of the tropical year, and for want of inspiration they called their new discovery Rio de Janeiro – 'January River'. It turned out not to be a river at all but a deep, wide bay. By that time, however, the name had stuck, and January River was set to become one of the most famous misnomers in the world.

The Portuguese must have been impressed by the tall, spiky granite peaks that thrust their way out of the forest right down to the ocean, but what made Rio's location eye-catching also made it commercially unpromising. There were much flatter, wider sites on which to plant sugar. But the pioneering Portuguese navigators had started something, and accounts of their discoveries accompanied by the new maps they'd compiled were luring other Europeans to the 'new land' of Brazil. The French were the first to take a serious interest in Rio de Janeiro and in the 1550s, led by Huguenots keen to flee persecution at home, they sought to establish a settlement in Guanabara Bay, called, with characteristic Gallic understatement, 'France Antarctique'. Belatedly the Portuguese, now well established higher up the coast, moved south to clear out the French interlopers and, after bloody battles fought in the shadow of Sugar Loaf Mountain, they re-established Portuguese supremacy; and, leaving a small garrison to look after Rio, they decamped to Salvador where the real money was to be made.

Four hundred and fifty years later, and with a population of some six and a half million people, or eleven million in Greater Rio, the spectacular physical beauty of the city is celebrated worldwide. Its inhabitants call it, modestly, Cidade

1

2

3

Maravilhosa – the Marvellous City. The wide bays, beaches and forested slopes first glimpsed by the Portuguese caravels remain an essential part of the cityscape, but the most prominent features are the granite plugs that rise dramatically from the heart of the city, their impressiveness uncompromised because they are too steep and sheer to build on. Or that's what they thought until 1931, when one of the most iconic statues in the world was raised on Corcovado, 'Hunchback Mountain', at 706 metres the second tallest of Rio's sharp summits. It is a massive figure of Christ, in concrete faced with soapstone. His arms are outstretched, and his head inclined downwards to take in the city below. It is known as Cristo Redentor, Christ the Redeemer, and it adds a further thirty metres to the top of Corcovado Mountain.

A few days from now there will be celebrations to mark the anniversary of the triumphant 'unveiling', in October 1931, of what has become the symbol of Rio, and I'm in a garden in the leafy western suburb of Gávea with the great-granddaughter of the man in charge of its design and construction, an architect and engineer called Heitor da Silva Costa.

Gávea, now a desirable residential area, was a farm until quite recently and nature is abundant. The house is squeezed right up against the forest, which is luxuriant and encroaching, with mango trees and bamboo stands spreading shade and the fiery red flowers of a banana tree filling one end of the small yard where we sit. On one side of us are supermarkets, shopping malls and a hospital. On the other, snakes and monkeys and screeching parakeets. On a round table are stacks

of books, letters, newspaper clippings and photographs relating to Heitor da Silva Costa, who seems always to be immaculately suited and, with his starched white collars and wavy hair, bearing more than a passing likeness to Scott Fitzgerald.

Bel Noronha, a documentary film-maker, with dark good looks etched with tiredness, seems as nervous about what's to happen on the top of Corcovado in a couple of days as her great-grandfather would surely have been, this time eighty years ago.

Bel has a lot on her hands. A bust of Heitor is to be placed at the base of the statue on anniversary day. She's worried about how she'll get it up there, and breaks off for voluble phone calls with the sculptor and others. Then there's the problem of the Landowski connection. Paul Landowski was a French sculptor who created the maquettes, or working models, of the face and hands of Christ, and recently members of the Landowski family have been trying to make money from the licensing of this iconic image. Bel is outraged. Ownership of the statue for commercial gain was something her great-grandfather always opposed. The statue was raised by public subscription and was for all the people.

Heitor's memorabilia reveals some fascinating insights. Early designs for the Redentor had Christ holding a cross, taller than himself, in the crook of one arm, with a globe in the other. This was rejected as being difficult to see at a distance. Heitor came up with the outstretched arms idea when he'd been up on the site and had looked across at the horizontal beams of a communications mast on an adjacent hill. Until quite a late stage in its five-year construction, Christ was going

***Opposite:* 1** · *The building of a Brazilian icon. Heitor da Silva Costa (standing, left) shows work in progress inside the skeleton of the Redentor, 1930.*
2 · *Bel Noronha, Heitor's great-granddaughter, shows me the archive of her father's work.*
3 · *Christ shrouded in scaffolding.*
Above · *Photo opportunity. With Bel at the Redentor, eighty years after it was unveiled. The statue is made of concrete with a soapstone finish.*

Above · The view of Rio from the feet of Christ is reckoned to be the best of all.

to be looking straight forward. The decision to have him looking down meant a major engineering rethink to cope with the extra stress on the thirty-tonne head.

The modifications were successful. The strength of the final design is in its simplicity. Not only does the Redentor appear to embrace the people of Rio from his lofty perch, his wide outstretched arms can be glimpsed from all over the city below. In a country full of religious images, the Redentor is supreme. I ask Bel if her great-grandfather was a religious man. She shakes her head. 'No, he was an atheist,' she says, then adds, 'but by the end of his life, he was very religious.'

In the afternoon Bel takes us up to the top of Corcovado to see the Redentor close-up. It's not easy. During its five-year construction all the materials used to build the Christ were brought up on a cog railway, built in 1884. The railway still runs and the red two-car trains are still the best way to get to the top. There is an access road but parking is restricted. There is a path, but it's long and steep and on a hot day like today it's very much the adventure option. At the station below, there is nearly always a surplus of demand over supply and there are queues for each train. Patience is rewarded by an excitingly precipitous twenty-minute climb through the forest, and at the top it's an escalator ride to the feet of Christ. The figure, which looms thirty metres into the sky, has a colossal strength, but it's a strength that lies in restraint. The straight fall of the robe, the tilt of the head, the long shielding hands. The great skill of Heitor and Landowski is to have distilled a universal compassion. Though it is a likeness of Christ it seems to transcend any single religion.

Of course it's also a world landmark and everyone has their cameras out all the time. Including us. The serenity of the subject contrasts starkly with some of the behaviour below. People are lying flat and getting friends to spread their arms out like the Christ.

It is worth seeing up close, but the reward for climbing Corcovado is the magnificent view of Rio below. If you really want to orient yourself to the city this is the place to come. Forget puffing up the hill, this is what really takes the breath away.

Day 48 · Rio de Janeiro

A BIG STORM shakes the doors and rattles the windows in the early hours. Forked lightning over the Atlantic and dawn breaks over a colourless Copacabana Beach. Wisps of low cloud spread around the peaks and islets. Such a contrast from yesterday. And a contrast in subject matter too. We've been invited by Marjorie Marchi to accompany her to her place of work at the Governor's office. No leafy gardens or soaring statues today, just a grimy square close to Central Station. The rain, the rough sleepers, the rubbish in the gutters and the warning that this is a very dangerous area doesn't raise the spirits, but Marjorie seems on good form. She looks a little less hot and bothered than on the day of the parade, and is executively dressed in a white cotton blouse, black skirt, black stockings and black high-heeled shoes. Her wig is tied in a ponytail and she sports a pair of dangling diamante earrings. We cross the road, dodging in front of lines of buses three deep, dropping off the workers and picking up arrivals at Central Station. In front of us, behind tall, black railings, looms the State Governor's office. It's part of a huge complex, Art Deco in style and built, I should think, in the 1930s, not long after the Redentor first rose above Rio. It reminds me of another icon of the Great Depression, the Rockefeller Center in New York.

An absurd security problem at the main entrance. Although we are guests of a man dressed in women's clothes, our sound recordist is turned back for wearing shorts. Men in skirts are fine, but men in shorts apparently not. I suspect this is a clash of the systems. An old, bureaucratic dress code meeting the new respect for the minority rights, which a liberal State Governor sees as a vital ingredient of his policy of *cidadania* – citizenship. A man can wear women's clothing because Rio state law now recognizes and protects the right of a man to do so. In the rush towards tolerance and inclusivity it seems that men who choose to dress as men have been left behind.

Dulce, our Brazilian fixer, takes Seb off to buy some trousers at the nearby 'very dangerous' market, and the rest of us have no option but to wait in the yard in front of the building. The rain has lessened, but it's cold, and I never thought I'd feel cold in Rio. In the distance, across the square and rising behind the market, is an almost sheer hillside to which buildings cling tenuously. This is the *favela* of Providência. It's one of the worst, always in the news for clashes between drug gangs. Marjorie is deeply concerned about the new phenomenon appearing on Rio's streets. Crack cocaine. Addictive, destructive and, for now, very cheap. The drug gangs had kept it out of Rio for a long time because profits were so low. Now all that's changing.

'I am afraid,' says Marjorie. And she's not a woman who looks easily frightened.

Once inside the building she cheers up and ushers us briskly into a lift. As we emerge at the seventh floor, Marjorie's transformation is complete. She's in

control. This is her world. Red Aids ribbons decorate the elevator doors. 'Rio Sem Homophobia' is written in large letters across the wall ahead of us. As she walks down to her office Marjorie points out the various doorways. 'Lesbians in there. Transsexuals in there. Disabled over there.'

Everything seems to have been done to brighten up institutional passageways and wood-panelled walls, and everyone greets each other merrily; a less hysterical version of the atmosphere at the march on Sunday. Marjorie flirts and jokes so easily that it's hard to remember she's a large black man, something she confronts head-on as she settles us down in her office.

***Above** · Marjorie, President of the Association of Transvestites and Transsexuals of Rio de Janeiro State, inside her office.*

***Opposite** · The Panda, one of Rio's smarter love motels. The lovers' garage. Very discreet.*

'In my mind, I'm not a man. I'm a woman with a penis,' she declares. She's never wanted to have surgery and become a transsexual.

Marjorie has a rather impressive office. It has two big windows with Venetian blinds, a long desk with a panoramic photo of a Gay Pride March on the wall behind. The office furniture is from the 1950s and a very rough and ready modernization job has been done. Ducts and cables emerge from holes knocked through the walls and are carried across the room on a metal grid suspended from the ceiling. Coffee is brought in in small plastic cups and we talk. Marjorie's more relaxed and her English is much better today. She talks movingly about growing up as the son of an African-Brazilian mother and a German father. Her mother thought gay sex was a godless perversion, and it was her father who was the understanding one. Marjorie shows us a poster on the wall for an LGBT (Lesbian, Gay, Bisexual and Transgender – *Travestis*) fundraiser. It was demanding rights for those who had changed their sexual orientation to be able to use their adopted names on ID cards and work documents. The graphic on the poster is powerful. A woman emerging from a man's body holding an ID card aloft, whilst blood drips onto her skin.

Marjorie nods approvingly. 'We didn't want hearts or butterflies. We wanted to show the pain we felt.'

There are a hundred people working in the minority rights department on the seventh floor. The State Governor has recently authorized a multi-million *reais* advertising campaign to press home the message of sexual toleration. For people like Marjorie things seem to be going their way, but it's an uphill struggle. She is particularly worried by the growing strength of the Evangelicals. With their increasing representation in the Council of Deputies, they are seen by those on the seventh floor as the new enemy. But enemies seem to bring the best out of people like Marjorie. After plying us with free pencils and notepads she shows us to the lift. I wish her well. It can't be an easy ride, facing up to ignorance and prejudice on a daily basis, but I feel that the fight has a real soldier here. And we all kiss her goodbye.

Day 49 · Rio de Janeiro

IT'S CHILDREN'S DAY today and a public holiday. Despite the cloudy weather, volleyball nets and football posts are going up on the beaches, and the beachside avenues, partially closed to traffic, are taken over once again by an army of strollers, walkers, power-walkers, joggers, roller-skaters and skate-boarders, their bodies adorned with appliances – heart monitors, pedometers, headsets. The body, at all stages of life, is celebrated in Rio. And the display isn't just for the beaches, it's for the samba clubs and the nightspots. It's about making yourself attractive. It's about sex. And yet sexual display is less overt than in Europe. There's less nakedness in street adverts and topless sunbathing is still frowned upon. I see very few couples enmeshed on the beach. There's plenty of show, but not a lot of action. So where do these honed bodies go to enjoy other honed bodies? For all the apparent openness of Brazilian society sex is still at the heart of one of its more secret, lucrative and – from what I can gather – universal phenomena, the love hotels, or simply, the motels. Dotted all over the city, and indeed the country, are establishments where for anything from thirty minutes to thirty hours rooms can be rented for sex. And not necessarily sex with prostitutes. They're used by boyfriends and girlfriends seeking privacy away from overcrowded family apartments, husbands who fancy other people's wives and wives who fancy other people's husbands, or just lovers who prefer a bed to the back of a car. They cater for all incomes and all classes but the most important thing is that they're discreet. And discretion is not something I would have put high on my list of Brazilian qualities.

With curiosity and some trepidation I approach the entrance of the Panda Hotel (which, given the legendary inability of pandas to mate, seems an odd choice of name), set back from the road in a respectable residential neighbourhood

1

2

Above:* 1 · *Keeping it clean. Behind-the-scenes staff at the love motel.* 2 · *Celebrating Luhanna Melloni's birthday with a cake and a naughty room-service menu.* *Opposite* · *The Presidential Suite, with several bathing options.

near the Botanical Gardens. The first thing I notice is that there is no foyer of any kind. The only way in is via a security gate, from which a key is handed out and a steel mesh door lifted. I watch various cars, ranging from Mercedes with black glass windows to Golfs and Polos with street atlases on the back shelf, go through the process. Then, accompanied by Luhanna Melloni, presenter of a late-night TV sex show and, I should add, a six-strong film crew, I approach the entrance myself. The mesh gate lifts to reveal a long, murky stretch of underground garage, stretching way into the distance. Lines of carports run along each side. Wooden strips are lowered over the licence plates, an extra level of security after cases of wives being brought in by their lovers and seeing their husband's car already there. At the back of the carport steps lead, past decoratively tiled walls, to a room above. The tariff at the door indicates apartments rentable from 119 *reais* an hour, about £40, to a Presidential Suite for 360 *reais*, £125 pounds an hour.

Luhanna and I (and the film crew) check out the Presidential Suite, one of the very few rooms unoccupied on Children's Day. At the top of the steps leading from the garage a door opens to reveal a world of bright lights, mirrors and a softly gurgling jacuzzi. Besides a bed, and the aforementioned jacuzzi, Presidents also get a bathroom, a white marbled bathing area with plunge pool, a small disco floor with flashing lights and a dining room with a table laid, rather demurely, with china featuring British castles. White imitation leather armchairs are scattered about.

There are two room service menus beside the bed. One offering food and drink, the other a sex menu, aids and devices like vibrators, dildos, creams, lubricants and a seduction kit, as if that were really necessary. Everything that's ordered is delivered through a hatchway so the staff, and there must be hundreds of them in the bowels of the Panda, never come into contact with the punters. The whole place is most odd. An hermetically sealed village where no one knows anyone else's business.

Luhanna, a tall, droll, affable girl, whose twenty-seventh birthday it is, has, for the past three years, been presenting a show on a late-night cable channel called Papo Calcinha, literally 'Panty Chat', in which she and two or three other girls

talk 'about everything to do with sex'. They take a different theme each week, like group sex, or oral sex, or sex toys – just recently the star of the show was an incredibly lifelike sex doll called Gladys. 'She was my size,' Luhanna adds, in some surprise.

Though Papo Calcinha has become very popular, especially amongst the young, it would, unlike in Europe, never be allowed on a mainstream channel. I return to Brazilians and their bodies. Is it just health or is it mostly sex? Luhanna considers for a moment. She nods. Yes, she thinks that Brazilians probably do have sex more often than most. The heat, the beaches, the lack of clothes (or 'clothies' as she pronounces them rather endearingly) all create a need for places like this. And they're in every neighbourhood, rich or poor. She herself has used them and many of her friends as well. The necessary secrecy may make for a rather sinister first impression, but the rooms are clean and comfortable and not expensive, and we both agree that it's much better to have sex above a car park than in a car park.

A bell sounds, indicating that what we've ordered from room service has arrived. It's a birthday cake for Luhanna.

When we step outside the Panda love hotel I take one last look at the forbidding frontage of grey stone and reflecting glass. A Toyota with darkened windows slips inside. Behind the Panda a mountain rises. At the top of the mountain is a statue of Christ the Redeemer spreading his arms out over us all.

Day 50 · Rio de Janeiro

FÁBIO SOMBRA is a man who lives, breathes and encapsulates Rio de Janeiro. He's a writer, artist, magician, musician and gourmet. And he still lives with his mother. A day in Fábio's company is a day spent on a very individual view of the city he loves. We start in one of his favourite parts of town, among the characterful, slightly faded glories of Santa Teresa. It's a neighbourhood, or *bairro,* which has seen fortunes come and go. In the nineteenth century it was a place of comfortable mansions, overlooking the city and built largely for newly wealthy coffee barons. In 1892 a tunnel was pushed through the mountains below, connecting two sleepy fishing communities called Copacabana and Ipanema with the rest of the city for the first time. The rich and successful moved down towards the newly accessible beaches and Santa Teresa's heyday was over. After years of neglect it has undergone something of a rebirth. The old timbered houses remain, some creaky and skeletal, glimpsed on the hilltops through dusty trees, together with some Art Nouveau touches on the streets lower down. Most Cariocans still ignore the area. It's overlooked by seven *favelas* and they don't think it's a safe place to live. But its architecture and the distance from the beach have attracted an arty interest. Santa Teresa has become cool and bohemian. Yellow open-sided trams rattle through the streets and the shops and restaurants are small and curious. It has the feel of a rambling, overgrown, free-thinking village.

It's wholly suitable then that our first port of call is the headquarters of the grandly named Brazilian Academy of the Literature of Cordel. It's in a lock-up garage halfway up a steep hill. Inside the garage, just wide enough for a single car, are shelves and tables full of books and, at the back, a typewriter, printing press and paper. Its hawk-nosed, thick-spectacled proprietor, Gonçalo Ferreira da Silva, who looks like a thin Dr Kissinger, gets up from his table and comes to welcome us. Cordel literature, a phenomenon of north-eastern Brazil, has its roots in Europe in the Middle Ages, when minstrels would travel the land singing verses to entertain people who could barely read or write. In Brazil this was taken a stage further and small books, all in verse, were produced as cheaply as possible and sold on strings in the villages of the back country. Hence the name Cordel, from the word for string. Producing these books is an old art, and Gonçalo's garage is probably the only place where it's currently practised. And practised with enormous enthusiasm. He produces his little offerings, more leaflet than book, on any subject he thinks people will be interested in – or, more to the point, any subject he thinks people should be interested in. Gonçalo has produced edifying works on Darwin, Gandhi, Newton and Copernicus, whilst keeping an eye on the popular market with 'Goodbye Princess Diana'. It's all admirably low-tech. In the back of the shop he cuts and folds sheets of the cheapest paper into thirty-two-page books. Many of the covers are made from wood blocks. It is a labour of love, but he is encouraged by figures that show that Brazilians are the biggest consumers of poetry in the world, and by his own delight in versifying. Above the garage is a balustraded terrace on which he and his fellow poets gather once a month to eat, drink and recite. Gonçalo will recite at the drop of a hat, and he gives us a fruity rendition of his own poem 'Ode to a Book'. 'Obrigado Senhor Livro...' Thank you Mr Book. Every line charged with feeling.

Opposite · Gonçalo Ferreira, champion of Cordel literature, declaims his 'Ode to a Book'.
Below · A period tram station in Rio's Santa Teresa neighbourhood.

Santa Teresa is something of a haven for eccentrics and lost causes. As we walk around Fábio points out an open-fronted grocery store, eye-catchingly decked out in blue and white *azulejo* tiles, whose owners are so rude that if anyone stops to take a photo they shout abuse at them. Almost next door is the Bar do Arnaldo, Ronnie Biggs's favourite restaurant, where he would retell his version of the Great

1   2

Above: ***1*** *· Tasting* jabuticaba *with Fábio at the fruit and flower market in Laranjeiras.* ***2*** *· At home with Fábio's friends Marcelo and Carol and their two children.* ***Opposite*** *· The Lapa Arches were built to carry water from the hill of Santa Teresa into the centre of Rio. Nowadays they carry a tramway.*

Train Robbery to anyone who would buy him a meal. The only thing that's missing today is the yellow trams. Apparently there was a serious accident only a few days before in which several people died when the brakes failed. Until questions can be answered satisfactorily all the trams have been withdrawn.

Fábio likes surprises and on the way to our next destination he shows me a uniquely Brazilian accessory, called Pocket Percussion. The samba rhythm seems hard-wired into every Brazilian. As those of other nations might unselfconsciously scratch their heads or pick their noses, the Brazilian will begin to shuffle a step back, a step forward, sway the hips a little and go into their own private samba. Pocket Percussion consists of a tiny box with two ball bearings in it, which, when shaken, gives instant accompaniment for your samba habit.

What he wants to show me next is one of the regular fruit markets that are held weekly in neighbourhoods all over the city. The one we end up in is Laranjeiras, a comfortable middle-class area. Stalls with striped awnings stretch halfway up the hill. I've never seen fruit sold in such abundance and variety as here in Brazil. For a papaya fan like myself the sight of succulent piles of them ten or twelve deep is like some mild hallucination. Passion fruit and mango, limes, oranges, custard apple and coconut of course are all in perfect condition. Fábio is keen to show me the more exotic varieties like the small red, cherry-sized fruit from the Amazon called *acerola*, in demand around the world now as a 'super fruit', with a hundred times more vitamin potential than any other. *Jabuticaba* is a black olive-like fruit which only grows in the area of Rio, Minas and São Paulo. Its name has passed into the language to mean something quintessentially Brazilian.

The throng of people, the insistent thumping of a drum and accordion one-man band and the consumption of fresh-made cheese pastries washed down with a cane juice and lime chaser has rendered me a little weary and I gladly take up the invitation to drop in on a young couple who are friends of Fábio.

Marcelo, in his thirties I should think, is a graphic designer, and his wife Carol produces interactive visual displays for exhibition spaces. They have two young daughters and a fine view from the eleventh floor of a well-kept 1930s apartment block. They look like the perfect modern Brazilian family, but when I ask them about the way the country's going, with the economy expanding by leaps and bounds in a way that makes us at home green with envy, I don't get the answers I expected.

Everything in Rio is expensive. Their rent has gone up sixty percent in the last year. Foreign buyers are snapping up property, hoping to make a killing when the World Cup comes to Rio in 2014 and the Olympics in 2016. Marcelo and Carol bemoan the dire state of public education in Brazil, echoing what I'd heard up in Salvador. Both their daughters are in private school, which is also expensive. Boom, it seems, can be as cruel as bust, if you're not among the fortunate few. But all is not gloomy. The children love Fábio and his books and his tricks and he makes a very good passion fruit *caipirinha,* which we drink on the balcony. Only as we're about to leave do I get the hint of another anxiety. I'm admiring the extent of thick, green forest which climbs up a steep, rather impressive mountain side close by them when Marcelo points out a structure at the very top of a V-shaped pass. That's the *favela,* he tells me, it's reached the top of the hill behind them and their fear, everyone's fear in this pleasantly affluent neighbourhood, is that it will spill over the top and spread down towards them.

Fábio takes me downtown where the big modern office blocks have sprung up. On the way we stop to see something very much older, and no less impressive, the Arcos da Lapa, the Lapa Arches. They carry an aqueduct built back in the sixteenth century to bring water from the slopes of Santa Teresa into the

centre of Rio. It was all constructed by Indian slave labour. According to Fábio the indigenous Indians were accomplished builders and engineers, but they were hopeless agriculturalists. Only the women worked the fields. So when the sugar plantations needed intensive hard labour it had to be brought in from Africa.

We end the day at the house Fábio shares with his mother and his new Czech wife Sabina. He shows me his latest paintings, lovely bright evocations of the good life of Rio. The only thing I'd quibble about is that in Fábio's paintings the sun is always shining. Tonight, as we look out from the balcony nursing *jabuticaba caipirinhas*, a thick, grey drizzle is falling all around us and the Cidade Maravilhosa is like Rotherham in November.

Day 51 · Rio de Janeiro

Above · *With Priscilla Ann Goslin, author of* How to be a Carioca. *I ask her how Cariocans cope with rain. 'They evaporate from the street,' she tells me.*

IT'S ALWAYS HARD to get under the skin of a big city. Beneath a spurious unity lurks a hotbed of contradictions. The citizens of Rio call themselves Cariocans, from the Tupi-Guarani Indian words *cari*, meaning 'white man', and *oca*, meaning 'home'. And yet half the population of Rio is black. Whatever the contradictions, one thing that Cariocans, like New Yorkers or Parisians, do agree about is that they are the centre of the world. They are specially blessed to live here. What makes those who live in Niterói, the city on the other side of Guanabara Bay, the luckiest people in the world? They wake up every day with a view of Rio.

To learn more about a city it's sometimes more instructive to look at how they see others rather than how they see themselves. In the same way that the Brazilians hate the Argentines, so the Cariocans hate the Paulistas, the people from São Paulo. In a handy, and very funny, manual called *How to be a Carioca* a Paulista is defined as 'Very sallow-skinned, always seen in business attire speaking Portuguese with an irritating accent. *Paulistas* tend to address each other with the term "*O meu*" ['Hey dude'].' *Mineiros* are similarly dispatched. 'Locals from the state of Minas Gerais. Males are known for doing away with their wives to save their honour.'

The author of such damning stuff is actually American. She's called Priscilla Ann Goslin, and she's made her home in Rio for more than thirty-eight years. Like a true Cariocan, she is wedded to the beach, pounding the sand every morning with her dog in tow. Today, however, the wind howls and the rain slants almost horizontally from the south-east so, instead of joining her on a run as I'd hoped to do, I end up sitting opposite her in a café in Leblon. She's slim, blonde, wears no make-up and looks a lot younger than her sixty-two years.

I ask her how Cariocans cope with the rain. 'They cancel everything,' she says firmly. 'They evaporate from the street.'

I look around and she's right. We're only a few blocks from Ipanema Beach and any other day the streets would be filled with shoppers, diners, drinkers and young men with surfboards. Today the tables are empty, and rain patters on the sunshades.

Priscilla thinks this is symptomatic of something deeper in the Cariocan psyche.

'They don't like bad news. They want to be happy.' She quotes as an example the radio traffic stations. 'The reports never say the traffic is bad. It's always "complicated".'

There's a line she picks out from one of her favourite Brazilian songs. 'It goes, "Don't be afraid, and don't be ashamed to be happy". They're serious people, but they're not afraid of the superficial.'

That's Brazilian, she adds, not just Cariocan. We talk about the Brazilian economy, bounding along like a happy dog whilst ours just lies in the kennel. She's known the years when Brazil was synonymous with inflation and currencies came and went and so she welcomes the stability. But there is the looming problem of personal debt. The middle classes are spending fifty percent of their income just making repayments. She fears the economic bubble will burst.

The gulf between rich and poor is starkly apparent in Rio. Priscilla and I are sitting in a street in Ipanema, probably some of the richest real estate in the city, but overlooking us from the heights behind is the *favela* of Morro do Cantagalo. I ask how middle-class Cariocans deal with this constant reminder of the yawning social gap.

'They only see what they want to see,' she says. 'If it's bad, they just don't notice it.'

Morro do Cantagalo is only one of hundreds of poor neighbourhoods that have grown up to house, in a fairly chaotic and unregulated way, the million or so poor people, often from the North-East, who have come to the city in the hope of work, wages and a decent chance for their children. For many it didn't happen. There was nothing on offer. The easiest way to make money was to deal drugs or be a runner for an existing drug dealer. The *favelas*, ignored by the city authorities, fell under the control of organized crime. Weapons were given to children as young as nine or ten. The book *Cidade de Deus* (*City of God*) by Paulo Lins, from which the viscerally powerful 2002 film of the same name was made, gives a flavour of life in poor communities that became war zones run by competing gangs, in which bullying and protection went hand in hand. Over the last two or three years, mindful of the damage this was doing to the city's reputation, and with the World Cup and Olympic spotlight about to turn on them, the authorities decided it was time to take back the *favelas* from the gangs and give control to the majority of law-abiding people who lived there, and without whom day-to-day life in Rio would grind to a halt. Of course, they should have done this a long time ago; but, like so many others, the police turned a blind eye for too long.

They call the new policy 'pacification'. It was first rolled out in 2008. It involves a concerted operation between civilian and military police moving in, ejecting the drug gangs and replacing them with a legitimate local organization bolstered by increased investment in housing, schools and services. A priority is the establishment of initiatives for those most vulnerable to the gang culture, the young men and boys. In Cantagalo, for instance, a surf school was set up to give all the younger people access to a sport previously confined to wealthy white boys. It was so successful that a popular Globo TV show made it their nominated charity and put in 10,000 *reais*. Surfing is an expensive sport that would have been beyond the means of almost everyone in the *favela*, but they make their own boards for half the price they cost in the shops, wetsuits are provided and, with the best waves on Ipanema Beach only a short walk down the hill, they can be for a while the equals of any other surfer from any other background. I walk along to watch them. There are boys and girls from up in Cantagalo ducking, diving, riding and tumbling with best of them. Jefferson, one of their top teachers, is only twenty-three and wise beyond his years.

Opposite: *1-2* *· At the Favela Surf Centre they make their own boards, for half the price they'd cost in shops.* *3* *· The surfers of Cantagalo set off for the beach.* *4-5* *· Surfing has traditionally been a rich kids' sport; once on the boards the* favela *kids show they're the equals of those much better off.*

'Surfing is a training for life,' he reckons. 'It's about knowing when to take your opportunity. It's about not being afraid.'

The removal of the drug gangs is one thing, but what matters most is keeping them from returning. This involves nothing less than reversing the long-term effects of a community that has become used to being controlled, and at the same time protected, by organized crime. There are many barriers to be broken down, much mistrust to be overcome, before the *favela* can be seen as a part of, not apart from, the rest of the city.

In a *favela* called Tabajaras, not far from Copacabana, we go to see a symbol of future hope in its most dramatic form. A building high up on the hillside that used to be the headquarters of the drug dealers is to be opened as a Community Centre. Entering a *favela* is not like crossing the road. Downtown, where the *favela* meets the rest of Rio, there is a lot of razor wire about, which creates an initial, threatening feeling of entering a community under siege. Then there are certain formalities that have to be observed. You must travel with a local contact and if in a minibus you must keep the windows open so people can see who's inside. Tabajaras, like many of the *favelas* in the south of Rio, is built on the side of a hill, and the narrow roads are steep. As we climb up the hill, where no one has property valuable enough to protect it with razor wire, Tabajaras becomes like any other poor area. Lively bars, small, crowded shops, lean dogs scavenging at uncollected garbage. Recently erected yellow signs hang from walls and posts, part of an initiative to give the streets names for the first time. It's thought that if they have names they'll be better looked after and therefore less dangerous. And presumably it'll be easier for the police to identify where people live.

As part of the celebrations for the new Community Centre a group called Abraço da Paz (Hug of Peace) is running a programme of street activities. Face-painting for children, story-reading, drawing, balloons and of course food and

1

2

3

4

5

1

2

Above: 1-2 · *Tabajaras is one of those shanty towns (favelas) once run by drug barons and now being rehabilitated. Children learn face-painting and making costumes, but basic services are still struggling to cope.* **Opposite: 3-5** · *In Tabajaras the drug gang's HQ has been converted into a Community Centre. At an opening-day party there's music from a police band, an actor's troupe, and a visit from the BBC.*

drink. 'You must give them something to eat or they won't come along,' one of the organizers tells me.

Juliano, one of those who started Abraço da Paz back in 2004, long before the place was pacified, is a tall, youngish man with dark floppy hair. He's a designer, white, in his thirties and grew up at the bottom of the hill. His group was set up after a particularly bloody period of gang warfare, in an attempt, as he puts it, to heal the wounds. They now work closely with the UPP, the specially trained police sent in to stabilize the pacified communities.

As we walk together up to the Community Centre he tells me that the most important thing is to bring communities like Tabajaras back into the mainstream of city life. To break down mutual mistrust that's grown over the years. Music is a good bridge-builder. He's brought 'very white' bands up here and they've been well received. He's persuaded a friend of his who's a chef in some smart downtown restaurant to come up to exchange ideas on food and cook with the locals. I ask him how all this has gone down with the *favelados*, the people who live here. He gives me a slow smile. 'The community is hugging us.'

We turn off the road and begin a long, steep climb up steps receding into the distance ahead of us. *Favelados* do this twice a day. Many of those who live on the hill take an hour or more to walk to work in the city below. They still have no mains water. A system of pipes collects water off the mountain and distributes it to blue plastic tanks on the rooftops. Unless these are kept securely covered, which they often aren't, breeding mosquitoes spread dengue fever. There is no sewage disposal system at all. Just open drains and gravity.

Two hundred and twenty steps later, we've reached what was once the hub of drug distribution in Tabajaras. From this eyrie, with its bird's-eye view out over the inchoate mass of shanty housing to the high-rises of Rio and the spectacular coastline beyond, a community of many thousands was run by the gangs and their leaders. Today this shell of concrete roofs and walls is full of the noise of children who've never had space like this before, shouting, chasing and eating, whilst well-intentioned charity workers try desperately to interest them in more constructive pursuits. Nothing confirms the change of ownership more starkly

3

4

5

than a police band, solemnly dressed in their blue uniforms, belting out jazz and samba at one end of this concrete cavern.

Outside, Rio looks forlorn in the ceaseless rain, but inside, all is hyperactive. It's as if no one can quite believe that they have this new home, and that it's no longer a place to be feared. A group of actors has taken to the stage and they're trying to engage the young audience in participation. Unfortunately someone has just given out whirling rattles. For the moment, anyway, exuberance has the upper hand over education.

Day 52 · Rio de Janeiro

ROAMING AROUND RIO for a day with no particular agenda, I try the public transport system. The buses are the preferred option for Cariocans. They're cheap and frequent, but they're driven hard, as if their drivers are operating fairground rides, so I opt instead for the gentler pace of the Rio Metro. The nearest station is four blocks back from the beach, about a ten-minute walk. It's called Cantagalo, after the mountain behind it, not the *favela* on its slopes. Unlike London, where many of the Underground lines are tunnelled through soft clay, the Rio Metro has been blasted out of granite and to get to the trains you walk through enormous chambers which contain both the access walkways and the trains. It's like being in the stomach of some great beast, with the entrails all around you. Opened in 1978, the Metro is cool, clean, airy and spacious, but it's a limited system, connecting twenty-five stations and covering just over twenty-five kilometres (sixteen miles) of the city (the London Underground covers just over 250 miles and serves 270 stations). There are plans to expand but it will only add some sixteen kilometres (ten miles) to the system before the city hosts the Olympics in 2016. The station at which I disembark, Cardeal Arcoverde, is like the Hall of the Mountain Kings. Its irregular jagged walls, sprayed with a covering of liquid concrete, rise high above our heads, disappearing into the darkness. Any Cariocan using the London Underground should certainly be warned about claustrophobia.

The transport system in Rio is co-ordinated from a compact, glossy box of a building sheathed in silver-green and completed in 2010. The Centro de Operacões is a showpiece and I'm not entirely surprised that it is where the Mayor of Rio has agreed to meet me. Inside, like a smaller version of a NASA control room, is a series of low-lit terraces at which operatives sit at computers in front of a fifty-metre wall of screens, transmitting pictures of traffic movement across the city. At the very back of this futuristic control room is a raised platform offering camera positions for the press and standing room for awed visitors like ourselves.

The Mayor, a popular man called Eduardo Paes, is delayed. There has been an explosion in a building somewhere in the city and there have been fatalities.

Opposite & Above ·
On the Rio Metro.
Small network,
huge tunnels.

He has rushed down to the scene. So we have plenty of time to sit and watch the seventy screens that make up the wall as they flick over, interspersed with weather reports and other information. No one else seems to be very interested. The staff, dressed in white mechanics' overalls that look very odd in this high-tech environment, are behaving in a very Brazilian fashion, laughing, talking, gossiping, joking whilst the city whizzes on in the background. Admittedly, it's not rush hour, but despite that I can't disguise a slight suspicion that this is all a bit of a cosmetic exercise, more about looking as if you're doing something rather than actually doing it.

The Mayor, when he eventually arrives, turns out to be a personable and enthusiastic man in his early forties who speaks excellent English. The explosion earlier is confirmed as being an accident caused by a gas leak. If this had happened in Europe, we both agree, one would have seen a much more alarmed response. Brazil, so far, is mercifully free from the threat of terrorism. It's a country that doesn't seem to have any enemies.

Eduardo Paes is a very modern politician. A qualified lawyer, he has form as the man who turned round the unprepared Pan-American Games which came to Rio in 2007. Dressed casually in a blue button-down shirt and chinos, he's very much aware of the value of public relations. Indeed he has suffered for it. His left arm is in a sling, broken when opening a new cycle lane. 'Three minutes after the press left,' he jokes ruefully.

He has an international perspective, and is modestly aware that Rio has a lot to learn from other cities. This flashy operations wall is designed by an Indian, and his liaison man with us is an Englishman born in Newcastle and now working

1

2

3

on the Mayor's staff. He's well aware that Rio's image as one of the world's most beguiling destinations will be put to the test when the World Cup and then the Olympics roll into town. He, like almost everyone else I've talked to, thinks that whatever happens, Rio will lay on a good party. He points out something which he feels characterizes Rio, as opposed to São Paulo.

'People meet here in public places. Maybe it's because of the beach, but this a good street-living city.'

Eduardo is up for re-election in a year's time and if he wins a second term then he will be the man steering his city through the most important years of its history. Behind him, as we talk, the city's roads and railways move smoothly. But the *favelas* continue to fill up, rising property prices are hurting the middle class, the airport is stretched and the hotels already overflowing. Some would consider taking the helm as a poisoned chalice. For Eduardo Paes it's the one thing he really wants to do.

Day 53 · Rio de Janeiro

MARACANÃ STADIUM, known simply to Brazilians as the Maracanã, is one of the most iconic names in world football. It is the beating heart of a nation obsessed with the sport. One day in 1950 the heart nearly stopped beating. It was the final of the first World Cup to be held in Brazil. Acknowledging its importance, Rio had invested in the largest football stadium ever built, and their ambition seemed to have paid off when 199,854 people (still the world record attendance at a football match) were packed in for the match. Brazil had coasted through the early rounds and the final was expected to be a formality. But their opponents, Uruguay, had not read the script. First they equalized the Brazilian goal, then, at exactly 4.33 on the afternoon of 16 July 1950, they went into a 2-1 lead. The vast crowd fell silent. According to Alex Bellos, in his book *Futebol*, the Uruguayan goal scorer Ghiggia recollected years later, 'Only three people have ... silenced the Maracanã. Frank Sinatra, Pope John Paul II and me.' Brazil were beaten in their own home. The psychological effect extended far beyond the football fraternity. It was a national disaster. The writer José Lins do Rego saw in it the confirmation of something preordained: 'it stuck in my head that we really were a luckless people, a nation deprived of the great joys of victory, always pursued by bad luck, by the meanness of destiny.'

The second World Cup final to be played in Brazil will take place on 13 July 2014, and it will be in the Maracanã again. Today I catch a glimpse of the great stadium, but only from a visitor area. The pitch that saw the Great Silence is full of trucks and cranes and diggers as the Maracanã undergoes a £270 million facelift. When the wonderful sweeping amphitheatre reopens in February 2013 it will have been reduced to a capacity of a mere 80,000, but they will enjoy state-of-the-art comfort. Meanwhile the closest you can get to the glory days of Brazilian football is a Visitors' Centre mock-up of the Calçada da Fama, the Pavement of Fame, where living legends like Zico, Pelé and Jairzinho have left an imprint of their bare feet.

It seems inconceivable, though ominously possible, that another national tragedy could take place in Rio in 2014. Brazil and soccer success are still inextricably linked. This is, after all, the country of Roza FC, the only team in the world entirely made up of transvestites, and of seventeen-year-old Milene Domingues, the 'keepy-uppy' phenomenon who kept a ball in the air for nine hours and six minutes. It's also the country where commentators vie for who can stretch the single word 'Goal!' out the longest. With Tim Vickery, an English football journalist who's lived in Brazil since the 1980s, I went to watch commentator André Henning, who screamed a superhuman twenty-three-second 'G...o....a ... l!' and without pulling a breath went straight into the rest of his patter. He tells me the record for the single word is held by a Romanian at twenty-nine seconds. Try it, it's not as easy as you think.

__Opposite__ · At Rio's state-of-the-art Operations Centre. __1__ · Something's happening... __2__ · With Eduardo Paes, young, energetic Mayor of Rio. He tells me he broke his arm whilst opening a new cycle lane. 'Three minutes after the press left,' he jokes. __3__ · Keeping a watchful eye on transport across the city.

1

2

Above: ***1** · The Visitor Centre at the Maracanã. The rebuilt stadium (seen here) will host the World Cup Final in 2014. Capacity will be 80,000. The old Maracanã squeezed in 200,000 for Brazil's World Cup Final in 1950. They lost one-nil to Uruguay.* ***2** · Not your average football club. Stained glass grandeur in the ballroom at Fluminense.* ***Opposite** · In the stands at Fluminense FC with Tim Vickery, an English football journalist. It's the oldest football club in Brazil.*

To help put football in Brazil in perspective, Tim takes me round to the Fluminense Football Club, one of the four big clubs of Rio – the others being Botafogo, Vasco da Gama (the first to introduce black players) and Flamengo, currently the most successful.

At the turn of the century one Charles Miller, son of a Scots engineer who'd come to Brazil to build railways, arrived in Rio and brought some footballs with him. Thanks to Miller and the local British contingent, Rio became the birthplace of Brazilian football. Fluminense was founded in 1902 by a wealthy Anglo-Brazilian called Oscar Cox. He and his friends saw it as much as a social club as a football club and it was always associated with the elite. And there is still the feeling that it's a club for the better-off.

The stadium we're in is set in the comfortable area of Laranjeiras and is the oldest football ground in Brazil, dating back to 1919. The stands have been well preserved and there's a lot of the original woodwork. But it's not a big ground, and nowadays it's only used for training games. It's the buildings attached to it that take the breath away. Built in French Belle Époque style, with wide staircases, vast mirrors, elegant ballrooms and stained-glass windows, they're quite unlike anything I've ever seen at a football club. There's an immaculate little garden and stucco decorations on the wall in Greek classical style. There is a modern club shop selling Fluminense strip and assorted merchandising. It's called, somewhat unfortunately, the Flu Boutique.

Tim draws an interesting contrast between the two great passions of Brazilian life – football and samba. Football started at the top and seeped very quickly down to all levels of society, whereas samba started at the bottom and became the ultimate in sophistication. There are other anomalies that he helps me try and understand. Why, if football is the national obsession, are average attendances in the Brazilian league only around 14,000? He has various explanations. The stadiums are old and inadequate. Games are played late in the evening when it's cooler, sometimes not kicking off till ten o'clock. This, along with a pretty poor public transport system, can mean a long walk home along often dangerous streets. He paints a bleak picture of fans getting home after the match. 'It's like a tropical

version of Napoleon's retreat from Moscow,' he says.

But Tim thinks there's a deeper reason, which accords with a number of things I've already heard about Brazilians. They like good news. They like the sun to shine. They like to be thought playful and easygoing, dwelling not on past or future but on the here and now. Alex Bellos quotes an historian, Sérgio Buarque de Holanda, as suggesting that the Brazilian contribution to civilization is 'cordiality'. The negative side to all this, thinks Tim, is a national inability, or simply disinclination, to deal with anything bad. Applied to football, this means that if your team's not winning you don't go to the ground. Club loyalty, says Tim, is another victim of what he calls the manic depressiveness at the heart of the Brazilian national character. 'It pats itself on the back effusively with every victory, and torments itself with every defeat.'

As if on cue, the rain starts to patter down on the roof of the stadium and there are long faces and big umbrellas at the gates of Fluminense Football Club. The slow steady rain makes me think of home. Which is not entirely inappropriate. It was at Fluminense's ground that Brazil's national team played their first game ever. It was against a touring British club side, Exeter City FC. In their first international Brazil beat Exeter 2-0. Just over a month later the First World War broke out in Europe.

A rather wonderful coda to this day of football. I go up to the guests' club room at our hotel to complain about the Wi-Fi reception. The lady is very helpful and confides that she knows who I am. Moments later a big, leather-bound guest book is brought out for me to sign. The paper is thick and luxurious. She finds a new page for me.

'There,' she says. 'You will be in good company.'

I check the page before mine. There, with a little drawing of a ball hitting the back of a football net, is the one word, Pele.

Day 54 · Rio de Janeiro

THE PACIFICATION POLICY, on which the politicians of Rio pin so much faith in addressing what the Mayor calls, somewhat euphemistically, 'the issue of social differences', is spearheaded by a crack paramilitary elite called BOPE. The Batalhão de Operacões Policiais Especiais (Special Operations Battalion). They are the hard men with whom the process begins. How it works is that the drug gangs are given advance warning that pacification is about to begin and that they should surrender or get out of the area. Some regard this as weakness, but the strategy is designed to avoid street battles in which innocent people could be involved and property needlessly destroyed. Such is BOPE's reputation – they're trained by Mossad after all – that the drug barons usually disappear rather than take them on. Once they have secured the streets then a specially trained police force, the PPU, occupy the *favela* on a much longer-term basis, and try to secure hearts and minds. BOPE, of necessity, project a highly secretive image, and it's with some surprise that we've heard that they have granted us access to their training centre.

__Above__ · The blood-curdling insignia of BOPE, the elite Special Operations Battalion. __Opposite: 1__ · Inside the HQ. Behind me a graphic of the hard men in action. __2__ · Some of BOPE's 470-man, six women crack squad, who spearhead the process of 'pacification' in high-crime favelas, *prepare to go out on patrol from their hilltop base. __3__ · Captain Marlisa, the PR face of BOPE, wearing an earring to die for. __4__ · The heavily armoured vehicles in which they enter the* favelas.

The rain has cleared away this morning and Copacabana is enveloped in a thick, swirling sea mist, which swathes the hotel like a warm duvet. As we wait to leave someone spots a small, confused furry creature nosing its way out of the ornamental bushes at the entrance to the hotel. It's a possum. No one knows where it's come from, but as it rubs itself up against the glass Seb, our sound man, goes to help it. One of the hotel's security men has other ideas. As the bewildered creature snuffles this way and that, he shakes his head, laughs and aims an almighty kick at it. Only a concerted yelp of protest from the entire film crew makes him pause, and instead of being sent flying onto the road and under the first car, the possum is escorted to relative safety.

A half-hour later I can relate to that possum as we wait at the security barrier of Brazil's most feared force. Above us is the unit's motto, 'Vá e Vença' ('Go and Win!') and alongside it the battalion logo, a pair of crossed handguns behind a venomous-looking skull with a knife embedded in it. Two guards, bristling with weapons and dressed head to foot in black, man the gate. They're the physical embodiment of a snarl. Whenever one of their men comes or goes through the barrier they give a very loud ritual shout and raise their assault rifles in an arc as the vehicle goes through. It is a convincing show of meanness and machismo, but at the same time there's something vaguely camp about the whole thing. The cut of the battledress and the intensity of the roar seem a little studied. We're eventually cleared to proceed up the hill to the base itself. This turns out to be a half-finished casino, a concrete shell with fine views out over Guanabara Bay, Sugar Loaf and the Santos Dumont domestic airport. Much closer to the base, indeed just below

1

3

2

4

it, are the rickety roofs and fragile walls of a *favela*. It looks almost as if it might be for training purposes. But it's real.

Outside the building are several all-black vehicles ranging from small patrol jeeps to a gigantic armour-plated snatch vehicle with bull bars on the front and room inside for twenty or thirty people. Inside the building, a physical fitness class is under way. In their Special Operations T-shirts and shorts, without combat gear or body armour, this feared elite looks reassuringly like anyone else. Not all hard men, not even big men. When they relax between exercises their default mode is not the snarl or the scowl. On their faces I can see uncertainty, humour, nervousness even. In the nearby canteen, heavy metal music blasts out to a sea of empty chairs.

Then the instructors call them to order and before they get down to the exercises there's a lot more ritual shouting. Group shouts are very big here. The technique of responses, bawled back and forth between a sergeant and his men, is intended presumably to strengthen solidarity and stimulate aggression.

As they start a workout – stretching, press-ups, twisting and turning – I take a tentative look at the place. No one seems to mind my nosing around these big wide open-plan floors. There isn't much furniture. But there is quite a lot on the walls. Emblems, symbols, mottoes: 'Nada é impossivel para o soldado do BOPE', even naïf paintings showing their big, black armoured vehicles pushing aside barricades. An enormous photomontage of their home base ringed by shots of the men in action has a long black bench in front of it, as if for contemplation of the brave deeds of BOPE. On one wall is painted 'A Prayer for the Special Forces'.

A pony-tailed girl in a T-shirt and sweatpants whom I'd taken for one of the catering staff turns out to be Marlisa, a Captain and public relations officer for BOPE. By the time of our interview, up on the roof of the building, she has been transformed into a black-booted, black-clad action woman with a glare which no smile can crack. It's only as the interview gets under way and we're discussing the risks to life and limb when they go into danger zones, that I become aware she's wearing a pair of dangly silver earrings. As she's telling me how the BOPE elite is made up of 470 men and six women and that women are not currently allowed on first-strike operations, I can't, of course, take my eyes off the earrings.

Marlisa is a good publicity officer. She thinks pacification is working, but that BOPE alone can do nothing. There has to be a will for change on everybody's part.

We have to abandon the interview for a time as a helicopter is coming in to pick up a young officer from the roof we're standing on. It swoops over from the east. Small, black and nimble, like the man climbing aboard. The engines keep running. The pick-up is effected and the helicopter drops down from the roof racing over the *favela*, deliberately and intimidatingly low. Marlisa warms up a little after this and by the end of the interview I feel emboldened to ask about the

earrings. She shows them to me and at last I can make out the design. It's a pair of crossed handguns behind a skull with a knife embedded in it. Perhaps noticing the expression on my face, Captain Marlisa briskly explains the finer points of the design. The knife, she points out, is coming out of the skull, not going into it. It's not about death, but victory *over* death.

Day 55 · Rio de Janeiro

OUR TIME IN RIO is nearly up and I'm aware that we have spent most of it in the landmark-studded Southside of the city – the Rio of the postcards and the ads, where you're lulled to sleep by the sound of the surf, and wake up every morning with a breathtaking beachside view. Where you're never far from the arms of Christ or the sight of the cable car looping up to Sugar Loaf Mountain. And it's all that most visitors ever see. Which is why I'm very curious about what we shall find as we leave our comfort zone and head north.

At first it gets only smarter. Our route skirts the affluent playground of Lagoa Rodrigo de Freitas, an inshore lake with smart and desirable residences around its shores, as well as all sorts of facilities supplying the ever-present need for sport and exercise. A seven-and-a-half-kilometre (four-and-a-half-mile) jogging and cycling circuit winds around it, and already at this early hour a number of rowing eights and individual scullers are out on the water. For those less energetic, there are pedaloes shaped like swans. And if you're a rich and successful Cariocan you can join the private sports clubs and play tennis behind high hedges. With mountain and forest framing the lake (the inconvenient *favelas* that once were here were removed in the 1960s and 1970s) it is a picturesque alternative to the more frenetic beaches. Past the lake, the road north takes us under the mountains through the long Rebouças tunnel, from which we emerge at brief intervals apparently having been transported in just over three kilometres from the city to the middle of the jungle. This is the Tijuca Forest, the world's largest urban forest, and yet another of Rio's natural wonders. The National Park that bears its name covers nearly forty square kilometres (fifteen square miles) of the city's boundaries. And it's big enough to get lost in. I'm told that people often do.

Opposite · BOPE helicopter approaches the roof of the half-finished casino they've taken over as their operating base. Panorama of Rio with Sugar Loaf Mountain in the background.

Emerging eventually from the last section of the tunnel, we head east and run along the edge of Guanabara Bay, by way of a beautifully landscaped parkway which leads up onto elevated highways with views of the docks. Though smaller ships still unload here, much of the area is now derelict. Soaring chimneys and silos give it a certain grandeur as do the long rows of warehouses, whose extensive blank walls have proved irresistible to the *graffitistas*, with some magnificent results. As in many cities around the world, the docks in Rio are seeing a new life as a cultural quarter. Beneath a flyover, in some dark, post-industrial canyon, I catch sight of queues already forming for another day of the Rio film festival.

Our journey's goal is to meet a young Englishman called Luke Dowdney who,

in 2000, launched Luta Pela Paz (Fight for Peace), one of the more successful of the initiatives that have been launched to help disadvantaged street children. He chose to locate it in one of the most notoriously dangerous communities, the Complexo da Maré, a *favela* that remains unpacified.

As we enter the Zona Norte the look of the city changes. The peaks are gone. The land flattens out. There are no lakes or green swathes of forest to break the urban sprawl. Trucks seem to outnumber cars as the roads roll, long and straight, through featureless, built-up areas. Our driver is unsure of himself. There are, as usual, no signposts indicating the presence of a *favela*. We keep pulling over. Phone calls are made.

Finally we turn off the main highway and park in a side street beside a packing and freighting plant. As delivery trucks reverse into loading bays, people trudge past us on the way to the main road. Old men, younger men, one or two stopping to look through a pile of rubbish in the hope of finding something recyclable, single women off to work in town, mothers with children. They all look very different from the people who walk the promenades of Copacabana. Their faces are resigned, their expressions sometimes hard, sometimes just dull. They're not walking for their health. They walk because they can't afford not to.

Our minders arrive, and once again we're warned to keep the windows of our vehicle open. This time there'll be no police to help us. Our safety is in the hands of whoever runs the *favela*. It's best not to ask too many questions. In fact Maré looks a lot more solid and substantial than the *favelas* that overlook Copacabana.

Opposite · *Giant graffiti on the wall of an abandoned warehouse in the old docks area, now finding new life as a cultural quarter.*
Above · *At the Fight for Peace gymnasium in Maré, a tough neighbourhood in Rio's Zona Norte. It was founded in 2000 by Englishman Luke Dowdney, talking to me whilst sparring goes on around us.*

Maybe it's just that it's built on the flat, maybe because it's been here longer. *Favelas* are not a new phenomenon. The first shanty town grew up here at the start of the century when they drained the swamp, and a lot of the workforce who built Rio's airport were settled here. The houses are of brick and plaster rather than scraps of wood and tin sheeting, and there are busy streets full of shops and businesses.

At the far end of the network of streets there's a patch of green open land, on one side of which runs the road to the airport, screened off by a high fence. The last building before this is the smartest in the *favela*. Tall, modern, with a curved metal roof and walls painted and tiled sky-blue, the legend 'Luta Pela Paz' boldly picked out on the front. Even before I go inside I can hear what it is that makes this particular charity so different. It's the sound of trainers squeaking on the floor and the thud and smack of boxing gloves. The door opens into a small lobby off which is a sparkling clean, state-of-the-art gym full of sparring couples. There are a number of girls among them. All wear expressions of serious concentration as they duck and jab and swing. There is some fast and very impressive punching. In amongst these almost entirely black faces is a tall, rangy white man. Luke Dowdney is in his mid-thirties. He is a boxer himself, a British Universities Middleweight Champion. His face looks as if it might have taken a few blows, but he was undefeated in eighteen amateur fights. Restless, ambitious and articulate, he runs through the history of this place as we sit together on the side of a boxing ring.

A dissertation on street kids for an anthropology degree at Edinburgh

University first brought Luke to Rio in 1995. He came back to work for a big Brazilian non-governmental organization and was frustrated at how hard it was to get through to children involved in street violence. 'If you walk out at night-time here, you'll see kids holding automatic weapons. They're working for the drug trade.'

From his previous experience of the sport, he had the idea that a boxing club might be an ideal way of luring these children off the streets, without expecting them to change their lives overnight. 'Boxing is about fighting, but without guns,' he says.

Created in 2000, the Fight for Peace formula proved its worth. Not only did the mix of boxing and martial arts offer an alternative to the drug trade, it's also been a success in itself. Last week they won gold, silver and bronze medals at the Brazilian National Championships and they have one man currently in the Brazilian Olympic team. And the boxing instruction comes with a commitment to education. Fight for Peace is not just a short-term diversion, it's a long-term attempt to change damaged lives. In partnership with the Brazilian Ministry of Education, they run courses in primary and secondary education, job-training and youth leadership. At the moment they have 275 people between the ages of sixteen and twenty-nine studying here. Success has brought in funds from charities like Comic Relief and Save the Children as well as company sponsorship from British Airways and the Brazilian oil company Petrobras.

Opposite: ***1*** *· Luke points out warring sections of the* favela. *His aim is to persuade them to fight with fists in the gym, not with guns on the streets.* ***2*** *· Bira, who came out to keep an eye on us. He was a bank robber who was shot in the back. Now he helps Fight for Peace talk youngsters out of crime.* ***3*** *· Telephone and electricity are taken off the public supply on leads. The clusters of leads are known as a* gato, *a cat. The local cat-man can connect you up.*

When Luke takes me up on the roof and points out the realities of life here, it all seems slightly surreal. Maré was the only *favela* in Rio where three of the city's four main drug factions had a base. He points out streets not far away – 'just over by that school' – where the walls are riddled with bullet holes, simply because it was on the front line between rival gangs' territory. One of the achievements of Fight for Peace has been to open outposts of the main building in other parts of the *favela*, so children can take advantage of what they offer without having to cross gang lines. Maré, like many other similar *favelas*, is being rebranded as a *bairro*, a community, but Luke says it'll take more than a new name to change the old image. The task, first and foremost, is to get the street kids away from their weapons.

'There are between 45,000 and 50,000 homicides in Brazil every year. Ninety percent of which are gun-related. There are a lot of guns on the street.'

He thinks the pacification policy has one big advantage going for it. Money. It's not just the Mayor and the police who want to improve things, it's the big companies as well. *Favelas* run by traffickers are not good for business. He's heard that Eike Batista, the fabulously wealthy mines-to-transport entrepreneur, is backing it. And there are rumours that Maré is already being prepared for occupation. The usual drop of leaflets and written warnings hasn't yet materialized, but BOPE have apparently begun operating here. Luke recalls that they were in the middle of shooting a video for British Airways when a fully armed BOPE assault group appeared round the corner. 'Very surreal moment,' he adds.

1

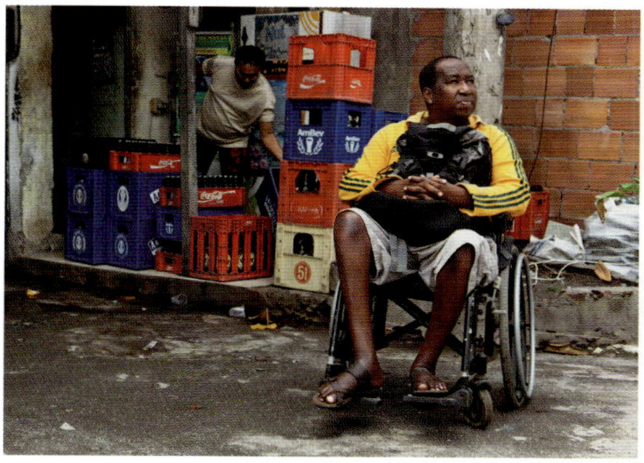

2

3

Right on cue, there is the sound of what could be distant crackling gunfire. Luke cocks his head. 'Firecrackers,' he concludes. 'That's how the gangs warn that there are police on the move.'

We go back downstairs. Outside, in the compound, Bira, a large middle-aged man wearing a gold Brazil football shirt, sits in a wheelchair surrounded by a group of NGOs from all over the world who've come here to see if there are lessons for their own countries' problems. Two of them are from the Congo. One is their national boxing champion despite only having one eye. He lost the other whilst a soldier in the children's army.

Bira too has a story. He was once a bank robber till he got shot in the back. Now, despite being wheelchair-bound, he is a figure everyone respects and a vital liaison between Luke and the local community. Someone asks Bira how he goes about trying to persuade others to give up a life of crime. He shrugs. 'What's good for me is good for them. That's all I can say. I'm not superman. I can't change things myself.'

He has an ambiguous attitude to pacification. He can see the reason for it but he still feels that he and others in Maré are being treated as special cases, just because they live in *favelas*. 'I want to be treated because I'm a citizen, not differently because I come from a *favela*.'

Which makes me aware of one of the frustrating truths about *favelas*. That the

1

2

3

4

5

predominantly peaceful, hard-working majority of *favelados* are damned for the actions of a small but ruthless minority. With Bira wheeling himself along ahead of us, we make a cautious sally out of the well-fenced compound and into the streets of Maré. There's a shoe black just outside, and a fruit seller, and as we go up the street, there is nothing more aggressive than some shouted greetings from acquaintances of Bira. Only when we hear the firecrackers again does Luke suggest we should be getting back. He sighs.

'Most of the bad stuff happens at night,' he says. But any weariness in his voice is more than made up for by his determination to stay the course. Things can get better.

Evidence of this is to be found only a short distance from Maré, in the huge, sprawling Complexo do Alemão. Almost a year ago, a battle was fought here between police and two drug gangs, Comando Vermelho (Red Command) and Amigos dos Amigos (the Friends of Friends). It was the most high-profile gang-busting operation and for the State Governor, Sérgio Cabral, it could not afford to fail. A similar operation in 2007, when nineteen people were killed, became known as the Complexo do Alemão Massacre, and the drug gangs remained in control. Three years later it was better planned and, though there were thirty-seven deaths in the action, this scattering of half a dozen *favelas* and 300,000 people were taken into police control. This time follow-up funds were poured in and outward and visible change has come amazingly quickly.

At Bonsucesso Station the railway into Rio connects with a brand-new cable car system, the Teleférico, which connects all the corners of the Complexo do Alemão. We're among the first people to travel on it, and several proud but wary officials escort us around, as does a highly articulate young journalist and blogger called Raul. Raul is twenty-two, clean-cut, with film star good looks. An advert for redemption. Raul grew up involved in petty crime. He didn't have a weapon, he claims, but 'he held one for others', as he puts it. As the shiny blue and white gondola swings us out over the rooftops he admits that it's going to take time for the people of Complexo do Alemão to get used to it. The young are already taking advantage, but, despite the fact that it's reduced the journey time to schools, shops and clinics from one and a half hours to fifteen minutes, the older people are still very wary of the buses in the sky. Raul's mother won't go near it. A few years ago something like the Teleférico would have been unthinkable. The only way you would have got this extraordinary view out over the *favela* would have been from a police helicopter.

When we get out at one of the spotless, freshly painted stations, we see military police in evidence, but they keep a discreet presence, standing almost shyly to one side wearing their turquoise baseball caps marked 'Forca da Pacificacão'. At the very heart of the Complexo, where narrow gullies crammed with precarious shanty houses converge, a very cool modern development is being completed. It's to be called Knowledge Square, and it consists of Cinema

***Opposite:* *1-4* · *The Teleférico and the view from above.* **5** · *New look for the favela; Einstein on the walls of Knowledge Square.*

***Preceding pages* .** *Complexo do Alemão. A big, sprawling, once dangerous neighbourhood, in the process of pacification. Key to the improvements is a shiny new six-station cable car system that connects the disparate parts of the community, and helps police keep an eye on the streets.*

Carioca, admission four *reais*, as opposed to twenty-five in the centre of Rio, a Digital Inclusion Centre for the locals to learn about the internet, new shops, a caged football pitch and a big mural of Albert Einstein. I see here something that seems so obvious, but which we haven't seen in any of the *favelas* we've visited so far, and that is well-designed social housing. 'Morar Carioca' the billboard announces. Carioca Living. The bright, attractive housing, the Teleférico and Knowledge Square are gleaming symbols of hope. The fact that armed gangs were in running battles with the police and the army here only a year ago shows how fast the renewal programme can move when it wants to. PAC, the Growth Acceleration Programme, which is organizing this initiative, is dear to the heart of President Dilma Rousseff and already a second-stage PAC 2 is being planned involving injections of billions of dollars into the infrastructure of Brazil's cities. How much it will have changed them by the time visitors pour in to the World Cup and the Olympics remains to be seen. The reality is that the drug dealers have not gone away for good. So long as there is a market for their product, so long as rich and aspiring Cariocans, and others further afield, demand their fixes, there will be drug dealers in Complexo do Alemão for some time yet. And the army knows this too. There are no plans to withdraw until well into next year.

What is beyond doubt is how the improved conditions can release the potential of those who have been neglected for so long. Like Bira in Maré, Raul is not leaving the community in which he learnt a life of crime, he's using his experience and his inside knowledge to change others the way he's changed. He runs a community blog, he's learnt excellent English and when I ask for some detail about the years of violence in his *favela*, he nods, smiles and brings out his iPad to look it up.

Day 56 · Rio de Janeiro

ONE OF THE inescapable impressions of this city, even on another glum day of squally south-easterly winds, is of a liveliness and openness to new ideas, particularly in the arts: the joyful ambition of the graffiti artists, the colour-saturated murals that liven up the concrete canyons, even the elaborate and complex sand sculptures which you see along the beach, with a bucket beside them to throw a coin in if you like them. It's all evidence of the public expression of an exuberant imagination. One Brazilian who typifies this is Vik Muniz, born in a *favela* in São Paulo fifty years ago, and now an artist with a worldwide following. His work delights in contrasts, in bringing together iconic images and doing something different with them, often using everyday materials that artists don't normally use, like dust and cotton and food and clothing. Muniz created a double Mona Lisa out of jam and peanut butter and a recreation of the Last Supper in chocolate syrup. He lives in New York these days, but works a lot in Rio and his latest project is to set up an art school in a beautiful location on a hill

***Above** · Vidigal, the Hill, looking down on Copacabana, the Asphalt.*

overlooking Ipanema and Copacabana. But, being Vik Muniz, there is a twist to the tale. The beautiful hillside location is already occupied by a rambling, unpacified *favela* called Vidigal. With Vik's contacts we're able to get up to the site where he hopes to locate his arts centre. As we look out, a man sits against a wall nearby, eyeing us benevolently, and cradling an AK-47.

The view is magnificent, a sweeping panorama of the finest beaches and the most sought-after property in the city. Vik notes the irony. 'Saint-Tropez surrounded by Mogadishu,' is how he describes it. 'Most of the people who live down there have never seen it from up here.'

There is, of course, an umbilical connection between the two, between what he calls the Asphalt and the Hill. Rio, says Vik, has one of the highest living standards in the world, because of the pool of cheap labour available in the *favelas*.

'And yet,' he says, 'you ask the people how often they've been to their maid's house or their nanny's house.' He spreads his arms 'They don't know where they live. They don't know anything about them.'

There is prejudice on both sides. Those down below imagine a place like Vidigal to be full of lawless bandits and drug dealers, and those who look down on the city are quite sure that anyone who can afford a twenty-million-dollar apartment in Ipanema must be a crook.

Vik is not short of evidence on both sides. He tells me some horrible tales of gang vengeance. Of a drug dealer beheaded by an opposing gang who then played

soccer with his head as a ball; of retribution by necklacing – forcing a rubber tyre over someone's head and setting it alight. But on the whole he's optimistic, not just that things are changing with pacification, but that the contrast between rich and poor, of the employers and the workforce, can be a productive one, especially for an artist. The life of people on the other side is where an artist like himself can flourish. Recently he completed a series of powerful images with material from Jardim Gramacho, the world's largest rubbish dump, on the outskirts of Rio. He worked with a group of *catadores*, highly organized scavengers who walk the tip, picking through the city's waste for recyclable materials.

As we walk back into Vidigal he worries that the fast-moving changes in the *favelas* might not always turn out to be the good things they're intended to be. He points out a huge bundle of wires attached to an overhead electricity supply cable.

'See that? They call that a *gato*. A cat. It's all the leads taking free electricity from the system. If you want a power supply you get in the cat-man, and he goes up there and finds you a connection.'

Building, likewise, is completely unregulated. Children don't leave home when they grow up, they just attach another room to the house. Vik calls the process, with a touch of admiration, 'practicality and confusion'.

When pacification restores order to these neighbourhoods, and brings shanty towns into the mainstream, the people will suddenly find themselves having to pay for electricity and satellite and cable. They'll have to find money to pay for that extra room. One of the cornerstones of the occupation policy is to give people deeds to their homes, to enfranchise them by making them property holders. Admirable in intention, but Vik sees many *favelados* deciding to sell up and move elsewhere and, in the case of Vidigal, leaving some very desirable real estate to some very undesirable people.

Back down the hill we walk together on Arpoador, one end of Ipanema Beach, which Vik describes as the most expensive real estate in the Southern Hemisphere. From here I take a last look up at Vidigal, as picturesque as a Mediterranean village. And the man with the AK-47 is probably still on his chair, looking back at me.

Everything in Rio seems to come back to the beaches. Vik agrees. Beach life typifies the Brazilian attitude. It is a place where everyone is equal, where the body-obsessed culture and innate sense of tolerance come together.

'The beach is free. Everyone can be what they want. Nobody knows who you are or what you do. Just that you have a pair of Speedos just like them.'

We end up not far from the sound of the sea, at one of Vik's favourite places, Rio's best Bahian restaurant. He entertains us with impressions of characters from the hugely popular TV soap operas that are the theme music to all Brazilian life. He talks about football and how he supports Flamengo if he's in Rio, and Corinthians if he's in São Paulo, and how everyone makes jokes about the 'country cousins' who come from Minas Gerais. But most of all, on this unseasonably cool, grey day, we relive the pleasures of *moqueca* and *acarajé* and the flavours of okra and vanilla and palm oil and imagine ourselves back on the sunny squares of Salvador.

Opposite · *On the beach with Vik Muniz.*
Below · *Farewell to Rio: Copacabana and the Sugar Loaf Mountain remain enduring images.*

Following pages · *Copacabana Beach. Sunday afternoon.*

PART 4 | SÃO PAULO & THE SOUTH

MATO GROSSO
BAHIA
São Fransisco
Araguaia
Alto Paraiso de Goiás
Tocantins
DISTRITO FEDERAL
Brasília
Cuiabá
Rondonópolis
GOIÁS
Goiânia
MINAS GERAIS
Planalto do Brasil
Taquarí
Paranaíba
Cardeal Mota
Barra Mansa
MATO GROSSO DO SUL
Belo Horizonte
Grande
Campo Grande
Ouro Preto
SÃO PAULO
Paraná
Tietê
Serra da Mantiqueira
Rio de Janeiro
São José dos Campos
Parati
Barra da Tijuca
São Paulo
Ivaí
Santos
PARAGUAY
PARANÁ
Curitiba
Morretes
Foz do Iguaçu
Pomerode
Blumenau
SANTA CATARINA
Uruguai
Florianópolis
Serra do Mar
RIO GRANDE DO SUL
ATLANTIC OCEAN
Porto Alegre
Lagoa dos Patos
Rio Grande
URUGUAY
0 200 400 600 kilometres
0 100 200 300 400 miles

Day 57 · Barra da Tijuca

ON AN ORDINARY DAY, almost anywhere in Brazil, there will be a television set tuned to a soap opera. Whether it be in hospital or hotel, airport or filling station, shop or café, *churrascaria, lanchonete,* or any one of a hundred million homes, the country will be watching itself in the painstakingly crafted parallel worlds of what their creators call *telenovelas.* There are three running concurrently, enthralling the nation and in the process earning unimaginable amounts of money for their production company, Rede Globo, known to all as Globo. Launched by Roberto Marinho in 1965, the privately owned company is now the fourth-largest broadcasting organization in the world.

The stories that have the nation in their grip are all produced in studios close to the booming suburb south and west of Rio called Barra da Tijuca, otherwise known as the Miami of the South. This morning, as we wind our way slowly along a busy coast road, the comparison doesn't do Miami any favours. Free of many of the planning restrictions of central Rio, and boosted by news that the 2016 Olympics will be sited here, tower blocks, stacked high with expensive apartments, are mushrooming all over Barra.

We turn off the main road and up into the wooded hills to an area called Jacarepaguá, which has an airport named after the founder of Globo, and which has given its name to Projac, the massive, multi-studio production complex from which Brazil's *telenovelas* are rolled out. After the hectic highways out of Rio there's a certain tranquillity up here. Over lunch at a smart, woody, studio restaurant, with the trees outside scattering sunlit shadows on the tables, I meet my host for the afternoon, a real-life soap star called Carolina Ferraz. She's in her early forties, and wears a pair of red-framed dark glasses and long dark hair pulled back in a ponytail. She has fine, regular features and the elfin build of a latter-day Audrey Hepburn. And, like Hepburn, Carolina began life as a ballet dancer before becoming an actor, and now a regular on the *telenovela* circuit.

We go on a buggy round to one of the sets of her latest hit, *Avenida Brasil.* It's a well-run production line, Carolina tells me, but they're expected to work hard. Which means putting in a ten- to twelve-hour shift, shooting an average of thirty to forty set-ups a day.

'It's like shooting a movie a week.'

We drive into the make-believe world of *Avenida Brasil,* passing behind houses, churches, whole shopping arcades, propped up with iron supports, before emerging into the centre of an utterly convincing run-down *bairro.*

'I'm a rich character. This is a poor area,' says Carolina, by way of introduction, adding tantalizingly, 'I'm going to lose everything and live here.'

The streets and buildings on the lot are labyrinthine enough to give a powerful sense of reality to this mocked-up world. Cars cruise back and forth convincingly and an army of extras, some eighty or ninety, Carolina estimates, are in position at

Above · *Touring the Globo back-lot with Carolina. Big blue screen on right is for computer graphic projections.*
Opposite: 1 · *Talking with Carolina Ferraz, soap star, between takes on the set of* Avenida Brasil.
2 · *Shanty town carefully constructed by the art department.*
3 · *Carolina Ferraz as herself.*

various parts of the action, like characters in a fairy story awaiting the prince's kiss to bring them to life. The director, a tall young man with a boyish look and a lick of hair across his forehead, sits in a darkened room off the main street, watching a bank of monitors and issuing his instructions through an old-fashioned hand-held microphone. He's one of four directors working simultaneously on different parts of the story.

The audience for these soaps is enormous. Carolina thinks that some seventy million people are tuning into *Avenida Brasil* every night. That's over fifty percent of Brazil's total TV audience. And they are from every kind of background.

'It's very democratic,' she says.

She sees the soaps as something more than just national wallpaper. They have, she thinks, a social obligation. To show me what she means we buggy across to another part of the lot where they have built a mock shanty town complete with wrecked cars and graffitied huts beside a huge, meticulously recreated rubbish dump. It's the sort of combination you'd find on the outskirts of any big Brazilian city. But in the new, caring Brazil these people are no longer ignored. Thanks to sympathetic books and films, there is growing interest in the scavengers. They've become new folk heroes, recycling the mountains of other people's rubbish, because they'd rather be in control of their own lives than live off handouts.

1

2

3

'There is no organic matter anywhere on the tip!' a Globo PR lady shouts reassuringly, as we walk across to investigate these skilfully crafted mountains of garbage.

One of the characters in Carolina's latest story is a woman who can only find work combing through the rubbish.

'She's raised in a place like this, but she breaks through, she becomes a hero,' Carolina explains. Then she adds, 'Imagine seventy or eighty million people discussing this every night.'

The difference between the soaps here and those in the UK or America is that Brazilian soaps have a finite lifespan. Instead of running on for thirty or forty years, they are limited to something like 196 episodes, lasting no more than nine months. Carolina approves. She thinks this is what keeps the audience's attention focused. And as an actor who's been in soaps for twenty-five years, it means that she can play a wide variety of characters.

Carolina is a good companion and I'm pleased that she wants to meet up again when we reach São Paulo. She commutes between the two major cities and has an interesting take on their differences.

'São Paulo is a male. Rio is a female. She's quite an old female. She's still sensual but a bit decadent. São Paulo is an older man. He's a little formal at first, but when you get to know him he can be very sweet to you.'

Day 58 · Parati

AS THE nineteenth century opened Brazil was firmly ensconced as a part of the Portuguese empire. Twenty-two years later, everything had changed. It all began with Napoleon. After his invasion of Portugal in 1807, the royal family, escorted by the British Navy, fled Europe and set up court in Rio de Janeiro. The Portuguese king, João VI, ruled his empire from Brazil for twelve years. In 1821 he returned home to Lisbon, leaving his son Dom Pedro behind as Prince Regent.

'That was my great-great-grandfather.'

I'm standing in front of a portrait embodying all the grandeur of European royalty. Beside me is a good-looking man with neatly trimmed beard and moustache, and more than a touch of an ageing Brad Pitt about him. He nods to the painting.

'He had a vision. A national vision, not a colonial vision. A vision that independence was the only way to keep this country together.'

On 7 September 1822, Dom Pedro declared himself Emperor of an independent Brazil and, as far as his great-great-grandson is concerned, saved it from the fragmentation and political instabilities that blighted the Spanish, the other empire in South America. He argues that the shape, size and stability of modern Brazil is due to the enlightened foresight of the stern-jawed figure who stands

1

2

3

***Opposite:* 1** · *With Dom João and Brazil's old royal family. Behind us the two princesses, Isabella and Leopoldina.*
2 · *Dom João flanked by his relatives, Leopoldina, sister-in-law of Napoleon, and Dom Pedro I, Emperor of Brazil.*
3 · *Immaculate colonial-style decoration.*
Above · *Dom João's house at Parati. Chinese influence in the door and window surrounds.*

before us in an elaborate gold-leaf frame, Emperor Dom Pedro I.

A partisan view perhaps, coming as it does from Dom João de Orléans e Bragança, who still calls himself 'Prince', but the man I'm talking to is a thoroughly modern Brazilian. A staunch republican who writes political articles for the newspapers, he is a noted conservationist, anthropologist, photographer and entrepreneur. And he seems on the best of terms with everybody.

He also has one of the most beautiful houses I've seen in Brazil. It dates from the 1820s and looks out onto the sea in the old colonial town of Parati, some 300 kilometres (186 miles) south-west of Rio. When gold was discovered up in the mountains of Minas Gerais, Parati became one of the boom towns of Brazil, the nearest port to which the gold could be carried, by slaves under armed escort, before being shipped to Europe. When this lucrative traffic switched to Rio de Janeiro, Parati began a stately decline before being rediscovered as a tourist destination, conveniently situated midway between Rio and São Paulo. It's been carefully restored and is now one of Brazil's most favoured cultural venues, home to all sorts of events including an International Literary Festival.

The elegant, shining white rectangle of Dom João's house stands looking out onto a flat foreshore, at a ninety-degree angle to the bay. The arches of the doors and windows are picked out in green. The 'raised eyebrow' style of their design shows Chinese influence, via Macau, a reminder of the global extent of the old Portuguese empire. Inside the house dark wood furniture and well-chosen antiques are perfectly placed and beautifully lit. A cool breeze blows across a floor of heavy stone paving and through the room which we share with Dom João's distinguished ancestors. Alongside Dom Pedro, the first Emperor, is his wife Leopoldina who was Napoleon's sister-in-law, and behind us, above a period writing desk, is their son Pedro II, Hapsburg jaw jutting proudly. Pedro was

only fourteen when he was crowned second Emperor of Brazil. He was able and enlightened and managed to steer Brazil clear of a series of local rebellions whilst the economy, particularly thanks to the world demand for coffee, began to grow and increasing numbers of European immigrants poured into the country. In the hallway hangs a charming portrait of two princesses. One of them, Isabella, Dom João's great-grandmother and Pedro's heir apparent, was fiercely opposed to slavery. She made secret visits to the communities of freed slaves they called *quilombos* and, in May 1888, despite strong opposition from big landowners, she signed the Lei Aurea, the 'Golden Law', which finally abolished slavery in Brazil. Her humanitarian action could be said to have spelled the beginning of the end for the only monarchy in America. Deprived of the support of the slave-owning landowners, the Brazilian monarchy was unable to resist a bloodless coup which deposed Pedro and his family. In November 1889 Brazil finally became a fully fledged republic.

Dom João maintains that the constitutional monarchy that his family set up was much more protective of civil rights than its successor. Under Pedro II and Isabella Brazil, in marked contrast to the general-run regimes in the rest of South America, enjoyed a civil government and freedom of the press. The republic that followed them brought in press controls and a military government. Having set the record straight, Dom João leads me out to a small courtyard at the side of the house where we discuss something that animates him just as much – the state of Brazil today. He talks about the false dawns of the 1940s and 1950s, when Brazil seemed set for great things, to the present when at last, he feels, Brazil 'has arrived in the future'. He seems to be very well informed. When the subject of Brazil's place among the BRIC countries comes up, Dom João bemoans the fact that I've just missed Jim O'Neill, the British economist who first coined the acronym.

'He was here yesterday!'

For the record, Dom João thinks Brazil is in a better position than the other BRICs. He cites a big internal market, a flourishing democracy and a lack of internal ethnic divisions as evidence. The miscegenation of the past has, he thinks, resulted in a degree of racial unity, and the bold economic policies pursued by Fernando Henrique Cardoso, President of Brazil for eight years before Lula, have dealt with the perennial problem of cripplingly high inflation. This proved a turning point for the country. Since then Brazil has succeeded in implementing what Dom João calls the biggest redistribution of wealth on earth.

'Forty-five million people brought out of poverty in the last fifteen years.'

He says I should meet the man responsible for it, ex-President Cardoso. FHC, as he's affectionately known. Another good friend of the Prince. But first he wants to show me a corner of the beautiful Mata Atlântica, the forest that once covered the mountains along Brazil's coastline. We drive up behind Parati and are enveloped swiftly in the balmy warmth of a stretch of secondary forest which is reclaiming an abandoned banana plantation. As Dom João points out, the Mata Atlântica has a richer biodiversity than the forests of the Amazon, but is in a much worse state of depletion. Because eighty percent of Brazil's population lives within 400 kilometres (250 miles) of the coast, the pressure on land for cultivation, housing, transport and industry has over the years reduced the Mata Atlântica to less than ten percent of its original size. What remains is subject to various degrees of protection, but here Dom João the conservationist dons his real estate hat and with hardly a pause for breath describes the hotel he plans to put up on the land we're walking through.

I can see why he's chosen this spot. It has the advantage of height and looks across the low-lying spread of Parati, squeezed between two rivers that spill out onto an enclosed bay of islands, hemmed in by forested headlands. The problem

Opposite · *The view out over Parati from Dom João's property in the foothills.*
Above · *Dom João, a keen environmentalist, walks me through the Atlantic rainforest.*

1

2

3

4

5

of celebrating nature and imposing on it at the same time is not just something the Prince faces. People with the money to be discreet are fuelling a considerable property boom in what's left of the Mata Atlântica.

It's Easter week. The hotels are full and Parati's little airstrip is busy accommodating the succession of private planes flying in from São Paulo. By the waterfront a tall black man in chains is describing the lot of the earliest visitors to Parati, the African slaves who arrived in this pleasant bay after weeks crossing the Atlantic in appalling conditions. When he's finished the gaggle of tourists applaud politely and drop a few notes into a small basket, before making their way into the network of attractive streets that is the heart of this town of 15,000 souls. The streets are not easy to negotiate as they're paved with big uneven stones which were originally brought over as ballast by boats come to pick up the gold. Parents help each other across the mini-boulders whilst their more nimble children trail behind looking bored.

It gets even more difficult later when all the street lamps are switched off for the first of the Easter processions. This begins at midnight after the Missa Lava Pés, a Mass at which the feet of twelve people, representing the twelve apostles, are ceremonially washed. The procession emerges from the imposing Church of Nossa Senhora dos Remédios and is led by priests in red capes chanting and surrounding a wooden platform carried on their shoulders and bearing a doleful image of Christ with reeds behind him. The congregation follows, carrying candles made of wax-filled bamboo. I'm given one but it won't stay alight, and a kind fellow celebrant takes it from me and gives me hers. That promptly goes out. By now it's clear that I'm not the only one who's having trouble. The one or two brightly burning flames are far outnumbered by flickering embers. Word is going round that it was a big mistake to let the children make the candles this year. I've given up on ignition and am trying to find out in which direction the by now semi-torchlit procession has gone. The extinguishing of the street lights causes much stumbling and stubbing of feet before I catch sight and sound of the celebrants up a side street. They've stopped at one of the Stations of the Cross, which are marked by small altars enclosed behind doors on the side of the road. It takes almost an hour for them to make their way round them all and by the time they reach the waterfront and the church of Santa Rita the functioning candles are so few that their bearers have acquired some quasi-religious charisma.

Once the image of Christ has been borne back to the Church the street lights come on again and the secular celebrations go on long into the night. I admire and rather envy the Brazilians' ability to eat, drink and be merry in public without feeling the need to be in any way aggressive or objectionable. By way of a nightcap I stop at a stall where I'm mixed a powerful cocktail with *cachaça*, brandy, vodka and an infusion of tree bark called *catuaba*. This is a Guaraní word meaning 'gives strength to the Indian'. The stallholder nods and winks and produces a long wooden phallus to stir it with. I get the picture.

***Opposite:** **1** · The Easter procession passes a piece of street sculpture, without looking at it too closely. **2** · Celebrants outside the Church of Nossa Senhora dos Remédios. **3** · The Easter procession, figure of Christ borne aloft, moves through the streets of old Parati. **4** · With my glass of catuaba at the end of the night. **5** · The procession returns to the church.*

1

Day 59 · Parati

IT'S GOOD FRIDAY, or Seixta-Feira Santa as they call it here. We're out early, to pick up some shots of this colourful little town before the streets fill up. A few horse-drawn carts are already out and about, their thick rubber tyres bouncing their occupants over the uncompromising cobblestones. And there are additional obstacles to negotiate this morning. After a high tide, the sea water has flooded a number of streets (as it was designed to do) leaving large puddles and a rather unpleasant smell of drains. But this is a small price to pay for walking largely unchanged eighteenth-century streets full of boldly painted houses. Deep grey next to bright yellow and pink next to purple. Bougainvillea spills over the walls and dogs scratch themselves on doorsteps. One door is ajar and I bend backwards as I pass and catch a tantalizing glimpse of lush gardens, and courtyards framed by tiled and trailer-clad verandas. As it's peak holiday weekend the town is busiest at the long jetty by the harbour, where a prodigious assortment of multi-coloured craft are drawn up offering trips around the bay, fishing expeditions or picnics on surrounding beaches.

Dom João, man of a thousand contacts, has asked me to join him aboard a fast white sport-fishing boat which takes us at sea-gouging speed to a small beach. There we transfer to a beautiful three-masted sailing boat where we have lunch,

2

3

4

5

swim to a another beach and scramble up amongst the trees to where our host, a big wheel in Brazil's television industry, plans to convert a small fisherman's house. The rule is that you can only build to the dimensions of property that already exists. It is very quiet here. No roads anywhere near. Butterflies rule. Walking trails wend through the forest and for the truly adventurous there's a tough four-day trek which follows the zigzag coastline back to Parati. Sadly, the bright and promising sunshine of the morning disappears and by late afternoon Parati is as grey and wet as England on a Bank Holiday.

Day 60 · Parati 🚌 São José dos Campos

A SPECTACULAR ROAD with steep hairpin bends leads north-west, away from the coast, up through the Mata Atlântica, skirting mighty boulders topped with tenacious epiphytes and blood-red bromeliads. Big blue butterflies flit between bushes thick with hydrangea and on either side the dense green forest is splashed with purple and yellow blossom. The road climbs, laboriously, from sea level up to the pass at 1,600 metres. Then it's over the top and into a very different Brazil. A land where the wilderness has been tamed. The broad green upland valleys have been turned to fields and pastures, and the only things resembling a forest are stands of eucalyptus trees, planted as and when they're needed.

The farms grow into villages and the villages into towns and three and a half hours after leaving Parati we funnel onto one big central valley highway, Route 116, which connects Rio and São Paulo, a distance of some 400 kilometres (250 miles). It's busy, well maintained, and they clearly take safety seriously. At intervals the smashed carcass of a vehicle has been hoisted onto a roadside platform with a billboard behind it and the single message 'Another Victim'. Not surprisingly the 116, connecting as it does Brazil's two biggest cities, has become a corridor of industrial research and development and some of the country's smartest companies are located along this strip. One of them is now the third-largest aircraft manufacturer in the world, Empresa Brasileira de Aeronáutica, better known as Embraer.

***Opposite:* 1** *· Good Friday morning. The stone-flagged streets of Parati have been washed by a high tide.* **2** *· Tourists venture out in a pony and trap.* **3** *· The sea water almost reaches the shop fronts.* ***Above:* 4** *· A traditional wooden-hulled boat is pulled clear of a sandbank in the harbour.* **5** *· Dom João and sports-boat-owning friend come to collect me for a trip along the coast.*

Day 61 · São José dos Campos

APART FROM the puzzling motif beside the main gate, of a small plane which has apparently crash-landed on top of a hedge, the approach to Embraer's huge plant feels remarkably cool and composed. More like a liberal arts college than a hive of industry. The gardens around the car park are lush and well tended and the polite security checks seem mainly concerned to warn against smoking and short trousers, both of which are banned anywhere on the site. We have been asked to arrive early as there is to be an official handing-over ceremony of a completed plane to KLM, the Dutch airline. The delivery building is modern, airy, elegant and blindingly white. The Dutch team, two pilots, two ground staff and a team sales leader, wear sweatshirts marked 'KLM City-Hopper Acceptance Team'. They've been here almost two weeks making pre-delivery checks. It's quite a tense time for both sides, as the aircraft, priced at some forty-five million dollars, has not yet been paid for. The Delivery Co-ordinator for Embraer is a tall, affable young woman called Thais and even at this late stage she and others are in hushed consultations at tables stacked high with specification files.

***Opposite:** 1 · With Thais and wearing my KLM clogs at the paling stall. **2** · Embraer's sales team and KLM's 'acceptance team' celebrate in front of their twentieth collaboration. **3** · Shiny new Embraer 195 awaits final tests.*

'The carpet issues are resolved,' says someone, and there is much satisfied nodding, 'and the seat plan has been discussed.' More nodding. Then something rather wonderful happens. The Dutch sales manager and his deputy disappear into an office and a few minutes later reappear wearing clogs, long striped aprons and bonnets. We follow them down to the hangar and pick our way between various other aircraft awaiting delivery until we find ourselves standing in front of an aircraft parts trolley that has been converted into a Dutch fish-cart. A striped awning has been attached, some pictures of Holland pasted on the front and plates of snacks have been laid out. The KLM team call me forward, present me with a pair of clogs and explain that this is Dutch Culture Lesson Number 20 (this being the twentieth aircraft they have ordered from Embraer) and that we are to be treated to a Dutch delicacy. It's oak-smoked eel, a speciality of Ijsselmeer in the north of the country. It's served on toast and its name is *paling*. Much laughter and I find myself in the bewildering position of being photographed with senior Dutch sales executives dressed as fish ladies and the Brazilian delivery team kicking their legs out whilst behind us forty-five million dollars' worth of aircraft awaits its most important test flight.

I ask Thais if this is normal behaviour at the handover of a new aircraft and, crunching on a bit of *paling* on toast, she confirms that the Dutch are particularly good at laying on something special, and the Brazilians, always keen on a party, encourage this side of the relationship.

'We become families, we become friends,' she says. And I think she really means it as she looks out to where the sleek, fresh-painted 195 waits to be taken to its new home. 'We represent Embraer, we represent Brazil... we're proud to do something that beautiful.'

1

2

3

It's not altogether a surprise that Brazil should be good at building aircraft. One of the country's heroes is Alberto Santos-Dumont, known to Brazilians as 'the Father of Aviation'. He spent much of his working life in France, where he pioneered the use of balloons and dirigibles and in 1901 won a 100,000-franc prize for flying between Parc Saint-Cloud and the Eiffel Tower and back again in less than thirty minutes. In 1906 Santos-Dumont made the first public manned aircraft flight of sixty metres. The Wright brothers are generally thought to have been the first to fly, but they had no official witnesses. Santos-Dumont returned to Brazil. He ended his own life in 1932. Some say he had been overcome with despair that the aircraft he'd pioneered were being turned into weapons of war.

1

2

4

3

5

Embraer, indeed, began as a military aircraft manufacturer in 1969, but had a chequered history and in 1994 the Brazilian government, faced with high inflation and an increasing economic crisis, refused to put any more money in. A private consortium saved the company with savage cost-cutting, reducing the workforce from 18,000 to 3,000. An astute policy of concentrating on feeder jets and private aircraft saw it gradually recover. By the end of 2011 the company had nearly 2,000 planes on its order books and the workforce is back up to 17,000.

The rest of the day is spent in the assembly sheds, where everything from nose cones to wing sections is made. The atmosphere is cool, well ordered and almost aseptically efficient. Quite un-Brazilian in fact. Most impressive sight of the day is a set of gigantic American-made milling machines which gouge out patterns in the aluminium alloy wing spars. These behemoths, each one as high as a house, move slowly and remorselessly down the aluminium blanks. Their massive motors enable the drill bits, each with five axles capable of turning in five directions, to carve out cavities in the hard metal with the precision of a tattooist. The delicacy of the work for some reason brings to mind something from my childhood – the motto on every can of Lyle's Golden Syrup, where, beneath the odd graphic of a lion with bees buzzing around it, were the words 'Out of the strong came forth sweetness'.

As I marvel at the sight of these hugely gentle machines, aluminium shavings flying out of them like sparks, I'm assured by my Embraer guide that these are now things of the past. For safety reasons, the new milling machines will be totally enclosed. Soon it will be impossible to see the biggest tattooists in the world at work.

__Opposite: 1__ · Engine assembly at Embraer. __2__ · Aluminium shavings are swept up after milling machines have done their precision work. __3__ · Cockpit assembly. There are ten 10,000 rivets in each jet. __4__ · Finished aluminium blocks glisten like Golden Syrup on the factory floor. __5__ · Fitting insulation panels.

Day 62 · São José dos Campos 🚌 São Paulo

SÃO JOSÉ DOS CAMPOS is a verdant city with plenty of skilled jobs in high-profile companies like Petrobras and General Motors. There's money here and a comfortable way of life if you're prepared to put the work in. This morning at Embraer I meet a young man whose attitude and ambition seem to symbolize the opportunities that today's booming Brazilian economy can offer. When I first encounter him he's in the paint shop, cracking jokes with his workmates, a lean, rangy figure with short black curly hair, *mestizo* colouring and eyes that take you in with a quick glance. His name's Felipe, he's twenty-seven years old and he gets up at 4.30 every morning to be at work by six. And he speaks pretty good English. He shows me the job he's about to do and asks if I've ever painted a tailplane before. The combination of his infectious enthusiasm and my indiscriminate curiosity soon has me swaddled in a protective coat and hood, and a mask and nose-clip fitted. We stand together on a platform whilst the tailplane of a Kazakh airliner is slid in alongside us. Felipe shakes his head. It's to be a deep blue colour.

'My nightmare,' he grins.

1

2

Above: ***1*** *· Tailplane being prepared for painting.* ***2*** *· Felipe supervises new recruit.* ***Opposite: 3*** *· The skill is to keep moving. He who hesitates is lost.* ***4*** *· In the workers' canteen with Felipe.* ***5-6*** *· The weird, ghost-like robot painters, which will eventually replace the likes of Felipe and me, set to work.*

It looks rather elegant to me, but Felipe explains that dark blue makes for a mirror-like sheen that highlights every blemish.

'I like white. White and green.'

He fills the spray-gun from a can and, after carefully adjusting the nozzle, he's ready to go.

'This is my weapon,' he shouts from behind a full-face mask. 'So now we go!'

After all the bravado, the application is quite a contrast. Felipe moves gracefully, like a dancer, with broad, slow, sweeping strokes, transferring his weight effortlessly from one leg to the other, keeping the nozzle pressure constant. Only when he invites me to have a go do I realize how easy he makes it look. The gun is heavy and yet the slightest dip in its trajectory makes an unsightly curve which Felipe has to adjust. But I make enough of a mark to be able say, when I'm next on my way to Almaty, that I sprayed the plane.

We lunch together in the canteen. Basic good buffet food for two or three *reais*, about a pound. It was here that Felipe first worked for Embraer, making coffee and distributing it round the factory. One of the departments he supplied was the paint shop and he knew as soon as he saw it that that was what he wanted to do. He took a three-month course in another town, then applied to Embraer and left his own engagement party when the phone call came to invite him for interview. He earns 3,500 *reais* (£1,250) a month, which he says is enough for a good life. He's bought a house and a car and with his wife Fabiana also working at Embraer they are comparatively well-off and thinking of starting a family soon. Felipe finishes his coffee and nods vigorously as he gets up.

'I believe in the future of Brazil. Sure.'

A curious sequence of events in the afternoon brings home to me just how well Felipe has done. We're invited to film a brand-new robot painting device in which the company has invested a fair bit of money. In a long shed behind a glass screen are two articulated arms, both wrapped in protective white sheeting, which move alongside a tailplane just like the one we worked on. Looking like two bandaged elephant trunks, they begin to apply the paint with tall arching movements, and in a fraction of the time it took us this morning. It's an American machine and there are two or three engineers from Detroit in attendance. But

3

4

the man who is doing all the work, mixing the paint, filling the tanks, checking the robot head and to whom everyone looks before giving the go-ahead, is none other than Felipe.

'I like to be a painter. That is enough for me,' was how Felipe had brushed off my question about his future when we ate lunch together. What he hadn't told me was that he was recently chosen from ninety other applicants to go to the States and learn how to operate the new robot painting equipment. That's why his English sounds like he'd learnt it from Hollywood movies. That's why he believes in the future of Brazil. Because quick, sharp, bright Felipe knows where that future lies.

We leave Embraer and head west to São Paulo along a toll road named after the great Brazilian sporting legend, Ayrton Senna. Only the Brazilians, one feels, would name one of their busiest highways after a racing driver. Like any major conurbation, the city limits of São Paulo seem ill-defined. The long, low slabs of logistic centres give way to long, low slabs of shopping malls and suddenly you're there, locked in some of the worst traffic in the world. The spirits sink to a new low as the rain comes down and the brake lights stab out across a half-dozen lanes of traffic ahead of us. Then our driver Caetano pulls us off up a slip road, through a *favela* and eventually onto another wide highway along which the traffic is still moving. Beside us a shallow, foul-smelling river runs in an open concrete conduit between a thick forest of tower blocks, stretching as far as the eye can see.

5

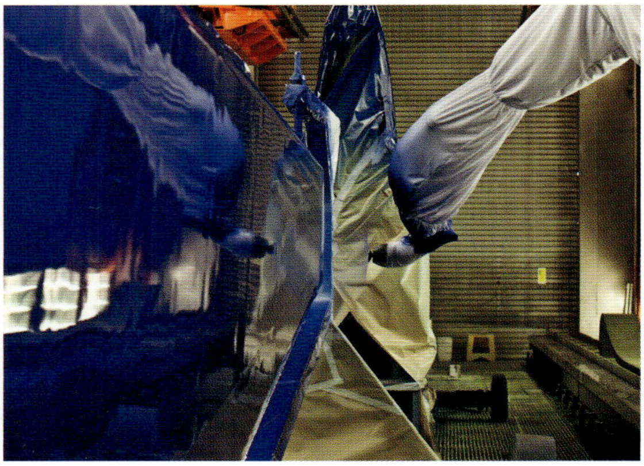

6

Day 63 · São Paulo

THE AMAZON BASIN occupies forty-two percent of Brazil's land area. Yet its combined population is less than that of New York City. The southern and south-eastern states of Brazil comprise only sixteen percent of the land area, but sixty percent of its population. Forty million people live in São Paulo State alone. Almost one in five of all Brazilians.

Being in São Paulo means being surrounded by other people, all the time. As far as the eye can see there are streets and blocks and highways and traffic. Planes and helicopters are constantly crossing the skies above. I now know what Marlene Dietrich meant when she famously said, 'Rio is a beauty. But São Paulo... São Paulo is a city.' Rio is defined by natural landmarks – the sea, the curving beaches, the mountains of Corcovado and Sugar Loaf – but São Paulo has nothing like that. There is, it seems, nothing here but the human race, in enormous numbers.

***Opposite: 1** · With Pedro Laurenço and hopefully inspirational collection of pink fabrics. **2** · Machining and **3** · hand-stitching in his mother, Gloria Coelho's workshop.*

***Preceding pages** · São Paulo skyline. Just one part of the largest city in the Southern Hemisphere.*

Difficult as it is to imagine, there was a time, 450 years ago, when São Paulo was very small. Two Jesuit priests, pursuing their quest to bring the local Indians to God, had slung their hammocks here, beside a small river. Not far away, bigger rivers had cut gaps in the high plateau, providing glimpses of the mysterious and possibly fabulous interior of this new land. Missionaries were joined by adventurers less interested in souls and more interested in shiny minerals. These *bandeirantes*, as they became known, found São Paulo a useful base for their expeditions, and a permanent settlement grew up beside the River Tietê. It wasn't until the late nineteenth century that São Paulo became something more than just another provincial town. The increasing world demand for coffee and the start of mass emigration from an overcrowded Europe coincided here. Industrious and ambitious Italians, Portuguese and Spaniards, having made some money in the coffee plantations, stayed on to set up businesses in the city. Their success attracted others, among them Japanese, Jews, Lebanese, Greeks and Koreans. By the mid 1950s São Paulo's population had reached over two million. But the immigrant boom was far from over. In the forty years between 1955 and 1995 the population of Brazil grew, staggeringly, from fifty-nine million to 172 million. São Paulo bore the bulk of this increase, and today it's the largest city in the Southern Hemisphere and the eighth-biggest in the world. No wonder there is a whole area of the city called Imigrantes.

To find why so many people seem happy to live here, you have to avoid making sense of the city itself and look instead at the fine detail. Halfway up a steeply sloping road in the middle of an anonymously built-up area is a building you might easily walk past without a second look, except that the brick walls are all sprayed silver and the staff all wear black. It was once a cutlery factory, and has now been intelligently restored to house one of Brazil's most successful fashion designers. And her son. The work of Gloria Coelho takes up most of the building,

1

2

3

but she is in danger of being upstaged by her precociously successful twenty-one-year-old son Pedro. Under the name Pedro Laurenço, he's one of Brazilian fashion's best-known names abroad. He's had four shows in Paris and his clothes sell in twenty outlets round the world. I meet Pedro as he works in a light-filled room at the top of the building where he's designing his new collection. He's fresh-faced, with short dark hair, big dark eyes and a quietly impressive grasp of both fashion and business. His English is immaculate. As he toys with a line of red ribbons and swatches of fabric, and then pins them onto one of his models, he's the personification of the work ethic. And that, he says, is what makes São Paulo so different from Rio.

'Rio's good for vacation, but São Paulo is good for work.'

I ask if there's any significant difference between Brazilian and European women that he has to bear in mind when designing. He pauses a moment, then looks up from his work. Brazilian women, he thinks, like to dress more daringly than their European counterparts. If they've got it they like to flaunt it?

He smiles and nods. As if I hadn't noticed that already. Cleavage seems almost obligatory in Brazil.

In the afternoon I renew acquaintance with Carolina Ferraz, who wants to take me to meet another young star from São Paulo. Only this time we're in a completely different part of the city. No silver walls or black-clad staff here. The streets are rough and run-down. The painted walls are smeared black and rubbish is piled up at the side of the road. This is Grajaú, an extensive neighbourhood which is home to 800,000 of the poorer Paulistas. We pull up at the doorway of a concrete shell of a house and ahead, waiting to greet us, is the man we've come to see. He's tall, lightly dark-skinned, quick on his feet and dressed in loose cotton trousers, a white T-shirt and trainers. He was born thirty-six years ago as Kleber Gomes, the son of migrant workers from the North-East of Brazil. Now he's a rapper, poet and composer and has taken the stage name Criolo, the Creole. Political protest is at the heart of his work, whether it be about police brutality, living conditions in the *favelas* or environmental policy. He's gained some formidable admirers, including the hugely respected singer and composer Caetano Veloso, who has described Criolo as 'possibly the most important figure on the Brazilian pop scene'.

Right now the coming man is leading us towards the house to meet his Mum and Dad. Dad is already waiting at the door, a solid man with greying hair and an instantly likeable face. Warm and wise. I notice Criolo untucking a corner of his father's shirt which has got stuck in the waistband of the older man's shorts. A quick bit of tidying up. Then Criolo goes ahead, loping smoothly up a flight of steps ahead of us. There's building work going on in the house and piles of breeze-block stand about.

The stairs lead out onto a roof with a panoramic view of Grajaú, stretching away on all sides. No one has built tower blocks out here, and there's a refreshing sense of air and sky. Criolo's mother is sitting out on the roof. She's a composed,

gently smiling, dark-haired woman wearing a pink cotton top and shorts. Carolina greets her with open arms and introduces us. On the way out here, Carolina had given me some background on this remarkable woman. She was born in a slum, worked as a maid, learnt to read from newspapers the meat was wrapped in and became a teacher, as did her son for a while. In 2006 she was diagnosed with some problem in her hand which made writing difficult and forced a change in her life. Two years ago she opened what she calls a philosophy café, to encourage people from the neighbourhood to come and talk about their lives and their problems. Criolo's Mum is a firm believer in thinking for yourself, in accepting responsibility for your own life.

Carolina translates for me.

'She has had a life that most poor Brazilians have had. But she learnt from the beginning how to dry her eyes and find a way out of whatever life had thrown at her.'

Criolo is less easy to talk to. He responds to questions with long silences. His big eyes and expressive face turn down into what looks almost like a pout. He moves his head away to one side.

I realize after an initial concern that it's not that he doesn't want to answer, it's just that he wants his answer to be thoughtful. I ask about his world and the poor neighbourhood in which he was brought up, and how he thinks it might change. The gist of his reply is that it's hard for people round here to stand back, look at their lives, and start to change them.

'You don't realize what's happening in the pen if you're stuck inside it.'

He uses a flock of birds wheeling restlessly above us as an image of Grajaú.

'They're flying all around but they don't know where to go. Everywhere is brick and concrete. They've lost their north.'

The pressure, he says, is so hard on families here. People have a two-hour bus ride into the city, an eight- to ten-hour job when they get there, and two hours' bus ride back. Parents and children become easily estranged. And the politicians are not interested. In fact they don't even notice. Criolo lets out a cry of frustration.

'How many poor people do we need to make one rich one?'

Opposite *· On a rooftop in Grajaú, Carolina Ferraz introduces me to Criolo and his mother.*

Above left to right *· Criolo's Dad, Mum and the man himself.*

1

2

Above: 1-2 *· Criolo sits in on a Sunday-night jam session in a Grajaú back street.*
Opposite: 3 *· At 'Musical Pagode da 27'. Spectators gather outside the bar.*
4 *· A guest vocalist steps up to the mike.*
5 *· The evening in full flow, with Criolo leading community singing.*

He is now an influential voice. People listen to him and he's becoming known outside São Paulo. But Criolo is no pedagogue, nor ever will be. His approach to social problems is not to dictate but to understand. He believes his songs and his poems connect with people because he's speaking at a primal level, identifying feelings of loss and loneliness. At this level there can be no leader. Like the philosophy café, his work sets out that real change cannot be achieved by a system or a great leader but by an individual's awareness of their own potential. Of which Criolo and his mother are prime examples.

I feel as if he and I are edging slowly towards each other, but the world still seems a dark place when suddenly the talk turns to music and, metaphorically anyway, the sun comes out. This is something that Grajaú does not have to be defensive about.

As Carolina puts it, 'Three things define a culture. The language, the food and the music.' She stands, gestures at the houses stretching off into the distance and speaks with real feeling, as though something is alive here that is missing in the polite middle-class world she moves in.

'And they have the most amazing music here. And they play it loud and it makes them happy. They're not ashamed to let go.'

Carolina is back on the *Avenida Brasil* set tomorrow morning, so she has to set off for the airport. And in doing so misses what turns out to be a great example of what she was talking about.

'Musical Pagode da 27' reads the sign above a strip-lit bar and café, number 27 in an ordinary-looking Grajaú back street. Criolo walks with me down the hill towards it. He's more relaxed now, full of bonhomie as he approaches the group of musicians setting up outside the bar. A blue plastic awning has been pulled tight across the street to protect them from the storms drifting across São Paulo tonight. Every Sunday these musicians, young and old, white and black, get together to play samba at the Pagode. Tonight Criolo is going to sit in with them. It won't be recorded, it won't be filmed. It's just what they do here on Sundays.

Criolo looks bashful as he settles in behind his music stand, in the midst of ten other players, all regulars. The line-up consists of guitars, sax, trumpet,

3

4

5

keyboard and a well-stocked percussion section – drums, tambourines and bongos. It takes a while for them to get going and even when they do there are no more than a dozen people standing around. They play softly to start with, the lilting music warming them up, getting them together. The infectiously persistent samba rhythm is irresistible. I break into a smile and my feet start to move around of their own accord.

People wander down from their houses and the crowd begins to grow. The sky is suddenly slashed with jagged lightning. Moments later a crack of thunder sounds, and it's not far away. When the inevitable downpour begins it seems to move the band up a gear, and as the rain swells the plastic tarpaulin, the music takes on a new intensity. Everybody's shimmying about now and when an old black man steps up to the mike there are cheers and applause. He sings softly, urgently, with a delicate swooning swing in the voice. After a couple of numbers he gives way to a portly white man in late middle age who whips up the audience with popular sing-a-long numbers. As the rain hurls itself at the street, there is a great and joyful surrender to the music. I can see why Carolina was so passionate when she talked about the importance of music to the Brazilians. Here in a modest street in the middle of a cloudburst, in one of the most disadvantaged areas of the city, music and song has, for a few hours, made everything all right. Whatever bad things may happen tomorrow, tonight has been very fine. I catch sight of Criolo, 'possibly the most important figure on the Brazilian pop scene', singing along in the back row.

Day 64 · São Paulo

SÃO PAULO IS A HELICOPTER CITY. As traffic mires the megalopolis in endless congestion, the rich and successful take to the skies, flying from building to building without ever having to touch the ground. No self-respecting tower block is built without a helipad and it's been estimated that there are some 400 licensed choppers making 1,700 flights a day across the city. Some might think they're over-reacting, others just point to the chronic inability of São Paulo's road network to deal with the demand. In 2009 *Time* magazine reported a traffic jam 200 miles long.

One habitual helicopter user is Wilson Quintela. He has made a fortune from rubbish. His company, Estre Ambiental, motto 'Lixo É Só O Começo' – 'Waste is Just the Beginning' – was founded in 1999. It now has 5,000 employees, manages thirteen landfill sites, in Argentina and Colombia as well as Brazil, and in the last financial year made a profit of 1.2 billion *reais* (£37 million). Wilson Quintela is evangelical about waste management and despite being one of the busiest men in Brazil he's agreed to take me out to see how he's dealing with the 40,000 tonnes of unwanted matter that is collected from São Paulo every day.

We glide surprisingly easily through the morning traffic to a tall, four-tower complex called the Condomínio São Luiz. It's a vertical city. A managed executive environment inside which, beside the offices, are attendant banks, bars, restaurants, gardens, laundries, physio and massage facilities and, of course, a helipad. In close proximity are residential apartments and everything else you might want, including schools, hospitals, hotels and shopping centres. Everything is clustered together for safety and security. It's like a medieval castle, but instead of the drawbridge there are road ramps, high spiked fences and a battery of CCTV screens, all co-ordinated from a well-staffed reception area. The message is, in an admirably polite way, that out there, where you've come from, is dangerous. And where you are now is safe. We have our photos taken and our passports thoroughly checked before we are escorted through the barrier and up to Estre's floor.

Here all is space and light, and with the spotless laminated white tables reflecting big blown-up photographs of trees and animals you could be forgiven for thinking that this was the HQ of some enlightened national parks agency rather than a waste disposal business. This is quite deliberate. The fact that the office is an obsessively clean environment mirrors Quintela's philosophy, as do all the books and pictures conveying images of man and nature in harmony. There's not a discarded tissue in sight.

Opposite · *No self-respecting tower block is complete without a helipad.*
Above · *The Tietê and Pinheiros are the two rivers of São Paulo. Flanked by highways and very smelly. A clean-up is under way.*

Wilson himself is the antithesis of the buttoned-up businessman. He's a deeply tanned, middle-aged man wearing jeans and an open-necked blue shirt revealing a tasteful gold amulet sitting snugly on his chest. He's in good shape and is relaxed and disarming as he greets us. He's also very busy, and after brief introductions we follow him into the lift and ascend, past floor after floor of accountants, to the rooftop helipad. It's a bizarre world up here where all these buildings reach the sky. It's like being in the rainforest canopy, except that the trees are man-made. Even up here, forty storeys above ground where you'd think no one would notice, the architectural details of the penthouses are full of twirls and flourishes, as if they were mansions built at street level and then jacked up into the sky.

The helicopter is due to arrive any minute. Wilson checks his watch and looks off into the distance. I ask him if he uses them because of security fears at street level. He shrugs and shakes his head. His life is spent on the move and, like many of his ilk in São Paulo, he uses company planes and helicopters to save time. Then he turns to me, frowning.

'But my children have to go to school in armour-plated cars and that's crazy!'

Whether this fear of robbery and kidnap is real, or just a spectre kept in existence by all who make money out of the security business, is something we

don't get far with as our helicopter swings down onto the roof, bringing with it its own little tempest of sound and fury. The rotors continue to whirr above us as we race out, climb aboard and with almost insolent ease are swung off and away.

As we head due north the monochrome mass of the city gives way to rolling hills of green grass and red earth, the colour palette of the high plateau. Down below are new and seemingly prosperous suburban towns of detached houses with gardens and big swimming pools. Beyond one of these, called Paulínia, we descend towards a great gash across the landscape, festering at the centre, but with extensive cosmetic surgery going on all around it. This is Estre's oldest and biggest landfill site.

Wilson drives us round it with the sort of pride and passion that other men might display in showing off their art collection. We watch the trucks coming in with the raw rubbish which slides down a chute into the maw of a machine that sorts it all into dry or humid waste. The dry waste is suitable for recycling and goes off to make rubber tyres or car bodies or whatever. The rest (and if Wilson had his way there would be no such thing as non-recyclable waste) is taken out to a conventional rubbish tip, complete with bad smells and circling vultures. We park as near to it as we can without asphyxiation. But this, Wilson explains, is no ordinary rubbish tip. Alongside the refuse trucks is another line of vehicles carrying earth to spread over the spoil. And at the same time he draws my attention to a team working to install a network of black pipes which will be threaded through the compacted waste to extract methane from the decomposing waste. Cue for us to drive over to Wilson's pride and joy, a series of stainless steel tanks in which the methane that has been removed is heated to $1{,}000^0$, at which point it turns

into carbon. The captured carbon can be traded as credit with some big polluting company in Europe.

It's reassuring to know that the garbage of a megalopolis like São Paulo is taken so seriously. And legislation is soon to be introduced which will make Wilson an even happier, and richer, man. At present only about three percent of São Paulo's waste is recycled. By 2014 this will have to rise to between fifteen and twenty percent in line with the rest of the country.

Wilson makes much of the statistic I've heard from others I've spoken to. That in the last twenty years almost forty million people have been taken out of poverty in Brazil.

'This means more consumption and more consumption means more waste and all this, with the change in the law to make twenty percent recyclable, is going to mean a revolution in Brazil.'

His eyes shine.

'It's a huge opportunity. Not just to make money, but to do something good for the society.'

Wilson seems genuinely concerned about the social obligations. In an echo of the issues raised by Carolina's soap opera *Avenida Brasil*, there is, on his hi-tech site, a low-tech facility, run by a co-operative, which provides manual sorting work for some twenty people. Originally this was a job done by the pickers who scavenged the dumps, and rather than put them out of business Wilson acknowledged their contribution by giving them employment, despite it being hopelessly uneconomic to sort by hand. Many of the original, unionized rubbish-pickers have since moved on and the majority of the workforce at Wilson's

Opposite · *All neat and tidy. The carefully drained, methane-extracted terraces of Estre's biggest landfill site.*

Above · *Where there's muck, there's money. With Wilson Quintela as São Paulo's waste is buried behind us.*

1

3

2

4

Above:* 1 · *Fresh off the streets, waste is unloaded at the first stage of the process.* 2 · *The old way. Recycling by hand at the co-operative.* 3 · *The carbon-capture tanks in which methane from the dump is heated to* $1,000^{0}$*.* 4 · *The education centre. Model for children of the whole waste disposal process.

co-operative shed are from the local jail. They are given a day off their sentence for every day they spend sorting here.

Wilson seems to revel in our curiosity. He's already rung ahead and cancelled his next meeting, giving us two more hours of his precious time, and now he wants to show his pride and joy. It's a very smart, bright, colourful education centre with a rather quaint, old-fashioned working model of the whole waste process. Over 60,000 children have visited and he says they've trained 4,000 teachers. He believes that it's vital for the future that children understand about waste and how to deal with it. And, most importantly for him, how best to make use of it. There is an enormous potential for turning waste into energy. He tells me that what he would really like is a Tyrannosaurus. For a moment I wonder if this could be the latest toy for the Brazilian who has everything, but it turns out to be a huge Finnish machine into which you put your waste and out comes fuel.

Like Embraer, Estre is a Brazilian company that wants to compete with the world. What they share is ambition but also a sense, dare I say, of altruism. What they do and how they do it seems as important as the profits.

São Paulo may seem like a city of Mammon – church towers break the skyline less frequently than anywhere else I've been in Brazil – but the undercurrent of revivalist religion that flows so strongly across the rest of the country has manifestations here as well. Tonight we drive across to the east of town to the *bairro* of Água Rasa where, in a narrow street, we find a steel-fenced modern building belonging to one of Brazil's most successful Evangelical churches, the Assembly of Jesus. Outside, security men cast wary glances as a procession of women, many of them young and apparently on their way back from work, hurry past them and up the stairs into a modern glass-fronted auditorium. A sign outside announces that a Sanctification Congress is in progress organized by tonight's visiting preachers, the Princess Cult.

We have been given privileged access. Privileged because we're men and tonight's service is strictly women only. There must be close on a thousand of them squeezed inside, but no one seems to notice as we file in. Their attention is entirely focused on the figure occupying the stage. She's a slim woman of medium height, probably in her late forties and dressed like a 1950s hat-check girl, in a bouncy black frock with a wide skirt and a white chiffon hem. There's a matching chiffon rose in her buttonhole and a black bow in her hair. She is playing the audience well, her manner by turns coquettish and cautionary. Her name is Sara Shreever, and she is the high priestess of the Princess Cult.

Below · *The Princess Cult packs a hall in São Paulo.*

Her message, roughly translated, and adoringly received by her audience, is that there are two different kinds of women in the world. There are the Princesses, who have values and know how to behave and how to present themselves, and there are the Bitches, who behave badly and are submissive to their men. She calls on the authority of the Bible to back this up with an Old Testament passage in which women are described as either doors or walls. The women who are doors are wide open, the women who are walls are resilient and strong and will have

1 

 2

***Above:* 1 · *Sara Shreever belts it out for her followers.* **2** · *Her audience spans all generations.* ***Opposite:* 3** · *The streets of Liberdade neighbourhood in São Paulo.* **4** · *Jehovah's Witness patrols the Praça Liberdade.* **5** · *Prayers to the Buddha on the first day of the flower festival.* **6** · *Japanese-Brazilian in a Liberdade café.*

silver towers built upon them. Sara is on record declaring that she has been ten years without sex.

'And nine without giving a kiss on the mouth. I'm radical. I was a nymphomaniac who could not live without a man. My soul was healed by Jesus.'

With a jarring kick of feedback, the first chords from an over-amplified keyboard scream round the room.

A guitar joins in and Sara segues smoothly into song. She may not have much to do with men, but she certainly understands the power of seduction. As you might expect from a former backing singer, she has a strong voice and the music is loud and insistent. Chord changes follow one another like waves on a beach and the response from the audience is fervent. Emotion wells up. There is pain and there is joy. Tearful faces are upraised, arms stretched out, palms of hands open to the stage. The message is that only through faith in God will they find that strength and belief to control their carnal desires until they meet the ideal man that waits out there for them. The Prince to their Princess.

The music crescendoes and dies. Arms are raised, there are shouts of hallelujah. Cheeks are wet and shining. It's what you might see at a Gospel concert, yet the women here are largely white Brazilians. Some quite elderly, the majority ordinary working women. They're not dowdy or severe, but they all seem fiercely attracted to this notion that men, and by extension sex, can somehow be limited, controlled and indeed sanctified by the infinitely greater power of God.

After arousing them with the music, Sara skilfully calms them down. She smiles and cajoles and soothes and then when she thinks the time is right she touches a nerve again. It's an extraordinary performance, and despite the heat of the night and the jam-packed hall she barely breaks sweat.

Later I speak to her about the cult and what it means to her, whilst her daughter, who is now her backing singer, sits beside her, looking nervous. It's not a surprise to me that Sara reveals a past of broken and betrayed relationships. But for now her eyes shine with conviction, with the inner light of implacable certainty. No wonder her daughter looks nervous. This is a woman of sublime self-belief using her considerable stage skills to manipulate the emotions.

It's a sign of the times that so many want to be manipulated.

3

4

Day 65 · São Paulo

JUN TAKAKI is a second-generation Brazilian. His grandparents were farmers who came out from Japan to Brazil to look for a better life. Their intention had been to stay for a while and make some money in the rapidly expanding coffee-growing business. But they never went back. Brazil became their home, as it has done for three million other Japanese immigrants. Jun, young, serious and polite, can speak little Japanese, and has never been to the home of his ancestors. But he thinks it important that younger generations of Japanese do not forget their culture, and he runs a coffee shop which tries to keep alive some of the old traditions.

I meet him in the central square of the Liberdade neighbourhood, home to some 10,000 of São Paulo's Japanese population. A statue of Tsuyoshi Mizumoto, the first leader of the Japanese community in São Paulo, his head half taken up by an enormous pair of spectacles, stares out at the constant bustle of people coming and going from the Metro station. Already a very nice old Japanese lady has engaged me in conversation, but it turns out she is a Jehovah's Witness wanting to sell me a copy of *Sentinela*, the Brazilian equivalent of *The Watchtower*. At one end of the Praça Liberdade a tent has been erected in which a number of worthies from the Japanese community are gathering to celebrate the start of Hanamatsuri, the annual flower festival. Priests in traditional dress are blessing a tiny figure of the Buddha which rests on a bed of flower petals inside a small

5

6

palanquin. Serious-looking men in suits are taking their seats in front of it. There's a small gathering of onlookers but it hardly seems to be lighting up the place. Jun explains that this ceremony, with the blessing of the Buddha, is much more for the older traditionalists. He expects more young people to turn out for the festival parade later in the week.

Jun is happy in São Paulo. He has lived in other parts of Brazil, in Florianópolis and Brasília, but São Paulo has 'lots to do, lots of life, lots of culture'. Over the years the strict codes of the Japanese, especially regarding intermarriage with different ethnic groups, have been relaxed.

'Now it's not a problem,' says Jun.

Though he will continue to remind people of their Japanese heritage, he, like thousands of Koreans and Italians and Chinese and Russians, is first and foremost a Paulista.

São Paulo prides itself on being in the vanguard of the Brazilian economic boom, and beneath the veneer of featureless sprawl there are pockets of sophistication, not least of which are some impressive hotels, such as the extraordinary boat-shaped, copper-clad Unique by Ruy Ohtake and João Armentano and the rather more classic Fasano, with its dark leather and wood veneers and its striking slabs of stone and granite. The architect here was Isay Weinfeld, who has a wry, very Jewish take on his adopted city.

'I think it's one of the ugliest cities in the world,' he says cheerfully, as we walk together down a tree-lined street close to where he lives, 'but it's a wonderful city to work in.'

He thinks that the lack of any architectural heritage, the lack of any conventional unifying beauty is paradoxically one of São Paulo's great advantages. It's a perfect city for experiment.

'It's a big mother of all kinds of architecture,' he enthuses, 'you can build Mediterranean, neo-classical, contemporary. The lack of personality of the city has become its personality.'

The other side of his love-hate relationship with the city is its lack of street-level diversity. He bemoans the lack of mixed-use areas. Residential blocks tend to be self-contained and heavily security-conscious, without the mix of small bars, cafés and shops that one would find in other cities. Nobody walks in São Paulo, Isay complains.

'This is the first time I've walked the streets in a month.'

Being an acute observer of his environment, Isay has chosen this street because he wants to show me a wall. It's a three-metre wall topped with iron fencing, and it looks as if it's been there a while.

He stands and points.

'In the beginning there was no wall at all. Then you can see,' – he indicates weathering marks a third of the way up the chunky, irregularly cut stones – 'they built the first wall, about eighty years ago. Then twenty years after that one metre

1

2

3

more.' He moves closer to show me another clear mark between light and dark stone. 'Then,' he points higher, 'forty centimetres more.' In concrete this time. 'And now, on top of that, a wire fence.'

We stand back and admire his wall thesis.

'This is an indicator of our vulnerability. A mark maybe of the violence of the city.'

Whether this violence is real or imagined, I can't tell, but it is an interesting phenomenon, this edge of fear that seems to accompany prosperity. He agrees with me that it shouldn't have to be like that, and hopes that initiatives like the Cidade Limpa (Clean City) campaign of the last three or four years will make a difference. For now he smiles and shrugs and admits a grudging affection for what he calls 'the chaos'.

I'm beginning to get the distinct feeling now of the difference that others have pointed out between Brazil's two biggest cities. Rio is indeed an outdoor, street-life town. A playground, by comparison to São Paulo. Rio is blessed by the rolling ocean; São Paulo, though only seventy kilometres (forty-three miles) from the Atlantic, is around 800 metres above it, on the cooler, cloudier plateau. In Rio the footwear of choice is flip-flops. I haven't seen a single pair up here. One thing that Paulistas believe makes a big difference between the two is in the sphere of politics and ideas. Perhaps it's because it's less sensually distracting that São Paulo is more conducive to intellectual activity.

__Above: 1__ · With Isay Weinfeld, top hotel designer, and the wall that shows the several stages of São Paulo security. __2__ · Isay at the bar of the Fasano, the hotel he designed. __3__ · The pleasures of São Paulo. Plenty of bookstores.

1

2

Above: 1 *· Talking with Fernando Henrique Cardoso, FHC, Brazil's President for eight years.* ***2*** *· FHC remembers being converted to the joys of soccer during his first Presidential campaign.* ***Opposite*** *· FHC signs my copy of his memoir* The Accidental President.

Fernando Henrique Cardoso, one of the most significant figures of modern Brazil, and recently voted one of the world's top hundred living intellectuals, has chosen São Paulo to set up an institute in his name where the important issues facing the country can be discussed, researched and debated. Apart from being a prominent intellectual, he's also one of a group called the Elders, independent international wise men brought together by Nelson Mandela 'to promote the shared interests of humanity'. He served two terms as President of Brazil and is credited with turning round the economy and building the foundations for all the progress the country has made since the bad old days of hundred percent inflation. He's agreed to meet me at his institute, in a tall building at the heart of downtown São Paulo, adjacent to City Hall.

The lift delivers us to a spacious open reception area on the sixth floor, furnished in the minimal-traditionalist style. It was once the home of the Automobile Club of São Paulo, from which it inherited a solidly elegant wooden bar with a long granite counter, as well as a shoe-shine chair, grandfather clocks, cane-bottomed chairs and a fine timber floor. Grafted onto this, very successfully, are glass-walled meeting rooms where young, bearded men are hunched over tables, deep in discussion. Cardoso, known to everyone by his initials, FHC, is eighty-one and just returned from a trip to Europe. He sits opposite me at the table, and I'm immediately put at ease. There is no power-play here, and none of the sense of self-importance that many lesser men than he can convey.

He's just short of medium height, neatly dressed, sandy-haired, bespectacled and compact. In his eyes there's both warmth and wariness. I quote back to him a passage in his book *The Accidental President* in which he admits to conveniently becoming an avid football fan during the World Cup of 1994, which coincided with his campaign for the Presidency. He knew that he was perceived as a more distant, academic figure than his man-of-the-people opponent, Lula. Hence Cardoso made sure that he was seen jumping up and down in front of the television, applauding every Brazilian goal. It was a gamble which paid off. Brazil won the World Cup and Cardoso beat Lula to become President, a position he held for the next eight years.

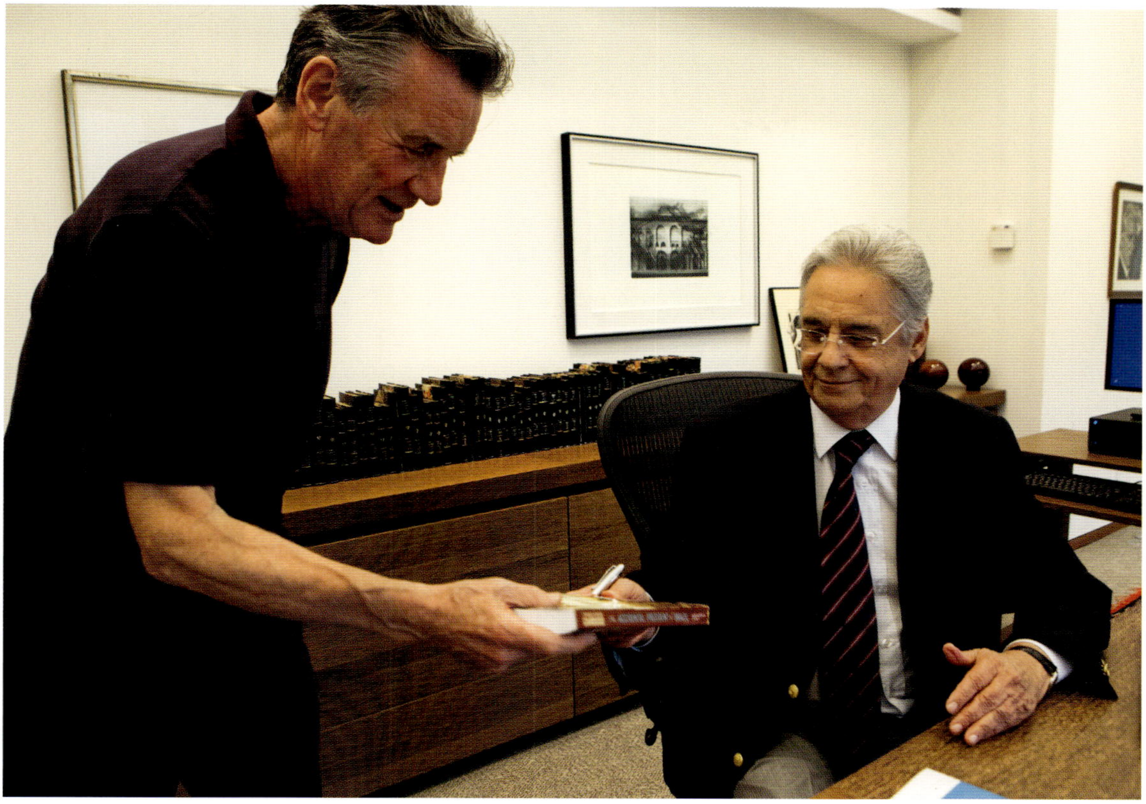

He smiles at the memory and admits that he was worried at the time that he might be seen as too stiff.

In Brazil, he says, 'If you want to be respected you have to be informal.'

Brazil's relaxed, less uptight attitude to life is something he thinks that Britain could benefit from. On the other hand, he adds, there is one significant thing that Brazil could learn from Britain and that is respect for the law. He frowns and gives a little shake of the head.

'We don't respect the law. The lack of respect for law is terrible.'

There is a Portuguese word for this – *jeito* or *jeitinho*, which he describes in his book as defining the way the Brazilians have of getting round the system. 'A particularly Brazilian way of breaking the rules in which, as long as you insist that you are obeying the law, you can get away with pretty much everything.'

It's almost shocking to hear an ex-President being so forthright about his country, but that is indicative of what he sees as one of the strengths of Brazil.

'We have a very strong civil society,' he says. 'An open press, independent universities, strong unions.'

Apart from the brief dictatorship of the generals in the 1960s and 1970s, he sees this openness as going back to the formative years of the country. He contrasts the integration of races and colours in Brazil with the USA, where black and white people lived together but didn't integrate, or the Spanish empire in America, which was much more hierarchical and arrogant.

'In terms of how we live with each other, it's more relaxing here. In Brazil it's much easier to be part of...' – he searches for the words – 'a similar confusion of things.'

Brazil's growing economic strength (growing more slowly, he warns, than is popularly thought) cannot obscure certain fundamental problems. Education and transport infrastructure, especially the big international airports, are poor; there is a real need for a rethink on energy policy: 'how we can use the junk from current forms of energy to fuel new ones'.

Then he smiles.

'We are like an adolescent. We are growing too fast and our clothes are a little tight.'

We make our way out into the square. As FHC told us, the only real problem of being so close to City Hall is the 'manifestations' – he uses the French word for large public gatherings. But they're never violent, he adds. Brazil doesn't have a history of social or political violence. A nearby strip of greenery is filled with histrionic classical statues, and old trolley-buses swing around the corner by the Teatro Municipal, its ornate, buttery cream facade completed in 1911. For a moment, standing here, I have a brief flash of what São Paulo must once have looked like.

Day 66 · São Paulo Santos

I PREPARE TO LEAVE São Paulo with mixed feelings. The size and scale of the city and the relentless roll and rumble of its traffic – on the ground and in the air – can sometimes give a sense of being trapped in some machine. At the same time I felt quite at home here. The neighbourhood round the hotel in Iguatemi, albeit quite a smart end of town, is not entirely anonymous. Contrary to Isay Weinfeld's experience, there are plenty of shops and cafés about. There are streets in front of the high-rise curtain on which I found bookstores, clothes shops, museums, health clubs. From outside São Paulo looks terrifying; but in the same way that smog seen from a distance seems to disappear when you're in the middle of it, so it is that once you've committed yourself to this monstrous place, the city rewards you with a stickily protective embrace. You can be what you want to be. As a result I can see how São Paulo has grown into one of the great sanctuaries of the world, receiving, housing and employing twelve million people in less than 150 years. It is a slightly soiled Promised Land, but a Promised Land none the less.

As we head south to Santos and the sea the city seems reluctant to let us go. It takes two and a half hours to cover the 100 kilometres (sixty miles) to the coast. A massive traffic jam tails back whilst above us the sun is blotted out by a low haze that quickly turns to fog. As we make our way down through the Serra do Mar we're hemmed in by walls of trucks bound for the port, their air-brakes hissing and wheezing as they inch through the mist.

Above · *Mist and mayhem. Traffic jam on the road to Santos.*

And things get no less hellish when we finally descend into Santos. Industrial plant, stacks of containers, rusting trucks on a railway track and all the mess of a dockside wasteland combine with the constant squeak and roar of heavy vehicles. Then, in a sort of replay of Rio, we're into a long tunnel from which we emerge into somewhere quite different, a recognizable residential city. A long avenue takes us to a wide beach with palm trees swaying in the wind and a bay with islands silhouetted against a stormy sky.

Santos itself is on an island and it has a long history. Its safe bay and the abundant water and shelter from the surrounding mountains made it a natural settlement. There is evidence of human activity going back 5,000 years. The Portuguese colonizers first made a base here in 1535 and later it became rich as an entrepôt for the coffee trade, connected to São Paulo by a railway built, financed and designed by the British. 'They brought a British aesthetic... a neat little railway that wouldn't look out of place in Surrey, Cumbria or Lanarkshire. Boilers came from Cornwall, carriages from Manchester and locomotives from the Avonside Engine Company. When the first trains started running [in 1867] they burned high-grade coal from Newcastle.' Thus Josh Lacey describes it in his book *God is Brazilian*.

The railway didn't survive for long and the picturesque coastline around Santos earned a reputation for severe industrial pollution. Petrochemical plants became a national scandal after mutant births at nearby Cubatão in the 1980s.

But the big stucco facades with blue louvred shutters on the sea front wouldn't look out of place on the Corniche at Nice, and it's clear that this part of Santos remains a flourishing holiday destination. Tonight, though, it just looks weather-beaten and as we eat a paella at a sea-front *choperia* the storm that has been brewing out to sea moves in and for two hours the heavens open with terrific force.

Day 67 · Santos

THE BRITISH brought something far more lasting to Brazil than the railways. They brought soccer. And Santos became one of the most famous soccer clubs in the world when, in the mid 1950s, they took on a promising fifteen-year-old named Edson Arantes do Nascimento, who under the less ponderous abbreviation Pelé became generally known as the greatest player in the history of the game. Despite tempting offers from Europe he continued wearing the black and white stripes of Santos FC until 1974, by which time he had scored 1,087 goals for the club in league and friendly games. It was Pelé who later talent-spotted another great Santos legend, Robson de Souza, aka Robinho, who led them to the Brazilian championship title before moving on to Real Madrid, Manchester City and AC Milan. Their current home-grown discovery, Neymar, is considered one of the hottest prospects in soccer. In 2011, he was voted South American Footballer of the Year. He was nineteen years old.

This morning, with the storm past and a hot, humid day developing in downtown Santos, we make our way to the training ground to see how this comparatively small club, with a stadium capacity of less than 20,000, keeps turning out such fine players. The Centro de Treinamento is up towards the mountains, with a road and a railway on one side and a *favela* on the

1

3

2

4

other. Beyond the wire fencing, a huge decomposing globe and other remains of Carnival floats are piled up. There is nothing very special about the training ground, no stands or flags or anything flashy. Every now and then one of the Santos buses, in black and white club livery, pulls in through the gates with another squad of young hopefuls aboard.

One of these is Pierre da Silva, a rangy thirteen-year-old whom everyone rates highly. This morning he's here with his mother, father and kid sister Arianna, a bright and busy little force of nature whose mother describes her as an earthquake. Like adolescent teenagers everywhere, Pierre seems a little shy in the presence of the family, eyes down and shifting uneasily from one foot to the other. His parents are fiercely supportive. They believe in him so much that they have reordered their lives around his future. His father Sebastião, who once harboured ambitions to be a professional himself, has stayed on in New York, where Pierre was brought up, whilst his mother Pilar, who's Peruvian, has moved to Santos to be with her son during his training. Sebastião, a Brazilian who speaks English with a pronounced Bronx accent, has rented out most of the family home in New York and lives down in the basement. The hardest sacrifice of all is living apart, but Pilar is unrepentant.

'I'm going to make it here,' she says fiercely.

But she knows that it's Pierre who is going to have to make it. And it'll be

Opposite *· Housing blocks form an unglamorous backdrop to the Santos training ground.*
Above: 1 *· The under 11s carry the goals for shooting practice.* ***2*** *· Training game in progress.* ***3*** *· Dodzinho, aka Dodo, big hope for the future, warms up at front.* ***4*** *· The teenagers work out.*

1

2

3

4

another two years before they know if he will be one of the very lucky few to be offered a contract. The club pay Pierre 450 *reais* (£160) a week, which helps. He trains from seven o'clock every morning and goes to school in the afternoon.

All three of the training pitches are now in action. Some of the games are exercises as well. In one, in which they concentrate on positional play, the ball is never kicked at all but thrown from one player to the other. I ask Pierre whom he rates at the club. Neymar, his first choice, is not unexpected, but his second choice is a tiny boy who plays in the under 11s called Dodzinho or Dodo. He points him out to me, a boy with a Neymar haircut, his long shorts coming almost down to his ankles, making him look like a little old man. Dodo doesn't fight for the ball, but when it comes to him he weaves and lays it off with precocious ease. And when Pierre strips down to his yellow vest and white shorts and joins in a game, I can understand why his parents think it's all worthwhile. He's a tall, fast, intelligent player, a winger with an accurate, powerful left foot.

Edi Marcel is one of the under 17s fitness coaches, married to a girl from Manchester. He explains the Santos philosophy. All-round support from the club for players from the earliest age. Schooling, medical check-ups, social assistants to help out with family problems, psychiatrists to help with behavioural problems. And on the pitch, the days are gone when the staff consisted of a manager and a trainer beside him with a sponge and a bucket. Santos provide

***Opposite:* 1** · *With Santos hopeful Pierre da Silva, and mum, dad and sister Arianna.*
2 · *The Santos flag and club crest.*
3 · *Pierre displays the tall, striding control which marks him out as a star of the future.*
4 · *Star of the past. Striking a penalty at Vila Belmiro.*
Above · *At Vila Belmiro, the stadium at which Pelé played for twenty years.*

doctors at every game as well as masseurs and physiotherapists. Despite their extensive and comprehensive youth programme, Edi estimates that on average only two players from each age group will stand a chance of a first-team place. That's maybe ten out of 200.

I drive back into town and go with Pierre and Pilar and Sebastião to the hallowed ground on which he one day hopes to make his debut. Vila Belmiro is not an intimidating ground. It's an intimate 18,000-seater, fitting snugly into an attractive neighbourhood of low, neatly painted stucco houses. There are cafés and restaurants on the corner opposite the main entrance selling scarves and photos and vests, and the only sign of rampant commercialism is a big likeness of Neymar on a shaving ad. Inside, the black and white colours of Santos are repeated in the seat patterns and the tiling, but there's nothing grand about the place. Guido, the Brazilian youth team goalie, has come along with us so we can see Pierre take a few penalties. And then they roll the ball out to me, and all I can think of is that I can now say I've struck a penalty from the same spot as Pelé. Except that he scored. And so did Pierre.

Say farewell to Arianna, Pilar and Sebastião, who, for the next two years at least, have given up their life for their son. They are good people and I hope so much that I've been sharing the penalty spot not just with a ghost of the past, but with the spirit of the future. One thing's for sure: from now on I shall be following Santos *and* Sheffield United.

Day 68 · Curitiba

Above · *The Eye at the Niemeyer Museum in Curitiba.* ***Opposite:*** *1 · The dramatic, apparently unsupported sweep of the ceiling at the Niemeyer Museum.* *2 · The spacious exhibition areas.* *3 · Scrubbing down an outdoor sculpture courtyard.* *4 · Artfully lit, an underground walkway leads to the Eye.*

FROM SÃO PAULO and Santos, Brazil extends almost a thousand miles further south, increasingly squeezed between Paraguay and Argentina on one side and the Atlantic on the other. This southern 'tail' of Brazil contains some of the richest land in the country and some of its most prosperous cities. If the North-East can be called African Brazil, then the South is predominantly European Brazil. Both were settled by immigrants. Forcibly in the North-East, voluntarily in the South. Curitiba, capital of Paraná State, and with a population of 1.75 million people, has its roots in Poland, Germany and Italy. And on this cool and overcast day you can feel the difference. Everyone seems to be going somewhere in Curitiba, many of them on the highly efficient bus network with its idiosyncratic shelters that look like bottles on their sides. There is little of the rambling street life of Bahia or the preening of Rio. Curitiba is a purposeful place, built on hard graft and earnestness. The roads are long and straight and sensible. A sign on the way into town proclaims 'A Proud World Cup City 2014', and in a street near our hotel is a supermarket simply called Big.

There *are* poor people here, people who haven't yet made it and probably never will. I see them pushing handcarts with caged sides in which they collect paper, packaging and other recyclables from the street, presumably to sell. And there are *favelas* in this tidy, rational place, but they're quietly, discreetly tucked away on the edge of town.

There's a feeling the city is trying hard to be cool, though the name of our hotel, the Slaviero Rockefeller Conceptual, suggests they're trying a bit too hard.

There is a museum and gallery in the centre of Curitiba which doesn't have to try to be cool. It just is. It was conceived by Oscar Niemeyer, Brazil's world-class architect, who has made his mark on so many of the cities we've travelled through. The Niemeyer Museum in Curitiba has all his trademarks: wide floors, breathtakingly long, low suspended concrete ceilings, sweeping access ramps, light-reflecting water tanks. At its heart is a most striking feature known as the Eye, a long elliptical pod of reflecting blackened glass, balanced several metres in the air on a yellow-tiled concrete plinth. Broad underground walkways connect the Eye with the rest of the museum. It feels young, light, bright and experimental. All the more impressive, then, that Niemeyer was ninety-five years old when he put the finishing touches to his designs.

The multifarious exhibitions of art, furniture and architecture have a cosmopolitan feel that seems to echo Curitiba's European heritage. There are some strikingly beautiful black and white photographs by Antanas Sutkus, a Lithuanian whom I'd never heard of before, and some of Goya's darkest and most fantastical drawings. Around the museum is a park, one of many carefully laid out green spaces that dot the city and earned Curitiba the title of World's Greenest City in 2007.

1

3

2

4

Day 69 · Curitiba → Morretes

APART FROM some commuter services in São Paulo and Rio, Brazil is a passenger railway wilderness. The railway-building boom in the second half of the nineteenth century was financed largely from Western Europe. In the mid twentieth century, the Americans had more money to invest, and the transport initiative swung to people like Henry Ford who saw the future in roads and motor cars. Railways never recovered and now Brazil is a country where those who move either fly or drive, or take enormously long bus journeys

Above · The Serra Verde Express crosses a bridge on the line through the mountains. ***Opposite:*** *1 · Epic view of the mountains and the Atlantic rainforest.* ***2*** *· At the bar with Fabio, the train manager.* ***3*** *· In the driving seat.*

Some surprise, therefore, to find that Curitiba has a working railway station, the Estação Rodoferroviária. And even more surprising to find that passenger trains run from here to the coast. But this is not a regular service, it's specially laid on for tourists. Still beggars can't be choosers and I climb gratefully aboard what's grandly billed as the Serra Verde Express. It consists of two aluminium-sheathed coaches. One is an American-made luxury coach called Iguaçu, fitted out with leather armchairs, a parquet floor, stout wooden tables and red and green velvet-covered seats. The other, more functional car is called Copacabana.

The reason we're able to embark on this adventure is that, although passenger rail travel may be virtually non-existent in Brazil, freight is thriving. Boosted by regular shuttle services like the iron ore trains I saw in Minas Gerais, almost thirty percent of all freight now goes by train. The line we'll be travelling on today is only there thanks to a private company called ALL, America Latina Logistica, who run and maintain the line. In return they have all the revenues from the lucrative freight business carrying soya, beef and other produce from Curitiba to the port of Paranaguá.

Today we'll be going as far as the town of Morretes, 110 kilometres (sixty-eight miles) down the line. Our journey will last a leisurely three and a half hours and there will be viewpoints at which we can stop and take photographs. All this is conveyed to us by Fabio, a big, burly man who's in charge of the train. He's not only unstoppable with the information, but also adept at multi-tasking, enabling him to make coffee and give his commentary at the same time. My travelling companion is Marcelo, a sculptor with dark Brazilian good looks and a deep interest in spiritualism. He lives in Curitiba but has to come to Morretes during the week to sell his work.

Leaving behind the anodyne skyline of Curitiba we pass by shanty towns and half-cleared construction sites. It's dull stuff and a disappointing hour has gone by before we enter a tunnel and find ourselves, quite suddenly and dramatically, swallowed up by the mountains. From here on, the narrow course of the railway

1

2

3

threads its way through a particularly dense and dramatic part of the Mata Atlântica, the Atlantic rainforest, whilst barely impinging on the majesty around it. We stop at a small, abandoned station to allow one of the long freight trains from the coast to toil past us on the single line. The station must have looked good once, with red gabled roofs, plain plastered buildings with chunky stone decoration around the arches. The air is clear and fresh and the combination of rocky pinnacles, crags from which water briefly catches the sunlight before cascading into some invisible chasm, the yellow butterflies and the purple blossom of the wild hydrangea make this somewhere very special. Far below we can see the red roof of the next station, which the railway will have to make a very tight turn to reach. For a moment time seems suspended, with only the subdued noises of the forest around us. The panorama of high peaks, tall trees and distant waterfalls reminds me of those American Sublime paintings which pitch man, the heroic pioneer, against nature at her most awesome.

1

2

I have a chance to see how brilliantly engineered the track is here when I'm asked up into the cab and given the controls for a while. (The driver obviously hasn't heard of my erratic landings in the aircraft simulator at the Embraer factory.) Clutching the single brake lever, I'm entrusted with bringing us round some tight corners, made a touch more terrifying by the fact that the wheels turn a beat or two before the train itself, giving the impression, for a brief heart-stopping second, that I've driven us all off into space.

It's early afternoon by the time we have emerged from the mountains and rolled into the small and picturesque town of Morretes. Marcelo and I go for lunch at a restaurant which serves the traditional dish of the area called *barreado* which means 'sealed'. It refers to the method of cooking brisket of beef in a ceramic pot with a manioc flour seal. Only salt and garlic are added and the whole lot is left over the fire for twelve hours. The recipe is centuries old and comes from the early settlers.

The sun is already edging behind the mountains we've just come through as I walk with Marcelo beside the horseshoe bend of the fast and shallow River Nhundiaquara, which snakes through this village full of brightly painted two-storey colonial houses, many of which are now art galleries or studios. The beauty of the place is clearly a big inspiration.

3

Opposite:* 1** *· With my friend, the sculptor Marcelo, in Morretes.* ***2 *· The hotel we're walking past is a favourite subject for Morretes' artistic colony.* ***3*** *· The Nhundiaquara River curves picturesquely through Morretes.* ***Above*** *· A new 'old-German' village for tourists in the heart of Blumenau.*

Day 70 · Blumenau

BLUMENAU, a city of a quarter of a million souls, is only 200 kilometres (124 miles) away from Morretes, but such is the difference between the two that you could be forgiven for thinking it was 10,000 kilometres (6,000 miles) and an entire continent away. Blumenau, founded by the philosopher Hermann Bruno Otto Blumenau, who with his fellow explorers sailed up the Itajaí River in 1850, is unequivocally German. It's not that there is German influence, or a hint of German in the mix; it is so German that the town hall is built in the style of a giant half-timbered chalet, and the big event of Blumenau's year is the Oktoberfest, the largest celebration of its kind outside Munich. In the centre of this very German town a pedestrianized mini-Germany has been built next door to a swirling road system. It's announced with a big sign reading 'Wilkommen' in very large letters, with the Portuguese 'Bem Vindo' added, rather cursorily, below it. Here, as the cars roar by, you can find temporary refuge in a Brothers Grimm world of cobbled streets and tall brick and timber buildings (in a style they call Enxaimel) with shutters open on either side of geranium-filled window boxes. Steins of beer are available and accordion music chortles out from artfully concealed speakers. Blumenau likes being German.

Some of the most popular products, not just of Blumenau but this whole corner of Santa Catarina State, are models. Not models of German town centres but models of the tall, leggy, photogenic sort. There is something about the southern Brazilian girls, with their mix of German bone structure and Italian elegance, that has become sought after worldwide. Gisele Bündchen, one of the most successful models of all time, is of German-Brazilian stock. I learn from Wikipedia that it was she who pioneered the 'horse walk', 'a stomping movement created when a model picks her knees up high and kicks her feet out in front'. (Not to be confused with the goose-step.) Since her success, agents have redoubled their efforts in this part of the world, and one of them, Giane Gregori, from an agency in nearby Florianópolis, is in town today. Giane, short, dark and round of physique, is the shapely antithesis of the girls, and boys, she's looking for, but quite comfortable with that. She's bright, alert and experienced, and refreshingly unpretentious and realistic about the talent-spotting process. She likes to see people in their natural environment, which means that, rather than set up a room or a smart studio for auditions, she prefers to walk the streets or sit and have a coffee in a shopping mall and watch the passing crowds. She's looking for a model-like figure, but most important to her is to find a face that is different and distinctive. If she sees someone she likes she will approach them, or their parents if they're young, and give them a card inviting them to come and see her. The youngest at which she will take them on is thirteen, but they can only legally take on paid assignments from the age of sixteen.

One of Giane's finds is Priscilla Falaster, born in Blumenau of second-generation German immigrants and fiercely, if inexplicably, proud of the town. Priscilla has the tall coltish looks of a classic model, with long reddish-brown hair, freckles and a slight Mick Jaggerish fullness of the lips. She's particularly in demand in Argentina and Tokyo. Like her mentor Giane, she's down-to-earth, happy to sit

1

2

3

and talk to me in the unglamorous surroundings of a pavement café in the busy centre of town. She recommends the sugar cane juice. Giane sits a little way off, casting an agent's eye over the afternoon shoppers of Blumenau.

It's not just the strong, long-limbed figure that Priscilla has inherited from her parents, both of whom still speak German – 'I speak it only so-so,' she says apologetically – it's also a hard-nosed sense of realism. Her mother insisted that she kept up her education and in between modelling assignments she's studying to be a pharmacist in Florianópolis. Though she thinks that, after seeing Gisele Bündchen's success, 'everyone wants to be a model', she credits Bündchen with having shown that being a model doesn't necessarily mean you lose your independence.

'Now they see you can have money and security and a real life.'

Most of all, though, she wants to sing the praises of her birthplace.

'It's so beautiful. The buildings and the culture.' When I ask her what it is that makes people come here in search of beautiful women, she replies quite positively 'German civilization.'

I know she doesn't mean this to sound the way it does, but I also know what she means.

Giane returns, smiling cautiously. She's given one card out, and she thinks she's found someone rather special in Blumenau this afternoon.

Later we eat at what we are advised is the best restaurant in the Blumenau area. It's run by Neapolitans and serves delicious Italian food. Back at the hotel I have to look at the map just to remind myself that I'm still in South America.

Opposite: 1 · *Priscilla Falaster, embodiment of the South Brazilian model.*
2 · *The glamorous world of international modelling. At the street café with Priscilla and Giane.*
3 · *Giane out talent-spotting on the streets of Blumenau.*

Day 71 · Blumenau 🚌 Pomerode

IF BLUMENAU is proud of its German heritage then nearby Pomerode is obsessed with it. If you've got it, flaunt it, and they do, welcoming visitors to 'the Most German City in Brazil'.

The most German city in Brazil is about half an hour's drive up the valley due north of Blumenau. At first the road passes a monotonous succession of suburban clutter. Car showrooms, filling stations, builders' yards full of blue swimming pool shells stacked high against the walls. When we turn off the main road the countryside changes and we're amongst gently undulating hills with lush green meadows studded, incongruously, with palm trees and stands of sugar cane, like a tropical Bavaria. They call this stretch of the Itajaí River the European Valley.

Pomerode, so named because its founders came mainly from Pomerania, sets out its stall very quickly. The main road has to pass through a recently built arched gateway, and as soon as it enters the town the surface changes to cobbles. There is a tourist office inside a brick tower and a crude statue, dated 1974 and dedicated to the *pioneiros alemães* – the German pioneers who first arrived here in 1863.

1

3

2

4

Of the 27,000 inhabitants nearly seventy percent have German ancestry and the majority still speak the Pommersch dialect. The local religion is sixty-three percent Lutheran.

Even the sport here is German. At the Hermann Weege Stadium, a rather grand name for what's little more than a sports field, the town is hosting an international Punhobol tournament. Punhobol is a game similar to volleyball, played with five on each side of a net over which a ball has to be hit using only the fists. The Germans call it Faustball or Fistball. Apparently it originated in Italy in the sixteenth century and is now played largely by Swiss, Austrians, Germans and South American countries where there is a German presence, particularly Brazil, Paraguay and Argentina.

All these nations are represented here as part of a three-day veterans' world championship which Pomerode is proudly hosting. The veterans begin at thirty-five, but there are one or two playing whose flowing white hair must put them at sixty or more. Herwig, an Austrian IT engineer, is here playing for his country. He likes the game.

'It's hard but you can't damage anybody.'

He grins.

'The ball can come at you pretty fast. A good smash travels at over 100 km an hour.'

Herwig was once a top volleyball player and he appreciates the fact that Punhobol remains a largely amateur sport.

'There aren't many games where you can sit down afterwards and shake hands with your opponents and have a drink with them.'

There's good nature in the air at the Hermann Weege Stadium. Five games are going on at once, four of them between various veterans' teams, another, at the far end of the ground, between two teams of Brazilian girls. They're great to watch because almost every time a point is scored they leap into each others' arms. The Brazilians love a good hug.

The public address system booms out. Fifty-year-old men walk around nursing red and calloused wrists, whilst others are in the massage tent being attended to by the local nurses. On one of the touchlines an elderly, white-haired lady waves a Swiss flag. Thuds and grunts and flying mud are everywhere.

Beyond the stadium, Pomerode presents a quiet, neat, reserved appearance that is at odds with almost everywhere else I've been in Brazil. We sit and have coffee and cake at a pink-themed German bakery which looks out over a well-kept garden with neatly trimmed topiary. Every now and then pony and traps go by, bouncing tourists over the cobbles. However weird, wonderful and inexplicable the Brazilian way of life might be, it's nearly always inclusive. Here I feel for the first time as if I'm an outsider pressing my nose against the glass. For this reason

Opposite:* 1** · *Brazilian girl attempts smash at the Punhobol Championships.* **2** · *A sportsman-like atmosphere prevails.* **3** · *Until the game starts. A smash has to be made with the wrist.* **4** · *Brazilian girls in a huddle.* ***Above · *A horse and cart takes me along a country lane in the lush 'European' Valley.*

I'm looking forward to lunch, which has been offered to us by an old-established German-Brazilian family in the hills above the town.

It's nice to get away from the oppressive neatness of Pomerode and onto the winding rural roads. They lead us up through thick woodland, interspersed with tidy farms where big, lazy, well-fed cows lie beside ponds and chickens strut amongst them. We eventually turn into a dark and well-sheltered driveway and find ourselves outside a long, low house with barns beside it, in which a pair of dusty old Volkswagens share space with ancient farm utensils. Though it's hardly past midday, the family guests are already sitting at tables along a shady veranda.

Our host, a small, stout, redoubtably energetic woman called Hanna Lora, is busy in a low-ceilinged old kitchen at the back of the house. Helped by daughters and daughters-in-law, she's putting the finishing touches to lashings of roast pork and duck filled with her own Pomeranian-style stuffing.

When everything is ready the local priest says grace and gives a short sermon at the same time. The excellent Sunday roasts are served up. There's jollity, encouraged by some very good beer, but it's quite contained within the family. Hanna Lora was born in Pomerode, one of fourteen children, to German-speaking parents. Her many children and grandchildren are all bilingual, but, unlike the majority of people in this country of immigrants, Hanna Lora remains wedded to the culture that her grandparents brought over with them. She is German first and Brazilian second. When I ask her how it is that the Germans, of all Brazil's millions of immigrants, have remained so homogeneous, she points to the fact that her forefathers who settled this part of Brazil knew exactly what they were doing. These were not chancers looking for a better life. They came in large numbers, were highly organized and motivated, had their own very strong culture and knew how they wanted to live. For them, rather like the Pilgrim Fathers, the New World was a place where the old world could be rebuilt the way they wanted it. Pomerode is very important to Hanna Lora. Though Santa Catarina State has always been a haven for German settlers, Pomerode remains the core, the heartland, of the German way of life. The schools are bilingual, the children learning subjects in both German and Portuguese. Other cities are changing, she

***Below:* 1** *· Hanna Lora in her kitchen.* **2** *· Her family and friends help themselves to Sunday lunch.* ***Opposite:* 3** *· At the dinner table with Dayse, in traditional dress, and Hanna Lora.* **4** *· Lunch draws to an end.* **5** *· Ingo Penz gives me a lift to the Carl Weege Museum.* **6** *· Riding sidecar on the* Choppmotorrad*, guarding fifty litres of Pilsner.*

1

2

3

4

says, becoming more integrated, less German, but the Pomerode city authorities are, like her, hardline and unwilling to compromise. It wasn't always like this. Hanna Lora can remember her father telling her of the days when it was very hard to keep their German identity. In the 1930s President Vargas's government pursued a vigorous policy of *abrasileiramento*, Brazilianization. The pleasant Itajaí Valley, where we are now, was described as a place of 'strange costumes, full of non-national Brazilians, a place of the disintegration of the national spirit'. She herself has met no discrimination and the German community is now free to live the way it wants to. There is a rather sad downside to all this, which I learn from my translator, Dayse. This well-kept, house-proud little city of Pomerode holds a melancholy record. It has the highest suicide rate in the country. (The suicide rate in Brazil, as in most other Latin American countries, is low, with 4.8 deaths for every 100,000 people. The homicide rate, by comparison, is very high, at 28.4 per 100,000.) It's hard to know why Pomerode should be particularly bad, but research suggests that hard-working Protestant, agricultural, conservative communities are the most at risk.

If the young people of the area are anything to go by, then the German-ness of Pomerode and its pretty rolling hills is unlikely to be abandoned any time soon. After lunch, at least thirty of them, in full national dress, stage some traditional dancing for us. We repair to the Carl Weege Museum, or the Casa do Imigrante,

5

6

1

2

4

3

5

as it's called in Portuguese, where the history of the first settlers, Weege being foremost amongst them, is commemorated. It's well done, with rooms decorated in early settler style – simple and well-made furniture, embroidered bedspreads and portraits of formidable, extravagantly mustachioed founding fathers.

Outside the museum the dancers, many of whom have already had a sharpener with their lunch, fill up their mugs with beer provided by the remarkable *Choppmotorrad* (*chopp*, pronounced 'sho-pee', being the word for draught beer in Brazil). It's a motorcycle sidecar driven by a portly photographer named Ingo Penz. He has adapted a 1950s Czech Jawa motorbike to carry, in the sidecar, a fifty-litre keg of iced Pilsner, and his wife. She, like he, is dressed in lederhosen, and both wear felt hats with feathers and badges as they dispense the beer. Ingo is a character, constantly coming up with ideas to show off yet another facet of German-Brazilian culture. One of his most recent is the magnificently named *Choppmotorradvereinmusikanten*, a musical group which preserves some of the instruments that the German settlers brought to southern Brazil, including the bandoneón, the *Mundharmonika* and the *Teufelsgeige*, the Devil's violin.

The traditional dances are done with great gusto. To the strains of a relentlessly jolly accordion, there's wood-chopping, in which young men with several steins of Pilsner inside them risk dismemberment whilst slicing into the wood with axes, mock-fighting and roundel dances which involve hoicking up the skirts of the girls. There's a bravura display of *Schuhplattler*, the Bavarian dance in which heels are kicked and thighs slapped at great speed, whilst yodelling at the same time. And behind them the sun slowly sinks beyond the hills.

Our evening in Pomerode is enlivened by an encounter with a thankfully rather different sort of band led by a man called Michael Lochner, a German who came to Blumenau for the Oktoberfest and fell in love with, and later married, a local girl. It's rather refreshing after a heavy-duty afternoon of Alpine culture to listen to a band which combines black and white musicians playing a fusion of rock, reggae, Bavarian and Brazilian music. It's a fusion of cultures which shows the lighter side of the European Valley.

A nice way to remember our day in the Most German City in Brazil, drinking beer brewed behind the bar and listening to this joyfully eccentric band play one of their more memorable numbers, 'White Sausage Samba'.

Opposite: **1** · *Young Brazilians celebrate their German heritage.* **2** · *Old Englishman joins them.* **3** · *Women dance on whilst men slap each other.* **4** · *The chopping dance. How did this get past health and safety?* **5** · *Wearing my German hat. A final salute to the motorized bar.* **Below** · *Pomerode lets its hair down. Michael Lochner, in drag, leads his very mixed band.*

Day 72 · The Pantanal

SOUTH-EASTERN BRAZIL is densely populated and can be quite claustrophobic so I'm very happy to find myself, 900 kilometres (560miles) north-west of Blumenau, on the final approach to a tiny bush airport in the Pantanal, the largest wetland on earth and one of Brazil's emptiest places. It's part of the enormous and equally empty Mato Grosso region, where the intrepid English explorer Percy Fawcett was last seen, and at whose northern end is the Xingu River system, home of the Wauja. Mato Grosso, meaning 'thick forest', is a better description of the North than of the state we're flying over now, Mato Grosso do Sul, in whose capital Campo Grande we spent last night. Much of the forest here has been cleared for cattle and soya production and much of it is confined to the dark green, geometric blocks we can see below us, or replaced altogether by fast-growing eucalyptus.

This is frontier country; the borders of Paraguay and Bolivia are only a couple of hundred kilometres (125 miles) to the west. It's also the watershed of two great river systems. One flows north to the Amazon, the other south, via the Paraguai and the Paraná, down to the Rio de la Plata, the River Plate. It's still early and as our single-engined Cessna flies west and north from Campo Grande, the great red sandstone rock-stacks and bluffs of the Planalto, the high plateau, look spectacular as the morning sun hits them. Soon they give way to a much flatter, very green landscape, with herds of cattle clustered below us, tiny as white maggots. The grassland becomes yellowy green and marshy. There are fewer cattle and more of the shallow brackish lagoons they call *salinas*. Just before half past eight we touch down on a bumpy grass runway at a *fazenda*, a farm, called Barra Mansa. It's an isolated estate that supplements its income by taking in a handful of visitors and giving them the Pantanal experience. In a happy coincidence the farm is run by the Rondon family, direct descendants of the great Brazilian explorer, Colonel Candido Rondon, who mapped and explored the Roraima border area where my journey began many months ago.

It is his great-grandson, Guilherme Rondon, a big, friendly man, who steps forward to greet us, along with his son Daniel and his daughter-in-law Pollianna, a lively, energetic blonde who runs the tourist side of the business. Her husband Daniel, who runs the farm itself, is taking our plane back to Campo Grande on business. The first thing I notice after two weeks in the deep South is just how hot it is here. The sun is strong and hats obligatory. As she leads us from the plane to the four-square red-roofed house where we shall be staying, she spreads her arm wide across what looks a healthily verdant landscape, and grimaces.

Opposite · *Dramatic escarpment on the edge of Brazil's high plateau.*

'We're having a very dry year, very different from last year. Between December and June we should get a flood, but not this year.'

I ask how much of a problem this might be.

'When the dry season comes in July, the grass, the pasture, will already be dry. The water in the field will evaporate and we won't have enough for the cattle, the horses and the wildlife.'

Farms are now having to dig down for water, or make artificial watering places. There's a very strong and proud Pantaneiro culture here and Pollianna and the Rondons are very keen that we should see it and understand what makes it unique. First of all, Pollianna has arranged for me to see the property the way it should be seen, on horseback. This is a cowboy culture.

'Gauchos?'

She shakes her head.

'We have some influence from the gauchos, but they were from the South, and up here the gaucho culture became the Pantanal culture because we had to adapt to the heat. There's no way to dress like the gauchos, no way to have the same habits as them. Because down there is cold, and up here it's hot.'

Before I can even mount the horse I'm shown the intricate preparations by three cowboys, or *peões*, as they call them in the Pantanal. Their names are Alex, Carlos and a much older man, rather splendidly called Vespasiano. Alex shows me the four layers of blanket and other covers that go on the horse's back before the saddle's even fitted. This is to make it as comfortable as possible for cowboys, who sometimes can be in the saddle for a hundred days collecting the cattle and moving them many miles to market. Pollianna remembers seeing runs of over 2,000 cattle being moved across country.

1

2

3

4

Whilst Vespa struggles to blow some sound from an enormous coiled horn, which I presume was some kind of pre-mobile phone cowboy communication, Alex trots out ahead of me keeping half an eye on me and half an eye on the hundred or so head of cattle which are his real responsibility. I've just begun to get the measure of my horse, Cambalo, when there's a sudden commotion up ahead. One of the cows breaks from the herd and races towards us, baying loudly. Carlos moves fast to head her off, but even my docile mount has reared back. What's happened is that keen-eyed Alex has spied a hobbling calf and Vespa has lassoed it and taken it out of the herd for examination. Alex, holding the calf down with his knee, finds claw marks in its side which have been inflicted by a jaguar. Whilst the mother is held at bay, Alex squeezes pus from the wound and then sprays it with anaesthetic. In the days before chemicals, he tells me, they would have used dried cow dung to protect the wound. With the calf returned to its mother, we press on. The morning sun is high and bright by now and I'm glad when Alex leads us on into a marsh-fringed lagoon to enable the horses to cool off. I get to drink too, a draught of *tenere*, cowboy tea, which can be made without getting out of the saddle. *Mate*, the dried and powdered leaves of the yerba plant, are dropped into a hollowed-out cow's horn about a metre long, decorated with a finely carved twisting motif. This is then lowered into the water on a length of rope. When it's filled up it's withdrawn and the tea drunk from a silver pipe that

***Opposite:* 1** · *Young calf is lassoed, to mother's evident distress.* **2** · *Alex applies antiseptic where the jaguar has attacked.* **3** · *Sounding the horn.* 4 · *Before antiseptic, the wounds would have been dressed with dried cow dung.*
Above · *With Vespasiano, carrying traditional curved horn, and Alex, taking a drink of mate in one of the wetland lagoons.*

runs, like a straw, down the side of the horn. The cool water is refreshing and the *mate* gives the system a caffeine-like hit. Which is very welcome as we now move on to the herding of the cattle, the most demanding part of my morning as a cowboy, as the heat builds up and the dust from hundreds of hoofs swirls around.

In late afternoon, with the sun less brutal and the light less harsh, we climb onto boats on the Rio Negro and set off upriver to see the wildlife. The birds are particularly rich. The Pantanal, the size of Belgium and Holland combined, stretches 950 kilometres (590 miles) north to south, through Brazil, Bolivia and Paraguay, making it twenty times larger than that much more famous wetland, the Everglades in Florida, and offers extensive, protected habitats. Even before we get to the boats I've spied the pygmy owl, or burrowing owl, a delightful little bird, standing on guard at the rim of a hole, and every now and then upending itself and sending a small cloud of dust flying out of the hole. Out on the river there are black hawks following our progress with interest as well as lapwings, herons and egrets along the banks and the elegantly beautiful yellow-headed caracara, perched up on the stump of an old tree. Occasionally we'll get a glimpse of a huge bird, the *jabiru*, or 'swollen neck', so called for the red collar at the base of its neck. It's the world's biggest stork and the adopted symbol of the Pantanal.

Below: 1 · A business-like capybara trots along the riverbank. 2 · Caimans prefer to sit in the sun. ***Opposite** · Trying my hand at piranha-fishing with the immensely patient Juan.*

Mammals are less diverse and spectacular. As Pollianna says with an apologetic grin, 'We have very small big game here.'

Jaguar are the most sought after of the Pantanal game, but they're famously discreet and seeing the claw marks on the calf this morning is probably the nearest I'll get to one. Reptiles are well represented by an abundance of alligators, or caiman as they're called here, but they're hardly exciting. Most of the time they sit motionless on the bank, often with their jaws wide open. This, I'm told, is part of their metabolism. Occasionally one of these long, scaly creatures, which can grow to nine metres long, will stir itself to slither into the water, where it continues to do nothing but look sinister, with only the eyes and the protruding bridge of the forehead breaking the surface.

For bank-side action we have to rely on the occasional sighting of a capybara, whose only claim to fame is that it's the biggest rodent in the world, weighing up

1

2

to seventy kilograms. And it's a rodent with webbed feet. If they're nervous, and they generally seem to be, they slip into the river, where they can remain hidden underwater for up to ten minutes. I ask my guide why they should be frightened in such a safe environment. The answer of course is that until recently they, and the caiman, were hunted for their skin. Now, with money available to pay for policing, poaching has greatly decreased.

An hour or so up this peaceful river, my guide Juan pulls into the side for me to do some hunting of my own. Piranha-hunting. It's not too complicated, just a stick with a line on the end. Juan baits the hook with a morsel of shrimp, and shows me where to drop it and what to do when I feel the tug of a fish. Again and again I steady myself in the bobbing boat, flinging the line out with repeated lack of success and feeling myself more and more like the old definition of a fisherman, 'A jerk on one end of the line waiting for a jerk on the other'. I do manage to hoist one of them clear, but with such force that it whips out of the water and thwacks the long-suffering Juan on the side of the head before bouncing back into the river. Encouraged nevertheless by at least seeing a fish, I bring the next bite in more gently, and suddenly there it is dangling above the tea-brown water, a fat, silvery body with an orange underbelly and lots of pointy teeth. My first, and almost certainly last, piranha.

I'm afraid to say we don't put it back to continue its happy life terrifying tourists. Instead we do the next best thing, which is to make it into sashimi. Juan skilfully beheads and guts the fish and whilst he attends to the slicing with meticulous care, he leaves it to me to dispose of the piranha debris. I spot a caiman, who until now has been watching this whole pantomime without the

1

2

Above: 1 · My piranha, about to become sashimi.
2 · The caiman, fastest waste-disposal system in the world.
Below: 3 · Racing back home as sun sets on the Rio Negro.
4 · End of the day. Sitting with Pollianna as Guilherme Rondon sings his songs.
Opposite · Morning on the lagoon. Heron and spoonbill friend.

slightest blink of interest. But when I toss the fish bits into the river he moves like a shot, opening his jaws and catching the remains before they've even hit the water. Finally, I have seen something terrifying.

The piranha sashimi goes down well and, leaving the black hawks to clean up whatever's left, we turn and head back down the river. As the light fades, Juan ups the speed to full throttle and we swing and curve round the corners, sending waves in a multi-coloured fan across the lacquered surface of the water. Above us a quite sensational sunset is being fashioned out of majestic clouds and red-gold bands of sinking sunlight. I can feel insects pepper my face as if I'm in a dust storm.

In the evening, as a distant thunderstorm flashes on the eastern horizon, Pollianna and Guilherme light a fire in the garden of the house and Guilherme sings folk songs he's written and recorded. They're soft and thoughtful and perfect for this quiet, starry, peaceful night. Pollianna is pleased that we are happy here. She makes much of the spiritual benefits of being surrounded by nature, but she's also practical and realistic about the disadvantages. Like the termites that eat away at the foundations of the houses, which have to be virtually rebuilt every fifteen years, the rodents who get at the food, and the bats that have to be treated with repellent every two weeks. Nothing, I'm glad to say, that stops me sleeping soundly.

3

4

Day 73 · The Pantanal

IT'S STILL DARK when we set out on a morning safari. The mosquitoes are worst just before the dawn, especially down by the water, but they seem to vanish with the sunrise. Birds are out in force, particularly waders like the roseate spoonbills, with their subtle pink glow and less subtle shovel-shaped beaks, the whistling ducks that pipe rather than quack and the little round jacanas which they call *cafezinho* here on account of their similarity to the dark brown coffee that all Brazilians seem to take at all times of day. Not much luck with the mammals. Two wild boar tear out of the undergrowth chasing cattle. Two capybara scoot into the water at our arrival, and that's about it.

Breakfast has been laid out for us in a great expanse of bushes, trees and grassland, with two *jabiru* in attendance nearby.

'They're dating,' Pollianna tells me, and points out their huge nests in the trees above. She looks around.

'In the rainy season we'd never be sitting here. The water will reach one and a half metres high. We have to come by boat.'

It seems almost unbelievable that so much water should spill across this plain each year. There are advantages, Pollianna thinks. One of them is that it makes it very difficult to build and maintain roads in the Pantanal. This saves it from

1

2

3

4

development. To my surprise she tells me that ninety-eight percent of the Pantanal is privately owned.

Pollianna and Guilherme are deeply concerned about change. Originally the Barra Mansa estate was part of 400,000 hectares owned by the Rondon family beside the Rio Negro. Over the years the land has been divided up between various children of various generations. The individual properties have shrunk and some have been sold off to what Pollianna calls 'foreigners' which, she hastily explains, means 'people from the city'. Not all of whom are so interested in preserving the habitat and the distinctive culture of the Pantanal.

There are farmers who want to clear trees in order to grow soya and other grasses, and in doing so alter the balance of nature. There are fires that are deliberately set for clearance and in the highlands of the Pantanal mercury used in gold-mining has been found in the stomachs of birds far downriver from the original mine.

By and large she thinks that interest in nature conservation has grown considerably in Brazil in the last twenty years and they have no trouble attracting people to a farm which is comfortable but hardly luxurious. On the other hand they do us what I would call a most luxurious farewell lunch of wild boar marinated overnight in salt, lime, vinegar and lots of garlic and cooked for two hours in a pit over an open fire, which leaves me with an unforgettable memory of the Pantanal. Sitting beneath a huge pimento tree overlooking the Rio Negro in which I'd just taken a dip, not fifty metres from basking and deeply uninterested alligators, with Vespasiano bringing over a spearful of fresh and beautifully tender pork. And talking to Guilherme and Pollianna about the importance of the simple life and how some rich clients check out early when they find there is no television and no spa at Barra Mansa. Guilherme's forefather, Colonel Rondon, mapped most of north and west Brazil. His maps defined this country. His foresight, in laying down telegraph lines and in instructing his military surveyors never to alienate the local people, contributed to the creation of the united, tolerant and largely good-natured place that Brazil is today. It's good to see that the current generations of Rondons are doing all they can to keep his flame burning.

***Opposite:* 1** · *Two hundred or more bird species live around Barra Mansa.* **2** · *Pollianna takes me on a walk in the wetland.* **3** · *Roseate spoonbills patrol the lagoon.* **4** · *The majestic jabiru. The stork that has become the symbol of the Pantanal.*

***Below:* 5** · *Vespasiano with second helpings.* **6** · *Last lunch in the Pantanal with Guilherme and Pollianna.*

5

6

1

2

3

Day 74 · The Iguaçu Falls

I STARTED my Brazilian journey up in the north, in the vast Amazon Basin, in which fifteen percent of all the river water in the world is contained, and I'm completing it 4,000 kilometres (2,500 miles) to the south, where another gathering of rivers creates a world record of a different sort – the biggest waterfall system in the world.

Up in the Pantanal we were between the south-flowing giants, the rivers Paraguai and Paraná. Looking at my map this morning I see that I'm now on the very edge of Brazil, where it meets both Paraguay and Argentina, only a few miles east of the Paraná River, and a few miles north of a town called Wanda, just across the Argentine border.

The River Iguaçu, on which I'm about to embark, is a comparative minnow in the Brazilian scale of things. It rises just outside Curitiba and flows, for some 1,200 kilometres (745 miles), to meet the Paraná, picking up speed and volume from tributaries along the way. Twenty-three kilometres (fourteen miles) short of the confluence of the two rivers, the placid Iguaçu plunges off the edge of a plateau, three kilometres (nearly two miles) long. This is what makes the Iguaçu Falls a world-beater. The Victoria Falls in Africa has the longest single curtain of water in the world but it is the sheer width of the Iguaçu spill that makes it special. When the river is full, there are nearly 300 separate waterfalls along its rim.

I'm heading up the Iguaçu, towards the falls, in a Zodiac dinghy in the company of Marina Xavier, a biologist from São Paulo who lives and works in the park. It's very warm and humid and the early morning cloud is breaking up and there is sporadic sunshine. Every now and then much bigger boats with powerful twin engines, and serried ranks of tourists strapped down inside, race past us, anxious to get to the falls as soon as possible. The wooded riverbanks rise steeply on either side of us and though this is not the wettest time of year, the river is splashing and bouncing over the rocks around us.

Marina says that the Iguaçu National Park is more a conservation area than a tourist area. Only three percent of this protected stretch of tropical rainforest is regularly visited, despite the great diversity of wildlife. Earlier, as we waited at a lodge to get our tickets, there was a lot of activity above us from coatimundi, scurrying creatures with black striped tails and long black noses, leaping about in the branches, and not far off was an armadillo, nose down, searching for something. But, as in the Pantanal, the jaguar remains the king of Brazilian wildlife. The beast that everyone wants to see. Marina smiles. Yes, they're beautiful, and they are the symbol of the park, but they're hardly ubiquitous. She's only seen one in the seven years she's worked here.

I ask her about the threats the park service has to face. Rather surprisingly, she names the palm heart business as one of the worst culprits. Obtaining this delicacy involves destroying an entire tree, and as palm seeds are an important

***Opposite:* 1** *· Coatimundi capering in the branches.* **2** *· Setting out for the falls with Marina Xavier.* **3** *· The majesty of Iguaçu. This is one of almost 300 separate falls along the rim.*
Below *· The crazy ones. Tourists pay good money to get very wet indeed.*

part of the animals' diet this is having quite an impact. Then there's poaching, of course. Poaching as opposed to legal hunting, I ask?

Marina shakes her head.

'There's no hunting allowed,' she says firmly. 'Anywhere in Brazil.'

I ask about the collaboration between the Argentines and the Brazilians, who have joint responsibility for the park. Do they get on well?

'On biodiversity, yes.' Then she smiles and adds, 'Soccer, never!'

The first waterfalls we see are on the Argentine side of the river. There must be forty or fifty of them, tumbling eighty metres down the gorge wherever they can find a path through the cracked and fissured rocks. And at last, directly ahead, I can see the big falls on the Brazilian side, where the water never touches the sides and the spray from the crashing impact rises back to form a white cloud over the lip of the falls. We edge a little further forwards. Water is thundering down all around us. The river is thrashing and boiling, coming at us from all sides. The noise is relentless, and it's practically impossible now to hear each other speak.

The raw power of falling water has always mesmerized me. The way that a river can change character so instantaneously. From a languid stream full of bathing pools and fishing reaches to a hammering inferno. From a ripple to a roar. From the benign to the apocalyptic. The basin into which we're edging is named, entirely appropriately, Garganta do Diabo, the Devil's Throat. High above me I can see lines of tiny figures, emerging every now and then from the clouds of

spray as they make their way up to the viewing platforms. Marina shouts and points across the river. There are the thrill-seekers who roared past us earlier, dripping wet and shrieking with ecstatic terror as their helmsman moves the boat as close to the falling torrent as he dares. I feel a touch of that hysteria as the swirling, treacherous white water flings us about. It's the kind of exhilaration you only get from being on the knife-edge between safety and chaos.

The Brazilians love nicknames. It's part of the informality that colours life here. Whether it's footballers or politicians, a jokey abbreviation of the real thing – Pelé, Lula, FHC – is a sign of endearment. It's the same with these waterfalls. They're all called something. Sometimes it's religious, Adam and Eve, San Martin, Santa Maria; sometimes they're heroes of Brazilian independence, Deodoro, Benjamin Constant; sometimes literary, Dois Mosqueteiros, Two Musketeers, and its neighbour Três Mosqueteiros. It's a sign of how proud they are to have the longest waterfalls in the world on their border. The Iguaçu Falls are the one site that every Brazilian has to visit at some time in their life.

And that's unusual. As we've travelled round I've been struck by how little curiosity the Brazilians seem to have about their own country. Many times in my journey I've wanted to share with them the beauties we've seen here. The power of the Amazon, the splendour of the rainforest, the exuberance of an African festival on the North-East coast. And more often than not my Brazilian friends nod their heads politely and ask.

'What's it like?'

Above · *Journey's end. Taking in the sheer power of the falls.*
Opposite · *The Devil's Throat, where the stately Iguaçu River becomes an inferno.*

Following pages · *Where Brazil, on the left, meets Argentina, on the right, water plunges over a rim nearly two miles long, making the Iguaçu Falls the largest waterfall on earth.*

ACKNOWLEDGEMENTS

THERE ARE MANY PEOPLE without whose help and expertise *Brazil* would never have happened and to whom I owe enormous thanks. Steve Abbott and Paul Bird have been there from the start, along with others at my office, especially Sue Grant, and Juliana Schuch, Lyn Dougherty and Mimi Robinson. Roger Mills, in whose company I set off on the very first journey back in 1988, this time gave his support and guidance as Executive Producer.

Taking the central role in planning and shooting the journey were my two directors, John-Paul Davidson and Frank Hanly, with the invaluable help of Rebecca Harris, Dulce Continentino, Willow Murton and Roberta Fortuna. My magnificent film crew was Nigel Meakin and Sebastian Dunn. Throughout our journey we were met with the most generous and enthusiastic support from local people, many of whom already appear in the pages of the book. To all those Brazilians who gave their time and energy I give my wholehearted thanks.

Others without whom we could not have contemplated and completed the series were Charlotte Moore at the BBC, Peter Meakin on camera in the North-East, and the man who introduced me to Brazil, Steven Chew.

This book owes much to Michael Dover, my editor, and Basil Pao, who in addition to his usual great job as travelling stills photographer, also took on the mantle of designer. Mary Spence has done a fine job on the maps. Thanks too to Alan Samson, Linden Lawson, and all the team at Weidenfeld and Nicolson, and, as ever, to Angela Martin.

The *Footprint Guide* and the *Rough Guide* were my two main companions to Brazil, and I owe a great debt of thanks to John Hemming for his invaluable series of books on the Amazon and Brazilian history. Also hugely helpful were Greg Grandin's *Fordlandia*, Josh Lacey's *God Is Brazilian*, Alex Bellos's *Futebol: The Brazilian Way of Life*, Peter Robb's inspirational *A Death In Brazil*, the *Bradt Guide to Bahia* and the *Time Out Guide to Rio*.

1

2

3

4

5

6

7

8

9

10

11

1 · J.P. filming at the Barra Mansa ranch in the Pantanal. 2 · 'My Favourite Martian' Sabastian in Alcântara. 3 · The lads filming impromptu shoe shine at the Mercado São Joaquim in Salvador. 4 · Frank on a coffee break at the Pernambuco Yacht Club in Recife. 5 · Nigel filming on the streets of Salvador. 6 · Sebastian, Peter and Nigel chatting with a Bumba Meu Boi participant in São Luís. 7 · Basil rescuing his cameras from the squirrel monkeys at the Ariaú Towers on Rio Negro. 8 · Nigel and Sebastian filming a Wauja ceremony. 9 · Rebecca, Dulce and Frank at the Francisco Brennand Sculpture Park in Recife. 10 · Willow sharing sweets with Wauja children. 11 · With Roberta in Blumenau.

CREDITS & COPYRIGHTS

First published in Great Britain in 2012 by Weidenfeld & Nicolson.
1 3 5 7 9 10 8 6 4 2

A CIP catalogue record for this book is available from the British Library.

ISBN: 978 0 297 86626 8

Art direction & design • Basil Pao
Assistant designer • Esther Jacobs
Maps by Mary Spence
Digital image processing & artwork by Studio 8 Ltd., Hong Kong
Printed by Printer Trento Srl and bound by L.E.G.O. SpA, Italy

FSC www.fsc.org MIX Paper from responsible sources FSC® C015829

Weidenfeld & Nicolson
The Orion Publishing Group
Orion House
5 Upper St Martin's Lane
London WC2H 9EA

An Hachette UK Company

www.orionbooks.co.uk | *www.palintravels.co.uk* | *www.basilpao.com*